EGO &
ARCHETYPE

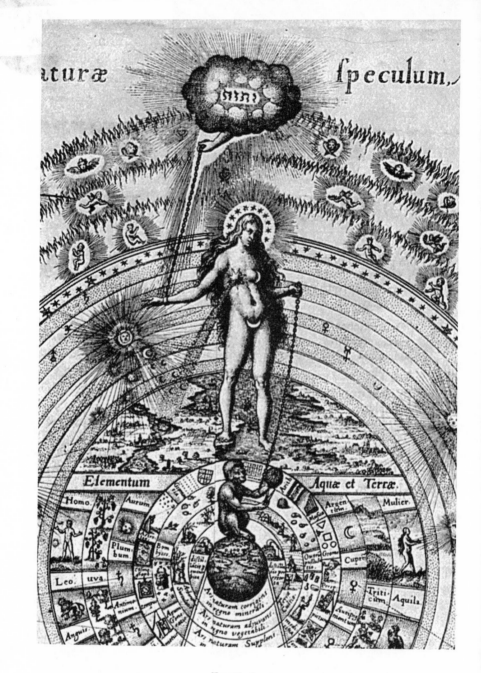

Frontispiece

THE WORLD SOUL by Robert Fludd. The anima as personification of
the ego-Self axis transmits guidance and support to the ego from the
archetypal psyche. (Detail)

EGO &
ARCHETYPE

*Individuation and the
Religious Function
of the Psyche*

Edward F. Edinger

SHAMBHALA
Boston & London
1992

SHAMBHALA PUBLICATIONS, INC.
Horticultural Hall
300 Massachusetts Avenue
Boston, Massachusetts 02115

SHAMBHALA PUBLICATIONS, INC.
Random Century House
20 Vauxhall Bridge Road
London SW1V 2SA

9 8 7 6 5 4 3 2 1

First Shambhala Edition
Printed in the United States of America on acid-free paper
⊗
Distributed in the United States by Random House, Inc., in
Canada by Random House of Canada Ltd, and in the United
Kingdom by the Random Century Group

LIBRARY OF CONGRESS CATALOGING-IN-PUBLICATION DATA
Edinger, Edward F.
   Ego and archetype: individuation and the religious function of
the psyche/Edward F. Edinger.—1st Shambhala ed.
      p. cm.
   Reprint. Originally published: New York : Putnam, 1972.
   "A C. G. Jung Foundation book."
   Includes bibliographical references and index.
   ISBN 0-87773-576-X
   1. Individuation (Psychology)   2. Ego (Psychology)   3. Archetype
(Psychology)   4. Psychoanalysis and religion.   I. Title.
BF175.5.I53   1991   90-53380
   150.19′54—dc20   CIP

CONTENTS

PART I / INDIVIDUATION AND THE STAGES OF
DEVELOPMENT   1

The Inflated Ego   3
1. Ego and Self   3
2. Inflation and Original Wholeness   7
3. Adam and Prometheus   16
4. Hybris and Nemesis   26

The Alienated Ego   37
1. The Ego-Self Axis and the Psychic Life Cycle   37
2. Despair and Violence   42
3. Alienation and the Religious Experience   48
4. Restitution of the Ego-Self Axis   56

Encounter with the Self   62
1. The Role of the Collective   62
2. The Breakthrough   69
3. The Book of Job   76
4. The Individuated Ego   96

PART II / INDIVIDUATION AS A WAY OF LIFE   105

The Search forMeaning   107
1. The Function of the Symbol   107
2. The Concretistic and Reductive Fallacies   110
3. The Symbolic Life   117

Christ as Paradigm of the Individuated Ego   131
1. The Acceptance of Separateness   131
2. The Ethical Teaching   135
3. The Self-Oriented Ego   146
4. Man as the Image of God   154

Being an Individual   157
1. The *A Priori* Existence of the Ego   157
2. The Monad and the Monogenes   163
3. Unity and Multiplicity   172

*The Trinity Archetype and the
Dialectic of Development*   179
1. The Three and the Four   179
2. Transformation and Development   187

PART III / SYMBOLS OF THE GOAL   195

Metaphysics and the Unconscious   197
1. Empirical Metaphysics   197

2. A Series of "Metaphysical" Dreams   199
3. Return to the Beginning   205
4. The Transcendent Dimension   209
5. Completion of the Opus   214

The Blood of Christ   225

1. Introduction   225
2. The Meaning of Blood   227
3. Christ and Dionysus   235
4. Extraction by Sacrifice   240
5. Attributes of the Blood of Christ   246
6. Relations to Alchemy   251
7. Modern Dreams   254

The Philosophers' Stone   260

1. Introduction and Text   260
2. Transformation and Revelation   265
3. The Fertility Principle   272
4. The Union of Opposites   274
5. Ubiquity   281
6. Spiritual Food and the Tree of Life   287
7. The One in the All   292

ILLUSTRATIONS

Page

Frontispiece. THE WORLD SOUL by Robert Fludd.   ii
Picture 1. Sequence of Gestalts.   9
Picture 2. Painting by a seven-year-old girl.   10
Picture 3. PARADISE AS A VESSEL from an Italian manuscript.   17
Picture 4. THE EXPULSION OF ADAM AND EVE by Massaccio.   19
Picture 5. THE FALL OF ICARUS by Pieter Breughel.   28
Picture 6. IXION BOUND TO THE WHEEL, Ancient Vase Painting.   30
Picture 7. WHEEL OF LIFE, Painting, Tibet.   35
Picture 8. HAGAR AND ISHMAEL IN THE DESERT by Gustave Doré.   45
Picture 9. ISRAELITES GATHERING MANNA from *The Hours of
    Catherine of Cleves.*   49
Picture 10. ELIJAH BEING FED BY THE RAVENS by Washington
    Allston, Detail.   50
Picture 11. ST. ANTHONY AND ST. PAUL THE HERMIT BEING FED
    BY A RAVEN, Dürer.   53
Picture 12. THE PENITENCE OF DAVID. Illumination from a
    Byzantine manuscript.   57
Picture 13. JACOB'S DREAM by Gustave Doré.   71
Picture 14. THE ANNUNCIATION by Botticelli.   72
Picture 15. THE ECSTASY OF ST. THERESA by Bernini.   73
Picture 16. PATIENT'S DRAWING.   74
Picture 17. DISKOBOLOS by Myron, c. 460-450 B.C., Roman Copy.   74
Picture 18. PIETA by Michelangelo.   75
Picture 19. ALCHEMICAL DRAWING.   75
Picture 20. VARIETIES OF THE THREE-FOOTED SUN WHEEL.   76
Picture 21. THE CONVERSION OF ST. PAUL, Woodcut 1515.   77
Picture 22. THE FIRE OF GOD HAS FALLEN FROM HEAVEN.
    Etching for the Book of Job by William Blake.   79
Picture 23. THE TOWER, Tarot Card, Marseilles Deck.   82
Picture 24. FIRE RAINS FROM HEAVEN by Albrecht Dürer.   83
Picture 25. YAHWEH FRIGHTENS JOB WITH A GLIMPSE OF HELL,
    William Blake.   86
Picture 26. YAHWEH ANSWERS JOB OUT OF THE WHIRLWIND,
    William Blake.   90
Picture 27. YAHWEH SHOWS JOB THE DEPTHS (BEHEMOTH),
    William Blake.   92
Picture 28. JOB SACRIFICES TO YAHWEH, William Blake.   97
Picture 29. ST. CHRISTOPHER CARRYING CHRIST AS A SPHERE.
    Oil painting by the Master of Messkirch (?).   99

Picture 30. THE ANGEL GABRIEL HANDS MARY A LETTER. The
    Annunciation by Dürer. 123
Picture 31. A DOVE TRANSMITS THE DIVINE VOICE TO
    ST. GREGORY THE GREAT. Ivory Panel, 9-10th Century. 124
Picture 32. THE GREAT ZIGGURAT OF UR, Reconstruction. 127
Picture 33. MAYAN PYRAMID. At the top is a Temple of the God. 128
Picture 34. CRUCIFIXION WITHIN A FIELD OF FORCE.
    Detail of altar piece. 139
Picture 35. CRUCIFIXION AND DISMEMBERMENT. Woodcut made in
    Rennes, France, c. 1830. 141
Picture 36. BAPTISM OF CHRIST, Leonardo de Vinci and Verrocchio. 147
Picture 37. SATAN TEMPTING CHRIST WITHIN A CIRCLE,
    Rembrandt. 148
Picture 38. THE FLAGELLATION OF CHRIST, *The Hours of Catherine
    of Cleves.* 151
Picture 39. THE LIVERPOOL MANDALA, C. G. Jung. 177
Picture 40. THE AWAKENING GIANT by Michelangelo. 203
Picture 41. LION WITH HIS PAWS CUT OFF, Alchemical Drawing. 215
Picture 42. THE DISMEMBERED MAN, Alchemical Drawing. 217
Picture 43. BIRD IN SPACE, Brancusi. 222
Picture 44. THE CHALICE OF ANTIOCH. 236
Picture 45. CHRIST AS A CLUSTER OF GRAPES. 237
Picture 46. CHRIST CHUSHED AS A GRAPE. 240
Picture 47. AZTEC SUN GOD FEEDING ON HUMAN BLOOD. 241
Picture 48. CHRIST'S BLOOD SAVING SOULS FROM PURGATORY. 247
Picture 49. BIRD WRITING WITH THE BLOOD OF CHRIST, Painting
    of a patient. 255
Picture 50. HEART ON THE CROSS, Patient's Drawing. 257
Picture 51. THE ULTIMATE GOAL AS A MANDALA. 266
Picture 52. THE BOLLINGEN STONE. 271
Picture 53. THE MIRACULOUS GROWTH OF WHEAT, *Très Riche
    Heures de Jean, Duc de Berry.* 273
Picture 54. THE REGENERATIVE SYMBOL OE THE HALOA FESTIVAL,
    from a Greek vase. 275
Picture 55. THE SUN-MOON HERMAPHRODITE. 276
Picture 56. UNION OF SUN AND MOON—SULPHUR AND MERCURIUS. 276
Picture 57. VIRGIN TAMING A UNICORN. 280
Picture 58. THE CRUCIFIED SERPENT. 282
Picture 59. UBIQUITY OF THE STONE. 283
Picture 60. THE EYE OF GOD. 285
Picture 61. THE ALCHEMICAL TREE. 289
Picture 62. CHRIST THE SAVIOUR IN THE TREE OF LIFE. 291
Picture 63. THE END OF THE WORK. 296

PLATES

Plate 1. THE GARDEN OF EDEN AS A CIRCLE. From
    Très Riche Heures de Jean, Duc de Berry   Facing Page 16
Plate 2. DANAE by Titian   Facing Page 68
Plate 3. PAINTING BY A PATIENT. From C. G. Jung,
    The Archetypes of the Collective Unconscious   Facing Page 81
Plate 4. CHRIST IN THE GARDEN SUPPORTED BY AN
    ANGEL, Paolo Veronese, Detail   Facing Page 152
Plate 5. JACOB'S LADDER by William Blake   Facing Page 268

ACKNOWLEDGMENTS

This book is the result of a decade of thought and writing. Part I began as a small paper entitled "The Ego-Self Paradox" published in *The Journal of Analytical Psychology*, Vol. 5, No. 1, January 1960. It was later expanded and given as a series of lectures to the Analytical Psychology Clubs of New York (1962) and Los Angeles (1963), and in Montreal (1964). Chapters 4, 5, 6 and 8 originally appeared in *Spring*, published by the Analytical Psychology Club of New York. I am indebted to Mrs. Jane Pratt, previous editor of *Spring*, for her editorial work on the earlier versions of these chapters. The original version of Chapter 7 was delivered as a paper at the Second International Congress for Analytical Psychology in Zürich, August 1962. It was subsequently published in the Proceedings of that Congress entitled *The Archetype*, edited by Adolf Guggenbühl-Craig, S. Karger 1964. It was also printed in *The Journal of Analytical Psychology*, Vol. 9, No. 2, July 1964. Chapter 9 began as a lecture under the auspices of the C. G. Jung Foundation (1969) and Chapter 10 was originally a lecture given to the Analytical Psychology Club of New York (1969).

I am grateful to Doreen B. Lee for her skillful preparation of the manuscript, also to Rhoda Head, editor, and to the Publications Committee of the C. G. Jung Foundation. I acknowledge gratefully permission to use pictures from the following sources:

Musée Condé, Chantilly, for Plate 1 and Pictures 30 and 53.
Museo del Prado, Madrid, for Plate 2.
Princeton University Press for Plate 3, Pictures 3, 6, 7, 39, 41, 44, 45, 46, 47, 54, 55, 56, 57, 60 and 63.
Pinacoteca di Brera, Milan, for Plate 4.
British Museum, London, for Plate 5.
Offentliche Bibliothek der Universität Basel for the Frontispiece and Jacket.
National Press Books and Rhoda Kellogg for Picture 1.
Michael Fordham for Picture 2.
Church of the Carmine, Florence; photographer Alinari Fratelli, for Picture 4.
Museum of Fine Arts, Brussels, for Picture 5.
Pierpont Morgan Library for Pictures 9, 22, 25, 26, 27, 28 and 38.
Museum of Fine Arts, Boston, for Picture 10.
Dover Publications, Inc., New York, for pictures 11 and 24.
Bibliotheque Nationale, Paris, for Picture 12.
The courtesy of the Robert Lehman Collection, New York, for Picture 14.
Cabinetto Fotografico Nazionale, Rome, for Picture 15.
Phaidon Press Limited, London, for Pictures 17, 18 and 40.
Philosophical Library for Picture 25.

Offentliche Kunstsamtung, Basel, for Picture 29.
Kunsthistorisches Museum, Vienna, for Picture 31.
Penguin Books, London, for Picture 32.
To: Roloff Beny for photograph, Picture 33.
National Gallery, London, for Picture 34.
Uffizi, Florence, for Picture 36.
Staatliche Museen, Berlin, for Picture 37.
Peggy Guggenheim Foundation for Picture 43.
Library of the Chemistry Department, University of St. Andrews, Scotland,
    for Picture 59.
Robinson and Watkins Books, Ltd., London, for Picture 61.
Staats Bibliotheque, Münich, for Picture 62.

I am grateful, too, for permission to quote as noted from the following:

Abingdon Press, from Roland H. Bainton, *Here I Stand*.
Academic Press, Inc., from *Theatrum Chemicum Britannicum*.
Basic Books, Inc., New York, 1958—excerpt from *Existence: A New Dimension in Psychiatry and Psychology*.
Beacon Press, Boston, from *The Gnostic Religion*, copyright 1958, 1963, by Hans Jonas.
Guild of Pastoral Psychology, from Derek Kitchin, Guild Lecture No. 80, April 1954.
From "The Wasteland" in *Collected Poems* by T. S. Eliot, copyright 1936, by Harcourt Brace Jovanovich, Inc.; copyright 1963, 1964. Reprinted by permission of the publishers.
Harper and Row, Inc., New York, from Pierre Teilhard, *The Phenomenon of Man*.
Journal of Analytical Psychology, London, from Erich Neumann, "The Significance of the Genetic Aspect for Analytical Psychology."
Methuen and Company, Ltd., London, from H. G. Baynes, *Analytical Psychology and the English Mind*.
Northwestern University Press, Evanston, Ill., from Rivkah Kluger, *Satan in the Old Testament*.
Oxford University Press, Inc., New York, from F. H. Bradley, *Appearance and Reality;* Gilbert Murray, *The Rise of the Greek Epic;* Rudolf Otto, *The Idea of the Holy*.
Random House, Inc., New York, from Swami Paramandenda, *The Wisdom of China and India;* Nancy W. Ross, *The World of Zen;* C. G. Jung, *Memories, Dreams, Reflections*.
Simon and Schuster, Inc., New York, from G. Ginsberg, *Legends of the Bible*.
Tavistock Publications, Ltd., London, from G. Adler (Ed.), *Current Trends in Analytical Psychology*.
University Books, Inc., Hyde Park, New York, from Francis Legge, *Forerunners and Rivals of Christianity;* A. E. Waite (Ed.), *The Works of Thomas Vaughn*.
University of Nebraska Press, Lincoln, Nebraska, from John G. Neihardt, *Black Elk Speaks*.
The Viking Press, Inc., New York, from Jean Doresse, *The Secret Books of the Egyptian Gnostics*, copyright 1960 by Hollis & Carter, Ltd.

John M. Watkins, London, from G. R. S. Mead, *Fragments of a Faith Forgotten*.

And most particularly I wish to express my gratitude to the Princeton University Press for permission to quote liberally from the *Collected Works of C. G. Jung;* excerpts from Gerhard Adler, *The Living Symbol*, from M. Esther Harding, *Psychic Energy: Its Source and Its Transformation,* and from Erich Neumann, *The Great Mother* and *The Origins and History of Consciousness.*

EDWARD F. EDINGER

PREFACE

It is only beginning to dawn on the educated world, what a magnificent synthesis of human knowledge has been achieved by C. G. Jung. Starting as a psychiatrist and psychotherapist he discovered in his patients and in himself the *reality of the psyche* and the phenomenology of its manifestations at a depth never before observed systematically. As a result of this experience, he could then recognize the same phenomenology expressed in the culture-products of mankind—myth, religion, philosophy, art and literature. He has penetrated to the root source of all religion and culture and thus has discovered the basis for a new organic syncretism of human knowledge and experience. The new viewpoint thus achieved, is so comprehensive and all-embracing that, once grasped, it cannot fail to have revolutionary consequences for man's view of himself and the world.

Pronouncements are not sufficient to convey new levels of consciousness. The realization of the "reality of the psyche" which makes this new world-view visible, can only be achieved by one individual at a time working laboriously on his own personal development. This individual opus is called by Jung *individuation*—a process in which the ego becomes increasingly aware of its origin from and dependence upon the archetypal psyche. This book is about the process of individuation, its stages, its vicissitudes and its ultimate aim. I hope it will be a small contribution toward a goal that Jung's work has made eventually certain, namely, the reconciliation of science and religion.

*Man's consciousness was created to the end that it may (1) recognize its descent from a higher unity; (2) pay due and careful regard to this source; (3) execute its commands intelligently and responsibly; and (4) therby afford the psyche as a whole the optimum degree of life and development.**

* Jung's psychological paraphrase of a statement by Ignatius Loyola. Jung, C. G., *Aion*, Vol. 9 II, Collected Works, Princeton, N.J., Princeton University Press, (henceforth C.W.), par. 253.

Part I

INDIVIDUATION AND THE STAGES OF DEVELOPMENT

And if it is true that we acquired our knowledge before our birth, and lost it at the moment of birth, but afterward, by the exercise of our senses upon sensible objects, recover the knowledge which we had once before, I suppose that what we call learning will be the recovery of our own knowledge . . .

PLATO °

° *Phaedo*, translated by Hugh Tredennick, Collected Dialogues, Princeton, N.J., Princeton University Press, Bollingen Series LXII, 1961.

CHAPTER ONE

The Inflated Ego

The sun will not overstep his measures; if he does, the Erinyes, the handmaids of Justice, will find him out.

—HERACLITUS [1]

[handwritten: Major Problem: Which genetic structure goes with which archetype.]

1. EGO AND SELF

Jung's most basic and far-reaching discovery is the collective unconscious or archetypal psyche. Through his researches, we now know that the individual psyche is not just a product of personal experience. It also has a pre-personal or transpersonal dimension which is manifested in universal patterns and images such as are found in all the world's religions and mythologies.[2] It was Jung's further discovery that the archetypal psyche has a structuring or ordering principle which unifies the various archetypal contents. This is the central archetype or archetype of wholeness which Jung has termed the Self.

The Self is the ordering and unifying center of the total psyche (conscious and unconscious) just as the ego is the center of the conscious personality. Or, put in other words, the ego is the seat of *subjective* identity while the Self is the seat of *objective* identity. The Self is thus the supreme psychic authority and subordinates the ego to it. The Self is most simply described as the inner empirical deity and is identical with the *imago Dei*. Jung has demon-

[1] Burnet, John, *Early Greek Philosophy*, New York, Meridian Books, p. 135.
[2] Jung, C. G., *Archetypes and the Collective Unconscious*, C.W., Vol. 9, i. par. 1-147.

strated that the Self has a characteristic phenomenology. It is expressed by certain typical symbolic images called mandalas. All images that emphasize a circle with a center and usually with the additional feature of a square, a cross, or some other representation of quaternity, fall into this category.

There are also a number of other associated themes and images that refer to the Self. Such themes as wholeness, totality, the union of opposites, the central generative point, the world navel, the axis of the universe, the creative point where God and man meet, the point where transpersonal energies flow into personal life, eternity as opposed to the temporal flux, incorruptibility, the inorganic united paradoxically with the organic, protective structures capable of bringing order out of chaos, the transformation of energy, the elixir of life—all refer to the Self, the central source of life energy, the fountain of our being which is most simply described as God. Indeed, the richest sources for the phenomenological study of the Self are in the innumerable representations that man has made of the deity.[3]

Since there are two autonomous centers of psychic being, the relation between the two centers becomes vitally important. The ego's relation to the Self is a highly problematic one and corresponds very closely to man's relation to his Creator as depicted in religious myth. Indeed the myth can be seen as a symbolic expression of the ego-Self relationship. Many of the vicissitudes of psychological development can be understood in terms of the changing relation between ego and Self at various stages of psychic growth. It is this progressive evolution of the ego-Self relation which I propose to examine.

Jung originally described the phenomenology of the Self as it occurs in the individuation process during the second half of life. More recently we have begun to consider the role of the Self in the early years of life. Neumann, on the basis of mythological and ethnographical material, has depicted symbolically the original psychic state prior to the birth of ego consciousness as the *uroborus*, using the circular image of the tail-eater to represent the primordial Self, the original mandala-state of totality out of which the individual ego is born.[4] Fordham, on the basis of clinical observations

---

[3] For a further discussion of the Self as it appears in mandala symbolism, see Jung's essay "Concerning Mandala Symbolism" in *The Archetypes and the Collective Unconscious*, C. W., Vol. 9, i, Par. 627 ff.

[4] Neumann, Erich, *The Origins and History of Consciousness*, Bollingen Series XLII, Princeton University Press, 1954.

of infants and children, has also postulated the Self as the original totality prior to the ego.[5]

It is generally accepted among analytical psychologists that the task of the first half of life involves ego development with progressive separation between ego and Self; whereas the second half of life requires a surrender or at least a relativization of the ego as it experiences and relates to the Self. The current working formula therefore is, first half of life: ego-Self separation; second half of life: ego-Self reunion. This formula, although perhaps true as a broad generality, neglects many empirical observations made in child psychology and in the psychotherapy of adults. According to these observations, a more nearly correct formula would be a circular one, which could be diagrammed thus:

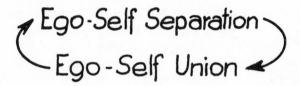

The process of alternation between ego-Self union and ego-Self separation seems to occur repeatedly throughout the life of the individual both in childhood and in maturity. Indeed, this cyclic (or better, spiral) formula seems to express the basic process of psychological development from birth to death.

According to this view the relation between the ego and Self at different stages of development could be represented by the following diagrams:

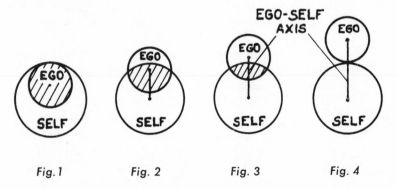

Fig. 1   Fig. 2   Fig. 3   Fig. 4

[5] Fordham, Michael, *New Developments in Analytical Psychology*, London, Routledge & Kegan Paul, 1957.

These diagrams represent progressive stages of ego-Self separation appearing in the course of psychological development. The
shaded ego areas designate the residual ego-Self identity. The line
connecting ego-center with Self-center represents the ego-Self
axis—the vital connecting link between ego and Self that ensures
the integrity of the ego. It should be understood that these diagrams
were designed to illustrate a particular point and are thus inac-
curate in other respects. For example, we generally define the Self
as the totality of the psyche, which would necessarily include the
ego. According to these diagrams, and to the method of this
presentation, it would seem as though ego and Self became two
separate entities, the ego being the smaller lump and the Self the
larger lump of the totality. This difficulty is inherent in the subject matter. If we speak rationally, we must inevitably make a distinction between ego and Self which contradicts our definition of
Self. The fact is, the conception of the Self is a paradox. It is simultaneously the center and the circumference of the circle of totality.
Considering ego and Self as two separate entities is merely a necessary rational device for discussing these things.

Figure 1 corresponds to Neumann's original uroboric state. Nothing exists but the Self-mandala. The ego germ is present only as a
potentiality. Ego and Self are one, which means that there is no
ego. This is the total state of primary ego-Self identity.

Figure 2 shows an emerging ego which is beginning to separate
from the Self but which still has its center and greater area in
primary identity with the Self.

Figure 3 presents a more advanced stage of development; however, a residual ego-Self identity still remains. The ego-Self axis,
which in the first two diagrams was completely unconscious and
therefore indistinguishable from ego-Self identity, has now become
partly conscious.

Figure 4 is an ideal theoretical limit which probably does not
exist in actuality. It represents a total separation of ego and Self
and a complete consciousness of the ego-Self axis.

These diagrams are designed to illustrate the thesis that psychological development is characterized by two processes occurring
simultaneously, namely, progressive ego-Self separation and also
increasing emergence of the ego-Self axis into consciousness. If this
is a correct representation of the facts, it means that ego-Self separation and growing consciousness of the ego as dependent on the
Self are actually two aspects of a single emergent process continuous from birth to death. On the other hand, our diagrams also

demonstrate the general validity of assigning awareness of the relativity of the ego to the second half of life. If we take *Figure 3* to correspond to middle age, we see that only at this stage has the upper portion of the ego-Self axis begun to emerge into consciousness.

The process by which these developmental stages unfold is an alternating cycle which is represented in the diagram (*Figure 5*, p. 41). As this cycle repeats itself again and again throughout psychic development it brings about a progressive differentiation of the ego and the Self. In the early phases, representing approximately the first half of life, the cycle is experienced as an alternation between two states of being, namely, inflation and alienation. Later a third state appears when the ego-Self axis reaches consciousness (*Figure 3*) which is characterized by a conscious dialectic relationship between ego and Self. This state is individuation. In this chapter we shall consider the first stage, inflation.

2. INFLATION AND ORIGINAL WHOLENESS

The dictionary definition of inflation is: "Blown up, distended with air, unrealistically large and unrealistically important, beyond the limits of one's proper size; hence, to be vain, pompous, proud, presumptuous." [6] I use the term inflation to describe the attitude and the state which accompanies the identification of the ego with the Self. It is a state in which something small (the ego) has arrogated to itself the qualities of something larger (the Self) and hence is blown up beyond the limits of its proper size.

We are born in a state of inflation. In earliest infancy, no ego or consciousness exists. All is in the unconscious. The latent ego is in complete identification with the Self. The Self is born, but the ego is made; and in the beginning all is Self. This state is described by Neumann as the uroborus (the tail-eating serpent). Since the Self is the center and totality of being, the ego totally identified with the Self experiences itself as a deity. We can put it in these terms retrospectively although, of course, the infant does not think in this way. He cannot yet think at all, but his total being and experience are ordered around the *a priori* assumption of deity. This is the original state of unconscious wholeness and perfection which is responsible for the nostalgia we all have toward our origins, both personal and historical.

[6] *Webster's New International Dictionary,* Second edition.

Many myths depict the original state of man as a state of round-ness, wholeness, perfection, or paradise. For instance, there is the Greek myth recorded by Hesiod of the four ages of man. The first, original age was the golden age, a paradise. The second was the silver age, a matriachal period where men obeyed the mothers. The third age was bronze, a period of wars. And the fourth age was the iron age, the period at which he was writing which was utterly degenerate. About the golden, paradise age, Hesiod says:

> (The golden race of men) lived like gods without sorrow of heart remote and free from toil and grief . . . They had all good things; for the fruitful earth unforced bore them fruit abundantly and without stint. They dwelt in ease and peace upon their lands with many good things, rich in flocks and loved by the blessed gods.[7]

In the paradise age, the people are in union with the gods. This represents the state of the ego that is as yet unborn, not yet separated from the womb of the unconscious and hence still par-taking of the divine fulness and totality.

Another example is the Platonic myth of original man. According to this myth, the original man was round, in the shape of a man-dala. In the *Symposium* Plato says:

> The primeval man was round, his back and sides forming a circle . . . Terrible was their might and strength, and the thoughts of their hearts were great, and they made an attack upon the gods . . . and would have laid hands upon the gods . . . the gods could not suffer their insolence to go unrestrained.[8]

Here the inflated, arrogant attitude is particularly evident. Being round in the initial period of existence is equivalent to assuming oneself to be total and complete and hence a god that can do all things. There is an interesting parallel between the myth of the original round man and Rhoda Kellog's studies of pre-school art.[9] She has observed that the mandala or circle image seems to be the predominant one in young children who are first learning how to draw. Initially a two-year-old with pencil or crayon just scribbles, but soon he seems to be attracted by the intersection of lines and

---

[7] Hesiod, "Works and Days," *The Homeric Hymns and Homerica*, translated by Hugh G. Evelyn-White, Loeb Classical Library, Cambridge, Harvard University Press, 1959, p. 11.

[8] Plato, *Symposium*, Dialogues of Plato, Jowett, B., Trans., New York, Random House, 1937. Sections 189, 190.

[9] Kellog, Rhoda, *Analyzing Children's Art*, Palo Alto, Calif., National Press Books, 1969, 1970.

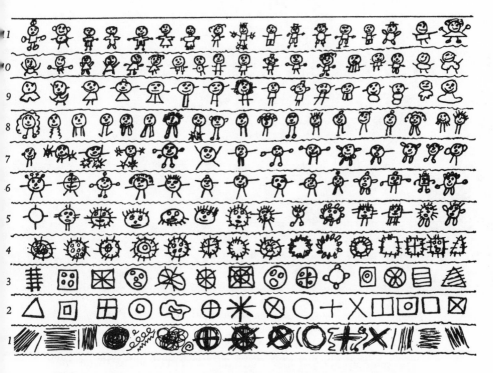

Picture 1. The sequence of Gestalts from bottom to top represent the probable evolution of human figures in the drawings of young children.

begins to make crosses. Then the cross is enclosed by a circle and we have the basic pattern of the mandala. As the child attempts to do human figures, they first emerge as circles, contrary to all visual experience, with the arms and legs being represented only as ray-like extensions of the circle (*Picture 1*). These studies provide clear empirical data indicating that the young child experiences the human being as a round, mandala-like structure and verify in an impressive way the psychological truth of Plato's myth of the original round man. Child therapists also find the mandala an operative, healing image in young children (*Picture 2*). All of this indicates that, symbolically speaking, the human psyche was originally round, whole, complete; in a state of oneness and self-sufficiency that is equivalent to deity itself.

Picture 2. This painting by a seven-year-old girl during psychotherapy marks reestablishment of psychic stability.

The same archetypal idea that connects childhood with nearness to deity is presented in Wordsworth's "Ode on Intimations of Immortality":

> Our Birth is but a sleep and a forgetting:
> The Soul that rises with us, our life's Star,
> Hath had elsewhere its setting,
> And cometh from afar:
> Not in entire forgetfulness,
> And not in utter nakedness,
> But trailing clouds of glory do we come
> From God, who is our home:
> Heaven lies about us in our infancy! [10]

From the standpoint of later years, the close connection of the child's ego with divinity is a state of inflation. Many subsequent psychological difficulties are due to residues of that identification with deity. Consider, for instance, the psychology of the child in

[10] Wordsworth, W., *Poetical Works*, London, Oxford University Press, 1961, p. 460.

the first five years or so. On one hand it is a time of great freshness of perception and response; the child is in immediate contact with the archetypal realities of life. It is in the stage of original poetry; magnificent and terrifying transpersonal powers are lurking in every commonplace event. But on the other hand the child can be an egotistic little beast, full of cruelty and greed. Freud described the state of childhood as polymorphous perversion. This is a brutal description but it is at least partially true. Childhood is innocent but it is also irresponsible. Hence, it has all the ambiguities of being firmly connected with the archetypal psyche and its extrapersonal energy, and at the same time being unconsciously identified with it and unrealistically related to it.

Children share with primitive man the identification of ego with the archetypal psyche and ego with outer world. With primitives, inner and outer are not at all distinguished. For the civilized mind, primitives are most attractively related to nature and in tune with the life process; but they are also savages and fall into the same mistakes of inflation as do children. Modern man, alienated from the source of life meaning, finds the image of the primitive an object of yearning. This accounts for the appeal of Rousseau's concept of the "noble savage" and other more recent works which express the civilized mind's nostalgia for its lost mystical communion with nature. This is one side, but there is also the negative side. The real life of the primitive is dirty, degrading and obsessed with terror. We would not want that reality for a moment. It is the symbolical primitive for which we yearn.

When one looks back on his psychological origin, it has a twofold connotation: first, it is seen as a condition of paradise, wholeness, a state of being at one with nature and the gods, and infinitely desirable; but secondly, by our conscious human standards, which are related to time and space reality, it is an inflated state, a condition of irresponsibility, unregenerate lust, arrogance and crude desirousness. The basic problem for the adult is how to achieve the union with nature and the gods, with which the child starts, without bringing about the inflation of identification.

The same question applies to the problems of child-rearing. How can we successfully remove the child from his inflated state and give him a realistic and responsible notion of his relation to the world, while at the same time maintaining that living link with the archetypal psyche which is needed in order to make his personality strong and resilient? The problem is to maintain the integrity of the ego-Self axis while dissolving the ego's identification with the Self. On this question rest all the disputes of permissiveness versus discipline in child rearing.

Permissiveness emphasizes acceptance and encouragement of the child's spontaneity and nourishes his contact with the source of life energy with which he is born. But it also maintains and encourages the inflation of the child, which is unrealistic to the demands of outer life. Discipline, on the other hand, emphasizes strict limits of behavior, encourages dissolution of the ego-Self identity and treats the inflation quite successfully; but at the same time it tends to damage the vital, necessary connection between the growing ego and its roots in the unconscious. There is no choice between these —they are a pair of opposites, and must operate together.

The child experiences himself quite literally as the center of the universe. The mother at first answers that demand; hence, the initial relationship tends to encourage the child's feeling that its wish is the world's command, and it is absolutely necessary that this be so. If the constant and total commitment of the mother to the child's need is not experienced, the child cannot develop psychologically. However, before long, the world necessarily begins to reject the infant's demands. At this, the original inflation begins to dissolve, being untenable in the face of experience. But also, alienation begins; the ego-Self axis is damaged. A kind of unhealing psychic wound is created in the process of learning he is not the deity he thought he was. He is exiled from paradise, and permanent wounding and separation occur.

Repeated experiences of alienation continue progressively right into adult life. One is constantly encountering a two-fold process. On the one hand we are exposed to the reality encounters which life provides, and which are constantly contradicting unconscious ego assumptions. This is how the ego grows and separates from its unconscious identity with the Self. At the same time we must have recurring reunion between ego and Self in order to maintain the integrity of the total personality, otherwise there is a very real danger that as ego is separated from Self the vital connecting link between them will be damaged. If this happens to a serious extent we are alienated from the depths of ourselves and the ground is prepared for psychological illness.

The original state of affairs—experiencing oneself as the center of the universe—can persist long past childhood. For instance, I recall a young man who thought quite naively: "The world is my picturebook." All the things he encountered he thought were put there for his purposes—for his amusement or his instruction. He quite literally considered the world to be his oyster. External experiences had no inherent reality or meaning except as they related to him. Another patient had the conviction that when he died the world would come to an end! In the state of mind that generates such an idea, identification with the Self is also identification with the world. Self and world are coextensive. This way of experiencing things does have a certain truth, a genuine validity; but it is a viewpoint which is absolutely poison in the early phases of development when the ego is trying to emerge from the original wholeness. Much later in life, the realization that there is a continuity between the inner and outer worlds can have a healing effect. Here is one more example of the *Mercurius* of the alchemists who may be the panacea to some and poison to others.

Many psychoses illustrate the identification of the ego with the Self as the center of the universe, or the supreme principle. For instance the common delusion among the insane that one is Christ or Napoleon is best explained as a regression to the original infantile state where the ego is identified with the Self. Ideas of reference are also symptoms of extreme ego-Self identity. In such cases the individual imagines that certain objective events have a hidden relationship to himself. If he is paranoid the delusion will be of a persecuting nature. For example, I remember a patient who saw men fixing the wires on a telephone pole outside her apartment window. She interpreted this as evidence that a wire tapping device was being installed to eavesdrop on her telephone calls and thus get evidence against her. Another patient thought that the news commentator on television was conveying a private message to him. Such delusions derive from a state of ego-Self identity which assumes that oneself is the center of the universe and hence attaches private significance to outer events which are in fact totally indifferent to one's existence.[11]

A common example of the inflated state of ego-Self identity is provided by what H. G. Baynes has called, "the provisional life." Baynes describes the state as follows:

> (The provisional life) denotes an attitude that is innocent of responsibility towards the circumstantial facts of reality as though these facts are being provided for, either by the parents, or the state, or at least by Providence . . . (It is) a state of childish irresponsibility and dependence.[12]

[11] For further psychotic manifestations of ego-Self identity see Perry, John Weir, *The Self in Psychotic Process*, Berkeley and Los Angeles, University of California Press, 1953.

[12] Baynes, H. G., "The Provisional Life" in *Analytical Psychology and the English Mind*, London, Methuen and Co. Ltd., 1950, p. 61.

M.-L. Von Franz describes the same condition as an identification with the *puer aeternus* image. For such a person, what he is doing:

> . . . is *not yet* what is really wanted, and there is always the fantasy that sometime in the future the real thing will come about. If this attitude is prolonged, it means a constant inner refusal to commit oneself to the moment. With this there is often, to a smaller or greater extent, a saviour complex, or a Messiah complex, with the secret thought that one day one will be able to save the world; the last word in philosophy, or religion, or politics, or art, or something else, will be found. This can go so far as to be a typical pathological megalomania, or there may be minor traces of it in the idea that one's time "has not yet come." The one thing dreaded throughout by such a type of man is to be bound to anything whatever. There is a terrific fear of being pinned down, of entering space and time completely, and of being the one human being that one is.[13]

The psychotherapist frequently sees cases of this sort. Such a person considers himself as a most promising individual. He is full of talents and potentialities. One of his complaints is often that his capacities and interests are too wide-ranging. He is cursed with a plethora of riches. He could do anything but can't decide on one thing in particular. The problem is that he is all promises and no fulfillment. In order to make a real accomplishment he must sacrifice a number of other potentialities. He must give up his identification with original unconscious wholeness and voluntarily accept being a real fragment instead of an unreal whole. To be something in reality he must give up being everything *in potentia*. The *puer aeternus* archetype is one of the images of the Self, but to be identified with it means that one never brings any reality to birth.[14]

There are numerous lesser examples of inflation, which we might call the inflation of every day life. We can identify a state of inflation whenever we see someone (including ourselves) living out an attribute of deity, i.e., whenever one is transcending proper human limits. Spells of anger are examples of inflated states. The attempt to force and coerce one's environment is the predominant motivation in anger. It is a kind of Yahweh complex. The urge to vengeance is also identification with deity. At such times one

[13] Von Franz, M.-L., *The Problem of the Puer Aeternus,* New York, Spring Publications, Analytical Psychology Club of New York, 1970, p. 2.

[14] A literary example of a *puer aeternus* is to be found in Henry James' novel *The Beast in the Jungle,* See: James, Henry, *Selected Fiction,* Everyman's Library, New York, E. P. Dutton & Co., 1953.

might recall the injunction, " 'Vengeance is mine,' saith the Lord," i.e., not yours. The whole body of Greek tragedy depicts the fatal consequences when man takes the vengeance of God into his own hands.

Power motivation of all kinds is symptomatic of inflation. Whenever one operates out of a power motive omnipotence is implied. But omnipotence is an attribute only of God. Intellectual rigidity which attempts to equate its own private truth or opinion with universal truth is also inflation. It is the assumption of omniscience. Lust and all operations of the pure pleasure principle are likewise inflation. Any desire that considers its own fulfillment the central value transcends the reality limits of the ego and hence is assuming attributes of the transpersonal powers.

Practically all of us, deep down, have a residue of inflation that is manifested as an illusion of immortality. There is scarcely anyone that is thoroughly and totally disidentified from this aspect of inflation. Hence, when one has a close call with death, it is often a very awakening experience. There suddenly comes a realization of how precious time is just because it is limited. Such an experience not uncommonly gives a whole new orientation to life, making one more productive and more humanly related. It can initiate a new leap forward in one's development, because an area of ego-Self identity has been dissolved, releasing a new quantity of psychic energy for consciousness.

There is also negative inflation. This can be described as identification with the divine victim—an excessive, unbounded sense of guilt and suffering. We see this in cases of melancholia which express the feeling that "no one in the world is as guilty as I am." This is just too much guilt. In fact taking on oneself too much of anything is indicative of inflation because it transcends proper human limits. Too much humility as well as too much arrogance, too much love and altruism as well as too much power striving and selfishness, are all symptoms of inflation.

States of animus and anima identification can also be seen as inflation. Arbitrary pronouncements of the animus are a deity talking, and so are the sullen resentments of the anima-possessed man who says in effect, "Be what I tell you to be, or I will withdraw from you; and without my acceptance you will die."

There is a whole philosophical system based on the state of ego-Self identity. This system sees everything in the world as deriving from and relating to the individual ego. It is called solipsism from *solus ipse*, myself alone. F. H. Bradley presents the viewpoint of solipsism in these words:

I cannot transcend experience and experience is *my* experience. From this it follows that nothing beyond myself exists; for what is experienced is its (the Self's) states.[15]

Schiller defines solipsism rather more colorfully "as the doctrine that all existence is experience and that there is only one experient. The solipsist thinks that *he is the one!*" [16]

3. ADAM AND PROMETHEUS

What follows the state of original inflation is presented vividly in mythology. An excellent example is the Garden of Eden myth which, significantly is called the *fall* of man. About this myth Jung writes:

> There is deep doctrine in the legend of the Fall; it is the expression of a dim presentiment that the emancipation of ego consciousness was a Luciferian deed. Man's whole history consists from the very beginning in a conflict between his feeling of inferiority and his arrogance.[17]

According to the account in Genesis, God put man in the garden of Eden saying: "You may freely eat of every tree in the garden; but of the tree of the knowledge of good and evil you shall not eat, for in the day that you eat of it you shall die." Then follows the creation of Eve from Adam's rib and Eve's temptation by the serpent who told her "You will not die. For God knows that when you eat of it your eyes will be opened, and you will be like God, knowing good and evil." So Adam and Eve ate the fruit. "Then the eyes of both were opened and they knew that they were naked; and they sewed fig leaves together and made themselves aprons." God discovered their disobedience and put the curse upon them following which are these significant words. "Then the Lord God said, 'Behold, the man has become like one of us, knowing good and evil; and now, lest he put forth his hand and take also of the tree of life, and eat, and live for ever'—therefore the Lord God sent him forth from the garden of Eden to till the ground from which he was taken. He drove out the man; and at the east of the garden of Eden he placed the cherubim, and a flaming sword

---

[15] Bradley, F. H., *Appearance and Reality*, London, Oxford University Press, 1966, p. 218.

[16] *Encyclopaedia Britannica*, 1955, xx, p. 951.

[17] Jung, C. G., *The Archetypes and the Collective Unconscious*, C. W., Vol. 9 i. par. 420 ff.

Plate 1
THE GARDEN OF EDEN AS A CIRCLE
From *Très Riches Heures de Jean, Duc de Berry*

which turned every way, to guard the way to the tree of life.

This is the myth which stands at the beginning of the Hebr branch of our cultural tradition and it is rich in psychologic meaning. The Garden of Eden is comparable to the Greek myın of the golden age and Plato's original round man. The Garden of Eden has certain features of a mandala with four rivers flowing from it and the tree of life in its center (*Plate 1*). The mandala-garden is an image of the Self, in this case representing the ego's original oneness with nature and deity. It is the initial, unconscious, animal state of being at one with one's Self. It is paradisal because consciousness has not yet appeared and hence there is no conflict. The ego is contained in the womb of the Self (*Picture 3*).

Picture 3. PARADISE AS A VESSEL from an Italian manuscript of the XV Century.

Another feature indicating original wholeness is the creation of Eve out of Adam. Clearly, Adam was originally hermaphroditic, otherwise a woman could not have been made from him. It is likely that we have here vestiges of an earlier myth in which the original man was definitely hermaphroditic. Undoubtedly this earlier myth was modified by the one-sided patriarchal attitude of

[18] Gen. 2-3, Revised Standard Version.

the Hebrews which depreciated the feminine component of the psyche, reducing it to no more than a rib of Adam. Adam's separation into masculine and feminine components is a process which is parallel and equivalent to his separation from the paradise garden. In any case the effect is that man becomes separated and alienated from his original wholeness.

The drama of temptation and fall begins when the original state of passive inflation turns into the active inflation of a specific deed. The serpent's whole approach and appeal is expressed in inflationary terms—when you eat of this fruit, your eyes will be opened and *you will be like God.* So the fruit of the tree is eaten and the inevitable consequences unfold. It all begins because Adam and Eve dare to act on their desire to be like God.

The myth depicts the birth of consciousness as a crime which alienates man from God and from his original preconscious wholeness. The fruit is clearly symbolical of consciousness. It is the fruit of the tree of the knowledge of good and evil, which means that it brings awareness of the opposites, the specific feature of consciousness. Thus, according to this myth and the theological doctrines that rest on it, consciousness is the original sin, the original *hybris,* and the root cause of all evil in human nature. However, others have understood it differently. The Ophites, a Gnostic sect, worshipped the serpent. They had essentially the same view as modern psychology. To them the serpent represented the spiritual principle symbolizing redemption from bondage to the demiurge that created the Garden of Eden and would keep man in ignorance. The serpent was considered good and Yahweh bad. Psychologically the serpent is the principle of *gnosis,* knowledge or emerging consciousness. The serpent's temptation represents the urge to self-realization in man and symbolizes the principle of individuation. Some Gnostic sects even identified the serpent in the Garden of Eden with Christ.

Eating the forbidden fruit marks the transition from the eternal state of unconscious oneness with the Self (the mindless, animal state) to a real, conscious life in space and time. In short, the myth symbolizes the birth of the ego. The effect of this birth process is to alienate the ego from its origins. It now moves into a world of suffering, conflict and uncertainty. No wonder we are reluctant to take the step to greater consciousness (*Picture 4*).

Another feature of the "fall" into consciousness is that Adam and Eve became aware of their nakedness. Sexuality and the instincts in general suddenly become taboo and objects of shame.

Picture 4.
THE EXPULSION OF
ADAM AND EVE
by Massaccio.

Consciousness as a spiritual principle has created a counterpole to natural, instinctive animal function. Duality, dissociation and repression have been born in the human psyche simultaneously with the birth of consciousness. This means simply that consciousness in order to exist in its own right must, initially at least, be antagonistic to the unconscious. This insight teaches us that all utopian psychological theories which assume that the human personality can be whole and healthy if only it is not subject to sexual and instinctual repressions in childhood are wrong. The innate and necessary stages of psychic development require a polarization of the opposites, conscious vs unconscious, spirit vs. nature.

But our survey of the myth of the fall is not complete if we leave it with the image of Adam and Eve sadly taking up their hard life in the world of reality, earning their bread by the sweat of their brow and bringing forth children in pain. There were *two* trees in the garden of Eden, not only the tree of knowledge of good and evil, but also the tree of life. And indeed Yahweh demonstrated some anxiety that man might discover the second tree and partake of its blessings. What can this mean? There is an interesting legend concerning the tree of life reported in Ginsberg's *Legends of the Jews* which offers some insight on the question:

> In paradise stands the tree of life and the tree of knowledge, the latter forming a hedge about the former. Only he who has cleared a path for himself through the tree of knowledge can come close to the tree of life which is so huge that it would take a man five hundred years to traverse a distance equal to the diameter of the trunk, and no less vast is the space shaded by its crown of branches. From beneath flows forth the water that irrigates the whole earth, parting thence into four streams, the Ganges, the Nile, the Tigris, and the Euphrates.[19]

Legends growing up around a myth often amplify and elaborate aspects left out in the original story, as though the collective psyche needed to round out the picture and clarify the full symbolic meaning. Such, I think, is the case with the legend quoted. The Biblical account gives a quite ambiguous picture concerning the relation between the tree of knowledge and the tree of life. This legend presents a much clearer and satisfying image. The legend presents the tree of life as an *omphalos* or world navel, analogous to the

---

[19] Ginsberg, G., *Legends of the Jews,* abridged version, *Legends of the Bible.* New York, Simon and Schuster, 1956, p. 37.

world tree Yggdrasil. The Bible tells us that the fruit of the tree
of life conveys immortality. Adam and Eve were immortal before
the fall, but they were also unconscious. If they can eat the fruit
of the tree of life after the fall, they have achieved both consciousness and immortality. Yahweh is opposed to any such infringement
on his realm and sets up the cherubim with the flaming sword as
an obstacle. However the Jewish legend quoted gives us some
hint as to how the tree of life can be found. It can be reached
by clearing a path through the hedge-like tree of the knowledge
of good and evil. That is, one must repeatedly accept the temptation
of the serpent, repeatedly eat the fruit of knowledge and in that
way eat his way through to the tree of life. In other words, the recovery of our lost wholeness can only be achieved by tasting and
assimilating the fruits of consciousness to the full.

The myth of the fall expresses a pattern and a process not just
of the original birth of consciousness out of the unconscious, but
also of the process that one goes through in one form or another
with every new increment of consciousness. I believe with the
Ophites that it is onesided to depict Adam and Eve just as shameful orchard thieves. Their action could equally be described as an
heroic one. They sacrifice the passive comfort of obedience for
greater consciousness. The serpent does indeed prove to be a
benefactor in the long run if we grant consciousness a greater
value than comfort.

We see fragments of this theme of the original fall of man in
a good many dreams in the course of analytic treatment. They are
very common at times when new conscious insights are being
born. The theme of encountering or being bitten by a snake is common in dreams. The latter generally has the same meaning that
the succumbing to the temptation of the serpent in the Garden
of Eden had for Adam and Eve; namely, that an old state of affairs
is being lost and a new conscious insight is being born. This is
often experienced as something alien and dangerous; hence it is
never a pleasant dream. But at the same time such a bite usually
initiates a whole new attitude and orientation. It is generally a
transition dream of considerable importance. Also, dreams of
having committed a crime may have the same meaning as the
original crime of stealing the fruit. What is a crime at one stage
of psychological development is lawful at another and one cannot
reach a new stage of psychological development without daring
to challenge the code of the old stage. Hence, every new step is
experienced as a crime and is accompanied by guilt, because the

old standards, the old way of being, have not yet been transcended. So the first step carries the feeling of being a criminal. Dreams of being given fruit to eat—apples, cherries, tomatoes—may have the same meaning. They are allusions to the theme of eating the forbidden fruit and represent an introduction to some new area of conscious awareness with much the same consequences as the original eating of the fruit.

The following is an example of a modern dream that strikes the old theme of the temptation in the Garden of Eden. It was dreamt by a man in his forties. He first came to see me with the complaint of "writer's block" and anxiety attacks. He was a talented man filled with creative ideas and inspirations. He could have the most amazing dreams, complete plays down to the last detail of costume and music, exit and entrance; but he could never get himself to do the hard work of putting them down on paper. It seemed as though the dream itself was adequate reality, as though just the fact that he could have such magnificent compositions in fantasy were sufficient reality to relieve him of any sense of obligation to realize them in fact. Such an attitude is an identification with the original unconscious wholeness, the provisional life, which avoids the hard work required to make the potential actual. Although he thought he wanted to write, fantasies were unconsciously considered sufficient reality in themselves. Such a person is afraid to make the commitment required to create something real. He would lose the security of anonymity and expose himself to disapproval. He is afraid to submit himself to judgment by being something definite. This amounts to living in the "Garden of Eden" state and not daring to eat the fruit of consciousness.

Here is his dream: *I am in a setting and atmosphere that reminds me of Kierkegaard. I go into a bookstore looking for a particular book. I find it and buy it. The title is* A Man Among Thorns.

Then the scene changes. My sister has made me an immense, black chocolate cake. It is covered with a thin covering of red icing that looks like red tights. Although chocolate has always been forbidden to me because I'm allergic to it, I eat the cake without bad effects.

Some of the dreamer's associations were the following. He saw Kierkegaard as a troubled figure, a man in conflict between antitheses, particularly the conflict between the aesthetic and religious attitudes. His book *Either/Or* represents the whole problem of opposites. The book title, *Man Among Thorns* reminded the dreamer of Christ and his crown of thorns. About chocolate cake the dreamer said he always considered it poison because it would make him sick. Red icing like "red tights" reminded him of "something the devil might wear."

This dream, although expressed in modern and personal imagery has a close parallel with the ancient myth of Adam's fall from paradise. On the basis of this archetypal parallel we can hypothesize that it represents a potential transition in this man's personal development. The most striking feature of the dream is the eating of the cake. It is black and has a red covering which associates to the devil. Black as the antithesis of white carries the implications of evil and darkness. In the dreamer's case the chocolate cake was considered poison indicating his conscious fear of the unconscious. To eat this poisonous cake is symbolically equivalent to being bitten by a serpent or eating the forbidden fruit. The consequence is the awareness of the opposites (knowing good and evil) and this means being thrown into a state of conscious conflict. With each new increment of consciousness, conflict comes too. That is how a new piece of consciousness announces its presence —by conflict.

Although the dreamer states that he ate the cake without ill effects, the consequences are presented symbolically in the first dream scene. It does not matter that this scene preceded the eating of the cake. Temporal sequence and causality do not apply in dreams. When a dream has several scenes they can usually be best understood as varying ways to describe the same central idea. In other words the stream of images in dreams circumambulates certain nodal centers rather than proceeding in a straight line as does rational thinking. Thus, being in a Kierkegaardian atmosphere and buying a book called "A Man Among Thorns" is only a symbolic variant of the image of eating a poisonous black cake. To eat the cake means to enter the Kierkegaardian experience of conflict and to understand the man among thorns—either Christ who endured the most extreme tension of opposites by being both God and man, or Adam who on being expelled from the garden was obliged to till the ground that brought forth thorns and thistles.

What did this dream mean practically for the dreamer? It led to no sudden insight or change. He was not aware of being different after the dream. But our discussion of it, together with subsequent dreams, did pave the way for a progressive increase in consciousness.

When this patient first entered psychotherapy he had symptoms but no conflict. Gradually the symptoms went away and were replaced by a conscious awareness of conflict within himself. He came to see that he didn't write because part of him didn't want to write. He came to realize that his anxiety was not a meaningless symptom but a danger signal trying to warn him that his prolonged residence in the Garden of Eden might have fatal psychological consequences. As the dream suggested, it was time to eat the fruit of the tree of knowledge of good and evil and accept the inevitable conflicts of being a conscious individual. And this transition is not all pain and suffering. The myth is onesided here. The paradise state, too long persisted in, becomes a prison; and expulsion is then no longer experienced as undesirable but as a release.

In Greek mythology there is a parallel to the Garden of Eden drama. I refer to the myth of Prometheus. In simplified outline it runs as follows:

Prometheus presided over the procedure of dividing the meat of sacrificial victims between gods and men. Previously there had been no need for division because gods and men ate together (ego-Self identity). Prometheus tricked Zeus by offering him only the bones of the animal covered by a layer of enticing fat. For man he reserved all the edible meat. Zeus, angered by this trickery, withheld fire from man. But Prometheus slipped into heaven, stole the fire of the gods, and gave it to mankind. In punishment for this crime, Prometheus was chained to a rock where every day a vulture tore at his liver and every night it was healed again. Punishment was also sent to his brother Epimetheus. Zeus fashioned a woman, Pandora, whom he sent to Epimetheus with a box. From Pandora's box emerged all the ills and sufferings that plague mankind—old age, labor, sickness, vice and passion.

The process of dividing the meat of the sacrificial animal between the gods and men represents the separation of the ego from the archetypal psyche or Self. The ego, to establish itself as an autonomous entity, must appropriate the food (energy) for itself. The stealing of the fire is an analogous image for the same process. Prometheus is the Luciferian figure whose daring initiates ego development at the price of suffering.

Considering Prometheus and Epimetheus as two aspects of the same image we can note many parallels between the myths of Prometheus and the Garden of Eden. Zeus withholds fire. Yahweh withholds the fruit of the tree of knowledge. Both the fire and the fruit symbolize consciousness which leads to a measure of human autonomy and independence from God. Just as Prometheus steals the fire, so Adam and Eve steal the fruit in disobedience to God. In each case a willful act is committed against the reigning authority. This willful act is the grasping for consciousness which is symbolized in each myth as a crime followed by punishment. Prometheus is cursed with an unhealing wound, and Epimetheus is cursed by Pandora and all the contents of her box. The unhealing wound is analogous to the expulsion from the Garden of Eden, which is also a kind of wound. The pain, labor and suffering that Pandora released are parallel to the labor, suffering and death that Adam and Eve met after they left the Garden of Eden.

This all refers to the inevitable consequences of becoming conscious. Pain and suffering and death do exist prior to the birth of consciousness, but if there is no consciousness to experience them, they do not exist psychologically. Distress is nullified if consciousness is not present to realize it. This explains the tremendous nostalgia for the original unconscious state. In that state one is freed from all the suffering that consciousness inevitably brings. The fact that Prometheus' liver is eaten by the vulture during the day and restored at night conveys a significant insight. The day is the time of light, consciousness. The night is darkness, unconsciousness. Each one of us at night returns to that original wholeness out of which we were born. And this is healing. It is as though the wounding influence is not active. This indicates that consciousness itself is the wound-producer. The eternally unhealed wound of Prometheus symbolizes the consequences of the break in the original unconscious wholeness, the alienation from the original unity. It is the constant thorn in the flesh.

These two myths say essentially the same thing because they are expressing the archetypal reality of the psyche and its course of development. The acquisition of consciousness is a crime, an act of *hybris* against the powers-that-be; but it is a necessary crime, leading to a necessary alienation from the natural unconscious state of wholeness. If we are going to hold any loyalty to the development of consciousness, we must consider it a necessary crime. It is better to be conscious than to remain in the animal state. But in order to emerge at all, the ego is obliged to set itself up against the unconscious out of which it came and assert its relative autonomy by an inflated act.

There are several different levels on which we can apply this understanding. On the deepest level it is a crime against the universal powers, the powers of nature, or God. But actually in everyday life it is generally not experienced in such religious categories, but in quite personal ways. On the personal level the act of daring to acquire a new consciousness is experienced as a crime or rebellion against the authorities that exist in one's personal environment, against one's parents, and later against other outer authorities. Any step in individuation is experienced as a crime against the collective, because it challenges the individual's identification with some representative of the collective, whether it be family, party, church, or nation. At the same time each step, since it is truly an inflated act, is not only accompanied by guilt but also runs the very real risk that one will get caught in an inflation that carries the consequences of a fall.

We encounter many people in psychotherapy whose development has been arrested just at the point where the necessary crime needs to be enacted. Some say, "I can't disappoint my parents or my family." The man living with his mother says, "I would like to marry, but that would kill poor old mother." And it might do just that because the symbiotic relationship that may exist can be a literal kind of psychic feeding; if the food is withdrawn the partner may well die! In such a case obligations to the mother are seen as too strong to envisage any other set of standards for living. The sense of responsibility towards one's own individual development has simply not yet been born.

We see the same theme operating at times in the psychotherapeutic relationship. Perhaps a negative or rebellious reaction has emerged towards the analyst. Such a reaction may be accompanied by a great deal of guilt and anxiety, particularly if the analyst is carrying the projection of archetypal authority. To express a negative reaction with genuine affect in these circumstances is felt to be very similar to the crime against the gods. It will seem to be a dangerous act of inflation certain to bring retribution. But at some point unless the forbidden fruit is eaten, unless one dares to steal the fire from the gods, he will remain stuck in a dependent transference and development will not proceed.

4. HYBRIS AND NEMESIS

There are many other myths that depict the state of inflation, for instance the myth of Icarus:

> Daedalus and his son Icarus were imprisoned in Crete. The father made them each a pair of wings, and with these they were able to

escape. But Deadalus warned his son, "Don't fly too high or the sun will melt the wax on your wings and you will fall. Follow me closely. Do not set your own course." But Icarus became so exhilarated by his ability to fly, he forgot the warning and did follow his own course. He went too high, the wax melted, and he fell into the sea.

In this myth the dangerous aspect of inflation is emphasized. Although there are times when an inflated act is necessary to achieve a new level of consciousness, there are other times when it is foolhardy and disastrous. One cannot presume to set his own course safely until he knows what he is doing. Dependence on the superior wisdom of others is often an accurate appraisal of the reality situation. As Nietzsche said, "Many a one hath cast away his final worth when he hath cast away his servitude." [20] I have spoken of a necessary crime of inflation, but it is a real crime and does involve real consequences. If one misjudges the situation he suffers the fate of Icarus.

I think that all dreams of flying have some allusion to the myth of Icarus; this is particularly true of the dreams of flight without any means of mechanical support. When one is off the ground the danger is that he may fall. Abrupt impact with reality, symbolized by the earth, may be dangerously jarring. Dreams or symptom-images of airplanes crashing, falling from high places, phobic fear of heights, etc. all derive from the basic psychic set-up represented by the myth of Icarus.

The following is an example of an Icarus dream. It was dreamt by a young man who was identified with a famous relative. He had borrowed wings constructed by another man and flew with them: *I was with people at the edge of a high cliff. People were diving off into very shallow water below, and I was sure they would be killed. While still in the dream or immediately upon waking I thought immediately of Breughel's painting, the "Fall of Icarus."*

Breughel's "Fall of Icarus" (*Picture 5*) is a painting of the Italian countryside. On the left farmers are plowing and going about their business. On the right is the sea with a few boats. In the lower corner one sees the legs of Icarus as he is disappearing into the water. One of the significant features of the painting is that the fate of Icarus on the right side is completely neglected by the figures on the left side, who are not aware that an archetypal happening is being presented before their eyes. The

[20] Nietzsche, F., "Thus Spake Zarathustra," I, 17, in *The Philosophy of Nietzsche*, New York, Modern Library, Random House, 1942, p. 65.

Picture 5. THE FALL OF ICARUS by Pieter Breughel.

dreamer commented on this aspect of the painting and it suggests that he himself is unconscious of the significance of what is happening to him. He was in the process of a fall from the heights of unreality but this insight dawned on him only later.

Another example of an Icarus dream is the following, dreamed by a woman: *I am travelling along a road and see a man, like Icarus, in the sky. He is holding up a torch. Suddenly his wings catch fire and everything flames up. Fire engines on the ground train their hoses on him and manage to put out the fire, but he falls heavily to his death, still holding up the torch. I see him land near me and am horrified, cry out "Oh God, Oh God!!"*

The dreamer was a victim of frequent, intense, idealistic animus projections. This dream marked the death of such a projection which had lured her into an inflated attitude about herself.

Another myth pertaining to inflation is the myth of Phaeton:

Phaeton was told by his mother that his father was Helios the sun god. In order to prove this to himself, he traveled to the place of the sun and asked Helios, "Are you in fact my father?" Helios assured him that he was and made the mistake of saying, "To prove it I will give you whatever you ask for." Phaeton asked to be permitted to drive the sun chariot across the sky. Immediately Helios regretted his rash promise, but Phaeton insisted and against his better judgment his father gave in. Phaeton drove the sun chariot, but because the task was quite beyond the youth's capacities, he crashed in flaming ruins.

Again the myth tells us that inflation has, as its inevitable consequence, a fall. Phaeton is the prototype of the modern "hot rodder." And perhaps the myth has something to say also to the indulgent father who against his better judgment puts too much power too soon in the hands of his son, whether it be the family car or excessive rights of self-determination, before it is balanced by an equal sense of responsibility.

I recall a patient with a "Phaeton complex." The initial impression he gave was that of a jaunty, cavalier attitude. The rules followed by others did not apply to him. He had had a weak father whom he did not respect, and consistently belittled or ridiculed figures who were in authority over him. He had several dreams of being in high places. In the course of discussing one of these dreams, the therapist told him the myth of Phaeton. For the first time in psychotherapy the patient was profoundly moved. He had never heard the myth before but immediately recognized it as *his* myth. He saw his life depicted in the myth and suddenly realized the archetypal drama which he had been living.

However, all mythical images are ambiguous. We can never be certain in advance whether to interpret them positively or negatively. For instance, here is a positive Phaeton dream dreamt by the same man who had the chocolate cake dream. He had this dream the night before a most significant experience in which for the first time he was able to assert himself effectively against an arbitrary and intimidating authority figure at his place of work. If this dream had happened after the event we might consider that it was "caused" by the outer experience. But since the dream came first, and the courageous encounter second, we are justified in thinking that the dream caused the outer happening, or at least created the psychological attitude that made it possible.

Here is the dream: *I am Phaeton and I have just succeeded in driving the sun chariot across the sky. It is a magnificent scene— brilliant blue sky and white clouds. I have a feeling of intense joy and accomplishment. My very first thought was, "Jung was right about the archetypes after all."*

Here the myth of Phaeton is incorporated into the dream but is changed to suit the dream's purposes. The dreamer Phaeton succeeds where the mythical Phaeton had failed. Obviously the dreamer was taking a step that was not beyond his powers. What he was doing is risky. It does involve some measure of inflation. However, coming after the prior dream, I understand it to refer to a necessary, heroic inflation that would relate the dreamer to a new level of effectiveness within himself, as indeed it did. It is surely evident by now that the whole question of inflation is an ambiguous one. On the one hand it is risky, and on the other hand quite necessary. Which aspect should be emphasized depends on the individual and the particular situation he is in.

Another myth of inflation is the myth of Ixion. Ixion's inflated act was his attempt to seduce Hera. Zeus foiled the attempt by shaping a cloud into a false Hera, with whom Ixion took his pleasure. Zeus surprised him in the act and punished him by binding him to a fiery wheel that revolved endlessly through the sky (*Picture* 6). In this case inflation manifested itself in lust and pleasure seeking. Ixion, representing the inflated ego, attempts to appropriate to itself that which belongs to the supra-

Picture 6. IXION BOUND TO THE WHEEL, Ancient Vase Painting.

personal powers. The attempt is doomed before it starts. The most with which Ixion is able to make contact is only a cloud-Hera, a fantasy. His punishment, being bound to a fiery wheel, represents quite an interesting idea. The wheel is basically a mandala. It connotes the Self and the wholeness pertaining to the Self, but in this case it has been transformed into an instrument of torture. This represents what can happen when the ego's identification with the Self lasts too long. The identification then becomes torture, and the fiery passions of the instincts become a hell-fire binding one to the wheel, until the ego is able to separate from the Self and to see its instinctual energy as a suprapersonal dynamism. So long as the ego considers instinctive energy its personal pleasure, he remains bound to Ixion's fiery wheel.

The Greeks had a tremendous fear of what they called *hybris*. In original usage this term meant wanton violence or passion arising from pride. It is synonymous with one aspect of what I am calling inflation. *Hybris* is the human arrogance that appropriates to man what belongs to the gods. It is the transcending of proper human limits. Gilbert Murray puts it well:

> There are unseen barriers which a man who has *aidos* (reverence) in him does not wish to pass. *Hybris* passes them all. *Hybris* does not see that the poor man or the exile has come from Zeus: *Hybris* is the insolence of irreverence: the brutality of strength. In one form it is a sin of the low and weak, irreverence; the absence of *Aidos* in the presence of something higher. But nearly always it is a sin of the strong and proud. It is born of *Koros*, or satiety—of "being too well off;" it spurns the weak and helpless out of its path, "spurns," as Aeschylus says, "the great Altar of Dike" (Agammenon, 383). And *Hybris* is the typical sin condemned by early Greece. Other sins, except some connected with definite religious taboos, and some derived from words meaning "ugly" or "unfitting," seem nearly all to be forms or derivatives of *Hybris*.[21]

Murray considers *Aidos* and *Nemesis* to be central concepts of the emotional experience of the Greeks. *Aidos* means reverence for the suprapersonal powers and also the feeling of shame when these powers have been transgressed. *Nemesis* is the reaction provoked by a lack of *Aidos*, i.e. *Hybris*.

A good example of the Greek's fear of going beyond reasonable human limits is presented in the story of Polycrates recorded by Herodotus. Polycrates was a tyrant of Samos in the 6th Century

[21] Murray, Gilbert, *The Rise of the Greek Epic*, London, Oxford University Press, 1907, p. 264 f.

B.C. He was an incredibly successful man. Everything he did worked out perfectly for him. His good luck seemed infallible. Herodotus writes:

> The exceeding good fortune of Polycrates did not escape the notice of Amasis (his friend the King of Egypt) who was much disturbed thereat. When therefore his successes continued increasing, Amasis wrote him the following letter and sent it to Samos. "Amasis to Polycrates speaks thus: It is a pleasure to hear of a friend and ally prospering, but your exceeding prosperity does not cause me joy, for as much as I know that the gods are envious. My wish for myself, and for those whom I love, is, to be now successful and now to meet with a check; thus passing through life amid alternate good and ill, rather than with perpetual good fortune. For never yet did I hear tell of anyone succeeding in all his undertakings, who did not meet with calamity at last, and come to utter ruin. Now therefore, give ear to my words, and meet your good luck in this way. Think which of all your treasures you value most and can least bear to part with; take it, whatsoever it be, and throw it away, so that it may be sure never to come anymore into the sight of man. Then if your good fortune be not thenceforth chequered with ill, save yourself from harm by again doing as I have counselled!" [22]

Polycrates took this advice and threw a treasured emerald ring into the sea. However a few days later a fisherman caught so large and beautiful a fish that he thought he could not sell it but must present it as a gift to King Polycrates. When the fish was opened, in its belly lay the emerald ring which the king had thrown away. When Amasis heard of this development it so frightened him that he terminated his friendship with Polycrates fearing he (Amasis) might be involved in the ultimate disaster that was sure to follow such uncanny good fortune. Sure enough, Polycrates eventually died by crucifixion following a successful uprising and rebellion.

The fear of excessive good fortune is deeply ingrained in man. There is an instinctive sense that the gods envy human success. Psychologically this means that the conscious personality may not go too far without taking the unconscious into account. The fear of God's envy is a dim realization that inflation will be checked. Limits do exist in the nature of things and in the nature of the psychic structure itself. Of course, sometimes the fear of

[22] Herodotus, *The Persian Wars*, trans. by George Rawlinson, New York, Modern Library, Random House, 1942, p. 231.

God's envy can be carried to quite excessive extremes. Certain individuals dare not accept any success or any positive happening for fear that it will lead to some obscure punishment. As a rule, this seems to be the result of adverse childhood conditioning; accordingly it needs re-evaluation. But beyond this personal conditioning there is an archetypal reality involved. Everything that goes up must come down. Oscar Wilde once said, "There is only one thing worse than not getting what you want, and that is getting it." Polycrates would be an example of that.

Emerson expressed the same idea. He discusses it in his essay *Compensation* which is a literary exposition of the theory which Jung later developed concerning the compensatory relation between the conscious and the unconscious. Here are a few passages from that essay. Emerson had been describing how every happening for good or ill has its compensation somewhere in the nature of things. He continues:

> A wise man will extend this lesson to all parts of life, and know that it is the part of prudence to face every claimant and pay every just demand on your time, your talents, or your heart. Always pay; for first or last you must pay your entire debt. Persons and events may stand for a time between you and justice, but it is only a postponement. You must pay at last your own debt. If you are wise you will dread a prosperity which only loads you with more . . . for every benefit which you receive, a tax is levied.[23]
>
> The terror of cloudless noon, the emerald of Polycrates, the awe of prosperity, the instinct which leads every generous soul to impose on itself tasks of a noble asceticism and vicarious virtue, are the tremblings of the balance of justice through the heart and mind of man.[24]

We find further expressions of the idea of inflation in the Hebrew and Christian theological concepts of sin. The concept of sin in the Hebrew scriptures apparently grew out of taboo psychology.[25] That which is taboo is considered unclean, but it also has the additional implications of being sacred, holy, and charged with an excess of dangerous energy. Initially, sin was the breach of a taboo, touching something that should not be touched because the tabooed object carried suprapersonal energies. To touch or

[23] *The Writings of Ralph Waldo Emerson,* New York, Modern Library, Random House, 1940, p. 181.
[24] Ibid.
[25] Burrows, Millar, *An Outline of Biblical Theology,* Philadelphia, Westminster Press, 1956, p. 165.

appropriate such an object was a danger to the ego because it was transcending proper human limits. Hence taboo can be seen as a protection against inflation. Later the taboo idea was reformulated in terms of God's will and the inevitability of punishment if His will is transgressed. But the idea of taboo and the fear of inflation still lurks behind the new formulation.

Christianity also practically equates sin with inflation of the ego. The beatitudes, approached psychologically, can be best understood as praise of the non-inflated ego. In Christian theology the concept of sin as inflation is beautifully presented by Augustine. In his *Confessions* he gives a vivid description of the nature of inflation. Recollecting his motivations as a child for stealing fruit from a neighbor's pear tree, he records that he did not want the pears themselves but rather he enjoyed the sin in itself, namely, the feeling of omnipotence. He then goes on to describe the nature of sin as the imitation of deity:

> For so doth pride imitate exaltedness; whereas Thou alone art God exalted over all. Ambition, what seeks it, but honors and glory? Whereas Thou alone art to be honored above all, and glorious forevermore. The cruelty of the great would fain be feared; but who is to be feared but God alone . . . Curiosity makes semblance of a desire of knowledge; whereas Thou supremely knowest all . . . sloth would fain be at rest; but what stable rest besides the Lord? Luxury affects to be called plenty and abundance; but Thou art the fulness never-failing plenteousness of incorruptible pleasures . . . Covetousness would possess many things: and Thou possessest all things. Envy disputes for excellence: what more excellent than Thou? Anger seeks revenge: Who revenges more justly than Thou? . . . Grief pines away for things lost, the delight of its desires; because it would have nothing taken from it, as nothing can from Thee. . . . Thus all pervertedly imitates Thee, who remove far from Thee and lift themselves up against Thee . . . Souls in their very sins seek but a sort of likeness of God.[26]

The same idea of inflation is implicit in the Buddhist notion of *avidya*, "not knowing" or unconsciousness. According to the Buddhist view human suffering is caused by personal craving and desirousness stemming from ignorance of reality. This state of affairs is represented pictorially by the image of man bound to the wheel of life which is turned by the pig, the cock and the

---

[26] *The Confessions of St. Augustine,* translated by Edward B. Pusey, New York, Modern Library, Random House, 1949, p. 31 ff.

Picture 7. WHEEL OF LIFE, painting, Tibet.

snake representing the various forms of concupiscence. (*Picture 7*).
The Indian wheel of life is paralleled by Ixion's revolving wheel
of fire; both signify the suffering which accompanies the ego's
identification with the Self when the former attempts to appropriate
for personal use the transpersonal energies of the latter. The wheel
is the Self, the state of wholeness, but it is a torture wheel so
long as the ego remains unconsciously identified with it.

Various states of inflation due to residual ego-Self identity are commonplaces of psychotherapeutic practice. Grandiose and unrealistic attitudes and assumptions of all kinds emerge as the therapeutic process uncovers the unconscious background. It is to these infantile-omnipotent assumptions that the theories and techniques of Freud and Adler have given almost exclusive attention. The reductive methods of these approaches is valid in dealing with the symptoms of ego-Self identity. Although even here one must never forget the need to maintain the ego-Self axis. The reductive method is experienced as a criticism and depreciation by the patient. And indeed those features are objectively present. An interpretation which reduces a psychic content to its infantile sources is a rejection of its conscious and evident meaning and hence causes the patient to feel belittled and rejected. This method may be necessary to promote ego-Self separation but it is a sharp sword to be used with care. The purpose is to deflate and it is this underlying purpose that is given expression in vernacular speech when the psychiatrist is called a "head shrinker." To those who resent the reductive method even when used judiciously, I would cite the words of Lao-Tzu:

> He who feels punctured
> Must once have been a bubble,
> He who feels unarmed
> Must have carried arms,
> He who feels belittled
> Must have been consequential
> He who feels deprived
> Must have had privilege . . .[27]

[27] Lao-Tzu, *Tao Teh Ching*, Verse 36. Translated by Witter Bynner as *The Way of Life*, New York, The John Day Co., 1944.

CHAPTER TWO

The Alienated Ego

Danger itself fosters the rescuing power.
—HOLDERLIN °

1. THE EGO-SELF AXIS AND THE PSYCHIC LIFE CYCLE

Although the ego begins in a state of inflation due to identification with the Self, this condition cannot persist. Encounters with reality frustrate inflated expectations and bring about an estrangement between ego and Self. This estrangement is symbolized by such images as a fall, an exile, an unhealing wound, a perpetual torture. Obviously, when such images come into play, not only has the ego been chastened, it has been injured. This injury can best be understood as damage to the ego-Self axis, a concept which now requires further discussion.

Clinical observation leads one to the conclusion that the integrity and stability of the ego depend in all stages of development on a living connection with the Self. Fordham [1] gives examples of mandala images in children which emerge as magical protective circles at times when the ego is threatened by disruptive forces. He also cites several occasions with children when the drawing of a circle was associated with the word "I" and which led to some effective action the child had previously been unable to take. A similar occurrence takes place in the psychotherapy of

° *Patmos, Wo aber Gefahr ist, wächst das Nettende auch.*
[1] Fordham, M., "Some Observations on the Self and the Ego in Childhood," in *New Developments in Analytical Psychology*, Routledge and Kegan Paul, London 1957.

adults when the unconscious may produce a mandala image which conveys a sense of calm and containment to a disordered and confused ego. These observations indicate that the Self stands behind the ego and can act as a guarantor of its integrity. Jung expresses the same idea when he says: "The ego stands to the Self as the moved to the mover . . . The Self . . . is an *a priori* existent out of which the ego evolves. It is, so to speak, an unconscious prefiguration of the ego." [2] Thus ego and Self have a close structural and dynamic affinity. The term ego-Self axis has been used by Neumann to designate this vital affinity.[3]

This ego-Self affinity is illustrated mythologically by the Old Testament doctrine that man (ego) was created in God's (the Self's) image. Also pertinent is the primordial name ascribed to Yahweh—"I am that I am." Do not the words "I am" also define the essential nature of the ego? We therefore seem on firm ground when we postulate a basic connection between ego and Self that is of crucial importance for maintaining the function and integrity of the ego. This connection is depicted in the diagrams on page 5 by the line connecting the center of the ego circle with the center of the Self circle and labelled ego-Self axis. The ego-Self axis represents the vital connection between ego and Self that must be relatively intact if the ego is to survive stress and grow. This axis is the gateway or path of communication between the conscious personality and the archetypal psyche. Damage to the ego-Self axis impairs or destroys the connection between conscious and unconscious, leading to alienation of the ego from its origin and foundation.

Before we consider how damage to the ego-Self axis occurs in childhood, a few preliminary remarks are necessary. Every archetypal image carries at least a partial aspect of the Self. In the unconscious there is no separation of different things. Everything merges with everything else. Thus, as long as the individual is unconscious of them, the successive layers we have learned to distinguish, i.e. shadow, animus or anima, and Self, are not separated but merged in one dynamic totality. Behind a shadow or animus problem or a parent problem will lurk the dynamism of the Self. Since the Self is the central archetype, it subordinates all other

[2] Jung, C. G. *Psychology and Religion: West and East*, C. W., Vol. 11, par. 391.

[3] Neumann, E. "Narcissism, Normal Self-Formation, and the Primary Relation to the Mother" in *Spring*, published by the Analytical Psychology Club of New York, 1966, pp. 81 ff. This seminal paper warrants careful study by all analytical psychologists.

archetypal dominants. It surrounds and contains them. All problems of alienation, whether it be alienation between ego and parent figures, between ego and shadow, or between ego and anima (or animus), are thus ultimately alienation between ego and Self. Although we separate these different figures for descriptive purposes, in empirical experience they are not usually separated. In all serious psychological problems we are therefore dealing basically with the question of the ego-Self relationship. This is particularly true of the child's psychology.

Neumann has suggested that the Self may be experienced in childhood in relation to the parents, initially the mother. Neumann calls this original mother-child relationship the primary relationship and says ". . . in the primary relationship the mother as the directing, protecting, and nourishing source represents the unconscious and, in the first phase, also the Self and . . . the dependent child represents the childish ego and consciousness." [4] This means simply that the Self is inevitably experienced initially in projection on to the parents. Thus the early phase of the developing ego-Self axis may be identical with the relationship between parents and child. It is precisely at this point that we must be particularly careful to do justice to both the personal historical factors and also the *a priori*, archetypal factors. The Self is an *a priori* inner determinant. However, it cannot emerge without a concrete parent-child relationship. Neumann has drawn attention to this and calls it "the personal evocation of the archetype." [5] During this phase of experiencing the Self in projection, the ego-Self axis is likely to be most vulnerable to damage by adverse environmental influence. At this time what is within and what is without cannot be distinguished. Therefore, inability to experience acceptance or rapport is felt to be identical with loss of acceptance by the Self. In other words, the ego-Self axis has been damaged, causing ego-Self alienation. The part has become separated from the whole. This experience of parental rejection of some aspect of the child's personality is a part of the anamnesis of almost every patient in psychotherapy. By the word rejection I do not mean the necessary training and discipline of the child that teaches him to restrain his primitive desirousness; I refer rather to the parental rejection that stems from the projection of the parent's shadow onto the child. This is an unconscious process experienced by the child as something inhuman, total,

[4] Neumann, E., "The Significance of the Genetic Aspect for Analytical Psychology," *Journal of Analytical Psychology* IV, 2, p. 133.
[5] Ibid. p. 128.

and irrevocable. It seems to come from an implacable deity. This appearance has two origins. In the first place the child's projection of the Self on to the parent will give that parent's actions a transpersonal importance. Secondly, the rejecting parent who is functioning unconsciously will be acting in his own area of ego-Self identity and will therefore be inflated in an identification with deity. The consequence from the child's standpoint is a damage to his ego-Self axis that may cripple his psyche permanently.

The Self as the center and totality of the psyche which is able to reconcile all opposites can be considered as the organ of acceptance *par excellence*. Since it includes the totality, it must be able to accept all elements of psychic life no matter how antithetical they may be. It is this sense of acceptance of the Self that gives the ego its strength and stability. This sense of acceptance is conveyed to the ego via the ego-Self axis. A symptom of damage to this axis is lack of self-acceptance. The individual feels he is not worthy to exist or be himself. Psychotherapy offers such a person an opportunity to experience acceptance. In successful cases this can amount to the repair of the ego-Self axis which restores contact with the inner sources of strength and acceptance, leaving the patient free to live and grow.

Patients with a damaged ego-Self axis are most impressed in psychotherapy by the discovery that the therapist accepts them. Initially they cannot believe it. The fact of acceptance may be discredited by considering it only a professional technique having no genuine reality. However, if the acceptance of the therapist can be recognized as a fact, a powerful transference promptly appears. The source of this transference seems to be the projection of the Self, especially in its function as the organ of acceptance. At this point the *central* characteristics of the therapist-Self become prominent. The therapist as a person becomes the *center* of the patient's life and thoughts. The therapy sessions become the *central* points of the week. A center of meaning and order has appeared where previously there was chaos and despair. These phenomena indicate that a repair of the ego-Self axis is occurring. Meetings with the therapist will be experienced as a rejuvenating contact with life which conveys a sense of hope and optimism. At first such effects require frequent contact and wane quickly between sessions. Gradually, however, the inner aspect of the ego-Self axis becomes increasingly prominent.

The experience of acceptance not only repairs the ego-Self axis but also reactivates residual ego-Self identity. This is bound to occur as long as the ego-Self axis is completely unconscious (condition represented by figure 2). Hence inflated attitudes, possessive expectations, etc. will emerge which evoke further rejection from therapist or environment. Once again the ego-Self axis will be damaged producing a condition of relative alienation. Ideally in psychotherapy and in natural development one would hope for a progressive dissolution of ego-Self identity so gentle that it would cause no damage to the ego-Self axis. In actuality this desirable condition scarcely ever occurs.

The process of the development of consciousness seems to follow the cyclic course represented in figure 5, page 41. As indicated in

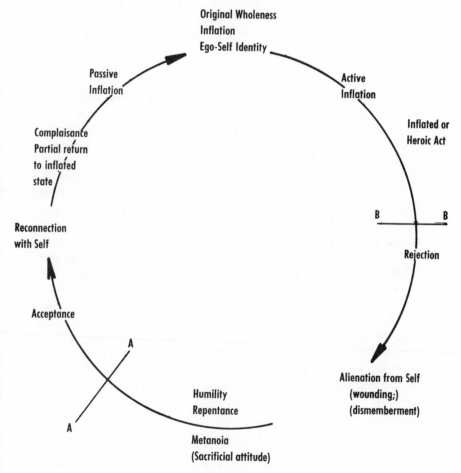

Figure 5. The Psychic Life Cycle.

the diagram, psychic growth involves a series of inflated or heroic acts. These provoke rejection and are followed by alienation, repentance, restitution and renewed inflation. This cyclic process repeats itself again and again in the early phases of psychological development, each cycle producing an increment of consciousness. Thus, gradually consciousness is built up. However, the cycle can go wrong. It is subject to disturbances, especially in the early phases of life. In childhood the child's connection with the Self is largely identical with his relation to the parents. Hence if this relationship is faulty the child's contact with his inner center of being will likewise be faulty. It is this fact that makes early family relationships so crucially important in personality development. If the interpersonal family relationships are too damaging, the cycle may be almost completely interrupted. It may be interrupted in two places (Points A and B in figure 5).

A block can develop if sufficient acceptance and renewal of love does not occur at Point A (figure 5). If the child is not fully accepted after punishment for misbehavior, the growth cycle can be short-circuited. Instead of completing the cycle and reaching the position of rest and reacceptance, the child's ego can be caught in a sterile oscillation between inflation and alienation that builds up more and more frustration and despair.

Another place a block can occur is at Point B. If the environment of the child is so totally permissive that he has no significant rejection experiences at all, if the parents never say "No," that also short-circuits the cycle. The whole experience of alienation, which brings consciousness with it, is omitted, and the child gets acceptance for his inflation. That leads to the spoiled-child psychology and contributes to the provisional life in which limitations and rejections have scarcely been experienced at all.

Figure 5 represents the alternation between inflation and alienation occurring in the early stages. It leaves out of account the later stage of development when the cycle is superseded. Once the ego has reached a certain level of development, it does not have to continue this repetitious cycle, at least not in the same way. The cycle is then replaced by a more or less conscious dialogue between ego and Self.

2. DESPAIR AND VIOLENCE

In the state of alienation, the ego is not only disidentified from the Self, which is desirable, but is also disconnected from it, which is most undesirable. The connection between ego and Self is vitally important to psychic health. It gives foundation, structure and security to the ego and also provides energy, interest, meaning and purpose. When the connection is broken the result is emptiness, despair, meaninglessness and in extreme cases psychosis or suicide.

The Bible presents several mythological figures representing the state of alienation. Adam and Eve are sad and estranged figures as they are expelled from the garden (Picture 4). Also Cain is a figure of alienation. We read in Genesis:

> Now Abel was a keeper of sheep, and Cain a tiller of the ground. In the course of time Cain brought to the Lord an offering of the fruit of the ground, and Abel brought of the firstlings of his flock and their fat portions. And the Lord had regard for Abel and his offering, but for Cain and his offering he had no regard. So Cain was very angry, and his countenance fell. The Lord said to Cain, "Why are you angry, and why has your countenance fallen?" [6]

Yahweh does not seem to realize that it was his own rejection of Cain and his offering that has caused the whole trouble.

> Cain said to Abel his brother, "Let us go out to the field." And when they were in the field, Cain rose up against his brother Abel, and killed him. Then the Lord said to Cain, "Where is Abel, your brother?" He said, "I do not know; am I my brother's keeper?" And the Lord said, "What have you done? The voice of your brother's blood is crying to me from the ground. And now you are cursed from the ground, which has opened its mouth to receive your brother's blood from your hand. When you till the ground, it shall no longer yield to you its strength; you shall be a fugitive and a wanderer on the earth." [7]

Thus Cain is banished to the wilderness, re-enacting on another level Adam's banishment from paradise. If we look at this myth objectively rather than traditionally, we see that the origin of the difficulty was God's rejection of Cain without apparent cause or reason. We are told that Abel was a keeper of sheep and Cain a tiller of the ground. Perhaps Cain was initiating agriculture in a society of herders. This could account for Cain's rejection. He was an innovator and suffered the characteristic fate of all who attempt to bring a new orientation to a fixed society that is fearful of change. At any rate Cain is an archetypal figure representing the experience of re-

[6] Gen. 4:2-6 RSV.
[7] Gen. 4:8-12 RSV.

n and alienation. His reaction to an excessive and irrational re-
a is characteristic, namely, violence. Whenever one experi-
an unbearable alienation and despair it is followed by
:e. The violence can take either an external or an internal
form. In extreme forms this means either murder or suicide. The
crucial point is that at the root of violence of any form lies the experience of alienation—a rejection too severe to be endured.

I recall a patient I encountered in a mental hospital who lived
out the Cain myth. From earliest childhood his greatest problem
and the central theme of his life experience was rivalry with his
older brother. His brother was successful in everything he put his
hand to and was the favorite of both parents. This favoritism was so
pronounced that the parents commonly referred to the patient by
his brother's name. This, quite understandably, infuriated him,
meaning, as it did, that he was not experienced as a separate individual and scarcely existed in their eyes. The patient was left in a
state of bitterness and frustration with a sense of utter worthless-
ness. How identified he was with "the rejected one" was revealed by
his reaction one time while attending a movie, *East of Eden,* based
on the novel by John Steinbeck. This story is a modernized form of
the Cain and Abel theme. There are two brothers in the story, one
the favorite of the father, and the other neglected and rejected. The
patient identified powerfully with the rejected brother and in the
midst of the movie he had such an extreme reaction of anxiety and
distress that he was forced to leave.

Later the patient married, but things did not go well between him
and his wife. His wife had an affair with another man. This situation then provoked the old rejection theme in full intensity, and he
made a murderous assault on his wife but did not kill her. Later he
attempted suicide. It was unsuccessful the first time but finally, on
his third try, he succeeded. Thus he lived out his mythological fate
to the bitter end.

From the inner standpoint there is very little difference between
murder and suicide. The only difference is in the direction in which
the destructive energy is moving. In the depressed state one often
encounters murderous dreams; the dreamer murders himself internally. Such dream images indicate that murder and suicide are
essentially the same thing symbolically.

Another Biblical figure, likewise a typical representation of the
alienated state, is Ishmael *(Picture 8).* Ishmael was the illegitimate
son of Abraham by the bondwoman Hagar. When Isaac, the legitimate son was born, Ishmael and his mother were cast out into the

Picture 8. HAGAR AND ISHMAEL IN THE DESERT by Gustave Doré.

desert. The theme of illegitimacy is an aspect of the alienation experience. Actual illegitimate children usually have a severe alienation problem, what might be called an Ishmael complex.

Melville's book, *Moby Dick*, is a beautiful example of the working out of an Ishmael complex. The name of the central character is Ishmael and the story depicts an alternation between the states of inflation and alienation. The first paragraph of *Moby Dick* reads:

> Call me Ishmael. Some years ago—never mind how long precisely—having little or no money in my purse, and nothing particular to interest me on shore, I thought I would sail about a little and see the watery part of the world. It is a way I have of driving off the spleen, and regulating the circulation. Whenever I find myself growing grim about the mouth, whenever I find myself involuntarily pausing before coffin warehouses, and bringing up the rear of every funeral I meet; and especially whenever my hypos get such an upper hand of me, that it requires a strong moral principle to prevent me from deliberately stepping into the street, and methodically knocking people's hats off—then, I account it high time to get to sea as soon as I can. This is my substitute for pistol and ball. With a philosophical flourish Cato throws himself upon his sword; I quietly take to the ship. There is nothing surprising in this. If they but knew it, almost all men in their degree, some time or other, cherish very nearly the same feelings towards the ocean with me.[8]

Everything that happens in the book follows logically from this first paragraph. The whole tragic drama of violence and inflation unfolds out of the initial state of alienated, suicidal despair. It is an example of a short-circuited cycle, a state of alienation that leads back to renewed inflation, having as its consequence still more disaster.

Other literary classics also begin with a state of alienation. Dante's *Divine Comedy* begins with these lines:

> Midway upon the journey of our life
> I found that I was in a dusky wood;
> For the right path, whence I had strayed, was lost,
> Ah me! How hard a thing it is to tell
> The wildness of that rough and savage place,
> The very thought of which brings back my fear!
> So bitter was it, death is little more so.[9]

[8] Melville, H., *Moby Dick*, New York, Hendrick's House, p. 1.
[9] Dante, *Divine Comedy*, Trans. Lawrence Grant White, New York, Pantheon.

Goethe's Faust likewise begins in a state of alienation. In the first scene he expresses his emptiness and sterility:

> Oh! am I still stuck in this jail?
> This God-damned dreary hole in the wall
> Where even the lovely light of heaven
> Breaks wanly through the painted panes!
> Cooped up among these heaps of books
> Gnawed by worms, coated with dust . . .[10]

Hölderlin expresses the transition from child to adult as from heaven to wasteland:

> Blest be childhood's golden dreams, their power
>   Hid from me life's dismal poverty;
> All the heart's good seeds ye brought to flower
>   Things I could not reach, ye gave to me!
> In thy beauty and thy light, O Nature,
>   Of all effort and compulsion free,
> Fruitful love attained a kingly stature,
>   Rich as harvests reaped in Arcady.
>
> That which brought me up is dead and riven,
>   Dead the youthful world which was my shield,
> And this breast, which used to harbor heaven,
>   Dead and dry as any stubble field.[11]

We do not lack for modern expressions of the alienated state. In fact they are so ubiquitous, our time could well be called the age of alienation. Consider for instance these passages from T. S. Eliot's *The Waste Land*:

> What are the roots that clutch, what branches grow   3
> Out of this stony rubbish? Son of man,
> You cannot say, or guess, for you know only
> A heap of broken images, where the sun beats,
> And the dead tree gives no shelter, the cricket no relief,
> And the dry stone no sound of water.
>   . . .
> Here is no water but only rock
> Rock and no water and the sandy road
> The road winding above among the mountains

[10] Goethe, *Faust*, Trans. L. MacNeice, London, Oxford Press.
[11] "To Nature," quoted in Jung, C. G., *Symbols of Transformation*, C. W., Vol. 5, following par. 624.

> Which are mountains of rock without water
> If there were water we should stop and drink
> Amongst the rock one cannot stop or think
> Sweat is dry and feet are in the sand
> If there were only water amongst the rock
> Dead mountain mouth of carious teeth that cannot spit
> Here one can neither stand nor lie nor sit
> There is not even silence in the mountains
> But dry and sterile thunder without rain.
> There is not even solitude in the mountains
> But red sullen faces sneer and snarl
> From doors of mudcracked houses.[12]

This powerful poem expresses the individual and collective alienation that is characteristic of our time. The "heap of broken images" surely refers to the traditional religious symbols which for many people have lost their meaning. We live in a desert and cannot find the source of life-giving water. The mountains—originally the place where man met God—have nothing but dry sterile thunder without rain.

Modern existentialism can be considered as symptomatic of the collective alienated state. Many current novels and plays depict lost, meaningless lives. The modern artist seems forced to depict again and again, to bring home to all of us, the experience of meaninglessness. However this need not be considered a totally negative phenomenon. Alienation is not a dead end. Hopefully it can lead to a greater awareness of the heights and depths of life.

3. ALIENATION AND THE RELIGIOUS EXPERIENCE

Just as the experience of active inflation is a necessary accompaniment of ego development, so the experience of alienation is a necessary prelude to awareness of the Self. Kierkegaard, the fountainhead of modern existentialism, recognized the meaning of the alienation experience in this passage:

> . . . so much is said about wasted lives—but only that man's life is wasted who lived on, so deceived by the joys of life or by its sorrow that he never became eternally and decisively conscious of himself as spirit . . . or (what is the same thing) never became aware and in the deepest sense received an impression of the fact that there is

[12] Eliot, T. S., Collected Poems, New York, Harcourt, Brace and Company, pp. 69 f. and 86 f.

Picture 9. ISRAELITES GATHERING MANNA from *The Hours of Catherine of Cleves.*

a God, and that he, he himself . . . exists before this God, *which gain of infinity is never attained except through despair* (italics mine).[13]

Jung says essentially the same thing in psychological terms:

The self, in its efforts at self-realization, reaches out beyond the ego-personality on all sides; because of its all-encompassing nature it is brighter and darker than the ego, and accordingly confronts it with problems which it would like to avoid. Either one's moral courage fails, or one's insight, or both, until in the end fate decides . . . you have become the victim of a decision made over your head or in defiance of the heart. From this we can see the numinous power of the self, which can hardly be experienced in any other way. For this reason *the experience of the self is always a defeat for the ego.*[14]

There are numerous descriptions of religious experiences which typically are preceded by what St. John of the Cross called "the dark night of the soul," what Kierkegaard called "despair," and what Jung called "defeat of the ego." All these terms refer to the

[13] Kirkegaard, S., *Fear and Trembling, the Sickness Unto Death,* Garden City, N.Y., Doubleday Anchor Books, 1954, p. 159 f.
[14] Jung, C. G., *Mysterium Coniunctionis,* C. W., Vol. 14, par. 778.

same psychological state of alienation. We find again and again in the documentation of religious experiences a profound sense of depression, guilt, sin, unworthiness, and the complete absence of any sense of transpersonal support or foundation for one's existence to rest upon.

The classic symbol for alienation is the image of the *wilderness*. And jt is here, characteristically, that some manifestation of God is encountered. When the wanderer lost in the desert is about to perish, a source of divine nourishment appears. The Israelites in the wilderness are fed by manna from heaven (Exodus 16:4) *(Picture 9)*. Elijah in the wilderness is fed by ravens (Kings 17:2-6) *(Picture 10)*. According to the legend, the desert hermit St. Paul was likewise fed by a raven *(Picture 11)*. Psychologically this means that the experience of the supporting aspect of the archetypal psyche is most likely to occur when the ego has exhausted its own resources and is aware of its essential impotence by itself. "Man's extremity is God's opportunity."

William James in his book *Varieties of Religious Experience*, gives a number of examples of the state of alienation that precedes a numinous experience. One of the cases he discusses is that of Tolstoy:

Picture 10. ELIJAH BEING FED BY THE RAVENS by Washington Allston, Detail.

At about the age of fifty, Tolstoy relates that he began to have moments of perplexity, of what he calls arrest, as if he knew not "how to live," or what to do. It is obvious that these were moments in which the excitement and interest which our functions naturally bring had ceased. Life had been enchanting, it was now flat sober, more than sober, dead. Things were meaningless whose meaning had always been self-evident. The question "Why?" and "What next?" began to beset him more and more frequently. At first it seemed as if such questions must be answerable and as if he could easily find the answers if he would take the time; but as they ever became more urgent, he perceived that it was like those first discomforts of a sick man, to which he pays but little attention till they run into one continuous suffering, and then he realizes that what he took for a passing disorder means the most momentous thing in the world for him, means his death.

These questions, "Why?" "Wherefore?" "What for?" found no response. "I felt," says Tolstoy, "that something had broken within me on which my life had always rested, and that I had nothing left to hold on to, and that morally my life had stopped. An invincible force impelled me to get rid of my existence, in one way or another. It cannot be said exactly that I *wished* to kill myself, for the force which drew me away from life was fuller, more powerful, more general than any mere desire. It was a force like my old aspiration to live, only it impelled me in the opposite direction. It was an aspiration of my whole being to get out of life.

"Behold me then, a man happy and in good health, hiding the rope in order not to hang myself to the rafters of the room where every night I went to sleep alone; behold me no longer going shooting, lest I should yield to the too easy temptation of putting an end to myself with my gun.

"I did not know what I wanted. I was afraid of life; I was driven to leave it; and in spite of that I still hoped something from it.

"All this took place at a time when so far as my outer circumstances went, I ought to have been completely happy. I had a good wife who loved me and whom I loved; good children and a large property which was increasing with no pains taken on my part. I was more respected by my kinsfolk and acquaintances than I had ever been; I was loaded with praise by strangers; and without exaggeration I could believe my name already famous. Moreover I was neither insane nor ill. On the contrary, I possessed a physical and mental strength which I had rarely met in persons of my age. I could mow as well as the peasants, I could work with my brain eight hours uninterruptedly and feel no bad effects.

"And yet I could give no reasonable meaning to any actions of my life. And I was surprised that I had not understood this from the

y beginning. My state of mind was as if some wicked and stupid
was being played upon me by some one. One can live only so
ʒ as one is intoxicated, drunk with life, but when one grows sober
cannot fail to see that it is all a stupid cheat. What is truest
₌₌₌ut it is that there is nothing even funny or silly in it; it is cruel
and stupid, purely and simply."
He is beset with unanswerable questions,
". . . What will be the outcome of what I do today? Or what I shall
do tomorrow? What will be the outcome of all my life? Why should
I live? Why should I do anything? Is there in life any purpose which
the inevitable death which awaits me does not undo and destroy?
"These questions are the simplest in the world. From the stupid child
to the wisest old man, they are in the soul of every human being.
Without an answer to them, it is impossible, as I experienced, for
life to go on." [15]

This is a good example of an acute attack of alienation. The questions that Tolstoy asks are the same questions that lie at the root of
every neurosis which develops in the mature years. Hence Jung can
say that he has never seen a patient past the age of thirty-five who
was cured without finding a religious attitude towards life.[16] A religious attitude, understood psychologically, is based on an experience of the *numinosum*, i.e., the Self. But it is impossible for the ego
to experience the Self as something separate as long as the ego is
unconsciously identified with the Self. This explains the need for
the alienation experience as a prelude to the religious experience.
The ego must first be disidentified from the Self before the Self can
be encountered as "the other." As long as one is unconsciously identified with God he cannot experience His existence. But the process
of ego-Self separation causes alienation because loss of ego-Self
identity also involves damage to the ego-Self axis. Hence the typical
"dark night of the soul" that precedes the numinous experience.
    Another example is John Bunyan's description of his alienated
state as reported by James,

[15] James, William, *Varieties of Religious Experience*, New York, Random
House, Modern Library, pp. 150 ff.
[16] Jung, C. G. *Psychology and Religion: West and East*, C. W., Vol. 11,
par. 509. The full quotation runs as follows: "Among all my patients in the
second half of life—that is to say, over thirty-five—there has not been one
whose problem in the last resort was not that of finding a religious outlook on
life. It is safe to say that every one of them fell ill because he had lost what
the living religions of every age have given to their followers, and none of them
has been really healed who did not regain his religious outlook. This of course
has nothing whatever to do with a particular creed or membership of a
church."

Picture 11. ST. ANTHONY AND ST. PAUL THE HERMIT BEING FED BY A RAVEN, Dürer.

"But my original and inward pollution, that was my plague and my affliction. By reason of that, I was more loathsome in my own eyes than was a toad; and I thought I was so in God's eyes too. Sin and corruption, I said, would as naturally bubble out of my heart as water would bubble out of a fountain. I could have changed heart with anybody. I thought none but the Devil himself could equal me for inward wickedness and pollution of mind. Sure, thought I, I am forsaken of God; and thus I continued a long while, even for some years together.

"And now I was sorry that God had made me a man. The beasts, birds, fishes, etc., I blessed their condition, for they had not a sinful nature; they were not obnoxious to the wrath of God; they were not to go to hell-fire after death. I could therefore have rejoiced, had my condition been as any of theirs. Now I blessed the condition of the dog and toad, yea, gladly would I have been in the condition of the dog or horse, for I knew they had no soul to perish under the ever-lasting weight of Hell or Sin, as mine was like to do. Nay, and though I saw this, felt this, and was broken to pieces with it, yet that which added to my sorrow was, that I could not find with all my soul that I did desire deliverance. My heart was at times exceedingly hard. If I would have given a thousand pounds for a tear, I could not shed one; no, nor sometimes scarce desire to shed one.

"I was both a burden and a terror to myself; nor did I ever so know, as now, what it was to be weary of my life, and yet afraid to die. How gladly would I have been anything but myself! Anything but a man! and in any condition but my own." [17]

Bunyan's state of mind has a distinctly pathological character. The same feelings of total guilt and impossibility of redemption are expressed in psychotic melancholia. His feeling himself the guiltiest man on earth is a negative inflation. However, it is also alienation. Bunyan's envy of animals is something that comes up again and again in the accounts of the alienated condition that precedes religious experience. This envy of animals gives us a clue as to how the state of alienation is to be healed, namely, by renewed contact with the natural instinctive life.

Although alienation is an archetypal and hence a generally human experience, exaggerated forms of the experience, such as Bunyan's, are usually found in people with a certain type of traumatic childhood. In cases where the child experiences a severe degree of rejection by the parents, the ego-Self axis is damaged and the child is then predisposed in later life to states of alienation which can

[17] James, *Varieties of Religious Experience.*

reach unbearable proportions. This course of events is due to the fact that the child experiences parental rejection as rejection by God. The experience is then built into the psyche as permanent ego-Self alienation.

In the context of Christian psychology, the alienation experience is commonly understood as divine punishment for sin. Anselm's doctrine of sin is relevant here; according to him sin is a robbing of God's prerogatives and thus dishonors God. This dishonor requires satisfaction. Anselm writes:

> Every wish of a rational creature should be subject to the will of God . . . this is the sole and complete debt of honor which we owe to God, and which God requires of us . . . He who does not render this honor which is due to God, robs God of his own and dishonors him; and this is sin. Moreover, so long as he does not restore what he has taken away, he remains in fault; and it will not suffice merely to restore what has been taken away, but, considering the contempt offered, he ought to restore more than he took away. For as one who imperils another's safety does not enough by merely restoring his safety, without making some compensation for the anguish incurred; so he who violates another's honor does not enough by merely rendering honor again, but must, according to the extent of the injury done, make restoration in some way satisfactory to the person whom he has dishonored. We must also observe that when anyone pays what he has unjustly taken away, he ought to give something which could not have been demanded of him, had he not stolen what belonged to another. So then, every one who sins ought to pay back the honor of which he has robbed God; and this is the satisfaction that every sinner owes to God.[18]

Sin is the inflated presumption of the ego which takes over the functions of the Self. This crime requires punishment (alienation) and restitution (remorse, repentance). But according to Anselm, full satisfaction requires the return of more than was originally taken. This is impossible since man owes God total obedience even without sin. He has no extra resources to pay his penalty. For this he must use the grace provided by the sacrifice of the God-man Jesus Christ. In the sequence of sin and repentance God himself pays the fine by an influx of grace. This corresponds to St. Paul's statement: "But where sin was thus multiplied, grace immeasurably exceeded it, in order that, as sin established its reign by way of death, so God's grace might establish its reign in righteousness, and

[18] St. Anselm, *Cur Deus Homo*, Chapter XI, in *Basic Writings*, La Salle, Ill., Open Court Publishing Co., 1962, pp. 202 f.

issue in eternal life through Jesus Christ our Lord." (Romans 5: 20, 21) Paul's following question, "Shall we persist in sin, so that there may be all the more grace?" is of course answered in the negative. Nevertheless, the question alludes to the uncomfortable fact that grace is somehow connected with sin.

Understood psychologically, these theological doctrines refer to the relation between the ego and the Self. Inflation (sin) is to be avoided when possible. When it occurs the ego can be redeemed only by restoring to the Self its lost honor (repentance, contrition) (*Picture 12*). This however is not sufficient for full satisfaction. Grace derived from the Self's self-sacrifice must complete the payment. There is even the hint that the ego's sin and subsequent penalty are necessary to generate the flow of healing energy (grace) from the Self. This would correspond to the fact that the ego cannot experience the support of the Self until it has been freed of its identification with Self. It cannot be a vessel for the influx of grace until it has been emptied of its own inflated fullness; and this emptying occurs only through the experience of alienation.

Martin Luther expresses the same idea:

> God works by contraries so that a man feels himself to be lost in the very moment when he is on the point of being saved. When God is about to justify a man, he damns him. Whom he would make alive he must first kill. God's favor is so communicated in the form of wrath that it seems furthest when it is at hand. Man must first cry out that there is no health in him. He must be consumed with horror. This is the pain of purgatory . . . In this disturbance salvation begins. When a man believes himself to be utterly lost, light breaks.[19]

4. RESTITUTION OF THE EGO-SELF AXIS

There is a typical clinical picture, seen very commonly in psychotherapeutic practice which might be called an alienation neurosis. An individual with such a neurosis is very dubious about his right to exist. He has a profound sense of unworthiness with all the symptoms that we commonly refer to as an inferiority complex. He assumes unconsciously and automatically that whatever comes out of himself—his innermost desires, needs and interest—must be wrong or somehow unacceptable. With this attitude psychic energy is dammed up and must emerge in covert, unconscious or destructive ways such as psychosomatic symptoms, attacks of anxiety or primitive affect, depression, suicidal impulses, alcoholism, etc. Funda-

[19] Bainton, Roland, *Here I Stand*, New York, Abingdon-Cokesbury, 1950, pp. 82 f.

Picture 12. THE PENITENCE OF DAVID. David, reproached by the prophet Nathan, repents at having abducted Bathsheba. On the right is a personification of repentence (*metanoia*). Illumination from a Byzantine manuscript.

mentally, such a patient is facing the problem of whether or not he is justified before God. We have here the psychological basis of the theological question of justification. Are we justified by faith or by works?—which puts into a nutshell the difference between the introverted and extraverted viewpoints. The alienated person feels profoundly unjustified and is scarcely able to act according to his own best interests. At the same time he is cut off from a sense of meaning. Life is emptied of psychic content.

In order to break out of the alienated state some contact between ego and Self must be re-established. If this can happen, a whole new world opens up. Here is a description of such an experience which I take from a case reported by Dr. Rollo May. The patient

was a 28 year old woman who had been an illegitimate child and
had suffered severely with what I would call an alienation neurosis.
She reports her experience in these words:

> I remember walking that day under the elevated tracks in a slum
> area, feeling the thought "I am an illegitimate child." I recall the
> sweat pouring forth in my anguish in trying to accept that fact. Then
> I understood what it must feel like to accept, "I am a Negro in the
> midst of privileged whites," or "I am blind in the midst of people
> who see." Later on that night I woke up and it came to me this way,
> "I accept the fact that I am an illegitimate child," *but* "I am not a
> child any more." So it is, "I am illegitimate." That is not so either:
> "I was born illegitimate(ly)." Then what is left? What is left is this,
> "I am." This act of contact and acceptance with "I am," once gotten
> hold of, gave me (what I think was for me the first time) the ex-
> perience, "Since I am, I have the right to be."
> What is this experience like? It is a primary feeling—it feels like re-
> ceiving the deed to my house. It is the experience of my own alive-
> ness not caring whether it turns out to be an ion or just a wave. It is
> like when a very young child I once reached the core of a peach and
> cracked the pit, not knowing what I would find and then feeling the
> wonder of finding the inner seed good to eat in its bitter sweetness . . .
> It is like a sailboat in the harbor being given an anchor so that, being
> made out of earthly things, it can by means of its anchor get in touch
> again with the earth, the ground from which its wood grew; it can lift
> its anchor to sail but always at times it can cast its anchor to weather
> the storm or rest a little . . .
> It is like going into my very own Garden of Eden where I am beyond
> good and evil and all other human concepts . . . It is like the globe
> before the mountains and oceans and continents have been drawn on
> it. It is like a child in grammar finding the *subject* of the verb in a
> sentence—in this case the subject being one's own life span. It is ceas-
> ing to feel like a theory towards one's self . . .[20]

May labels this the "I am" experience which is certainly descrip-
tively apt. It can also be understood as the restitution of the ego-
Self axis which must have taken place in the context of a strong
transference.

The following dream of a young woman in therapy also illustrates
the beginning repair of a damaged ego-Self axis. She dreamt: *I have
been banished to the cold, barren wastes of Siberia and am wander-
ing about aimlessly. Then a group of soldiers on horseback approached. They threw me into the snow and proceed to rape me
one by one. Four times this happens. I felt torn apart and paralyzed*

[20] *Existence*, May, R., Engel, E., Ellenberger, W. F., (Eds.), New York,
Basic Books, 1950, p. 43.

with cold. Then the fifth soldier approaches. I expect the same treatment but to my surprise I see pity and human understanding in his eyes. Instead of raping me he gently wraps me in a blanket and carries me to a nearby cottage. Here I am placed by the fire and fed warm soup. I know this man is going to heal me.

This dream occurred with the onset of transference. The patient had suffered as a child from a severe degree of rejection by both parents. Her father in particular neglected her completely after his divorce from her mother. This was a crushing blow to the patient's self-worth and left her alienated from the values carried by the father and ultimately a portion of the Self. The dream describes vividly her feeling of alienation or banishment and also her newly emerging experience of restoration: the ego-Self axis was being repaired. This happens with the dawning awareness of strong transference feelings. Such experiences are, of course, encountered regularly in psychotherapy, and are usually handled more or less successfully by means of good human feeling and established theories concerning transference. However, I believe, a realization that a profound nuclear process involving repair of the ego-Self axis is taking place gives an added dimension to the understanding of the transference phenomenon. Furthermore, one is then able to understand the therapeutic experience in the larger context of man's universal need for a relation to the transpersonal source of being.

Another example of the healing effect achieved by re-establishing the connection between the ego and the Self is found in a remarkable dream that was brought to me. The man who had this dream had endured severe emotional deprivation in childhood. He also was an illegitimate child, reared by foster parents who were near-psychotics and who provided practically no positive parental experience for the boy. As a result, he was left with an extreme sense of alienation in adult life. Though quite talented he was severely blocked in his efforts to realize his potentialities. He had this dream on the night following Jung's death (June 6, 1961). I mention this detail because he was quite affected by Jung's death and because in a certain sense the dream epitomizes one aspect of Jung's approach to the psyche. Here is the dream: *Four of us arrive on a strange planet. The four seems to be a quaternity in that we each represent different aspects of one being as though we were representatives of the four directions or of the four different races of man. On arrival we discover a counterpart to our group of four on the planet—a second group of four. This group does not speak our language, in fact each of the four speaks a different language.*

The first thing we try to do is establish some language in common. (This problem occupies much of the dream but I shall omit this portion.)

There is on this planet a super-order which is enforced on all its inhabitants. But it is not enforced as though by a person or a government but by benign authority which we suppose to be nature. There is nothing threatening to the individuality about its ability to exercise this control on everyone.

I am then distracted by something happening in an emergency chamber. One of the planet's four has had an attack. It seems that his excitement over our arrival has caused his heart to beat too fast. And it is in the nature of the super-order to intervene when things of this sort happen. He is placed in a semi-comatose state during which he is plugged into the master heart beat which will absorb the "overload" until he has been equilibriumized.

I begin to wonder if the four of us will be allowed to stay. Then we receive the information that we will be allowed to stay on the condition that we be placed on wavelengths so that the "Central Source of Energy Law" will be able to measure and detect when we get into what the planet calls "danger" and what the earth calls "sin." At the moment we enter into danger, the super-order will "take over" until the condition has been corrected. Danger will be whenever an act is performed for the immediate gratification of the ego or any conscious part of the personality rather than with reference to the archetypal roots of that act—that is, without relating that act to its archetypal origin and the aspect of ritual that was involved in the first root act.

The central feature of this most impressive dream is the "super-order" and "central source of energy law" that exists on another planet (the unconscious). This remarkable image is a symbolic expression of the trans-personal regulating process of the psyche and corresponds to our concept of the compensatory function of the unconscious. The dream states that danger arises "Whenever an act is performed for the immediate gratification of the ego . . . (without) reference to the archetypal roots of that act." This is an exact description of inflation in which the ego operates without reference to the suprapersonal categories of existence. Furthermore the dream equates this condition with sin—a precise equivalent to Augustine's view as quoted previously (page 34).

The dream tells us that the "super-order" goes into effect to remove the "overload" as soon as the ego becomes inflated—thus protecting against the dangers of subsequent alienation. This protective or compensating mechanism is a close parallel to Walter

Cannon's principle of homeostasis in physiology.[21] According to this concept, the body has a built-in process of homeostasis or self-regulation which will not permit the basic body constituents to get too far out of proper balance. For instance, if we ingest too much sodium chloride, the kidneys increase the concentration of sodium chloride in the urine. Or, if too great a concentration of carbon dioxide accumulates in the blood, then certain nerve centers in the brain increase the respiratory rate in order to blow off the excess carbon dioxide. The same self-regulating, homeostatic process works in the psyche providing it is free to operate naturally and has not been damaged. Like the body, the unconscious psyche has an instinctive wisdom which can correct the errors and excesses of consciousness if we are open to its messages. This corrective function derives from the Self and requires a living, healthy connection between Self and ego in order to operate freely.

Even for the "normal" man, alienation is a necessary experience if psychological development is to proceed because ego-Self identity is as universal as original sin. Indeed they are identical. Carlyle has put it cleverly. He says that happiness is inversely proportionate to the quantity of our expectations, i.e., how much we think we are entitled to. Happiness equals what we have, divided by what we expect. He writes:

> By certain valuations, and averages, of our own striking, we come upon some sort of average terrestrial lot; this we fancy belongs to us by nature, and of indefeasible right. It is simple payment of wages, of our deserts; requires neither thanks nor complaint; only such *overplus* as there may be do we account Happiness; any *deficit* again is Misery. Now consider that we have the valuation of our own deserts ourselves, and what a fund of Self-conceit there is in each of us,—do you wonder that the balance should so often dip the wrong way . . . I tell thee, Blockhead, it all comes of thy Vanity; of what thou *fanciest* those same deserts of thine to be. Fancy that thou deservest to be hanged (as is most likely), thou wilt feel it happiness to be only shot . . .
> . . . the *Fraction of Life can be increased in value not so much by increasing your Numerator as by lessening your Denominator,* Nay, unless my Algebra deceive me, *Unity* itself divided by *Zero* will give *Infinity.* Make thy claim of wages a zero, then thou hast the world under thy feet. Well did the Wisest of our time write: "It is only with Renunciation *(Entsagen)* that Life, properly speaking, can be said to begin." [22]

[21] Cannon, W. B., *The Wisdom of the Body,* New York, 1932.
[22] Carlyle, Thomas, *Sartor Resartus,* Everyman's Library, London, Dent and Sons, 1948, p. 144.

CHAPTER THREE

Encounter With the Self

*I look on this life as the progress of an essence royal;
the soul but quits her court to see the country. Heaven
hath in it a scene of earth, and had she been contented
with ideas she had not travelled beyond the map. But
excellent patterns commend their mimes . . . but whiles
she scans their symmetry she forms it. Thus her descent
speaks her original. God in love with His own beauty
frames a glass, to view it by reflection.*

—THOMAS VAUGHN [*]

1. THE ROLE OF THE COLLECTIVE

We have seen that the states of inflation and alienation, both
being parts of the psychic life cycle, tend to turn into something
else. The inflated state, when acted out, leads to a fall and hence
to alienation. The alienated condition likewise, under normal
circumstances, leads over to the state of healing and restitution.
Inflation or alienation become dangerous conditions only if they
are separated from the life cycle of which they are parts. If
either becomes a static, chronic state of being, rather than a part
of the comprehensive dynamism, the personality is threatened.
Psychotherapy is then called for. However, the mass of men have
always been protected from these dangers by collective, conventional (and therefore largely unconscious) means.

The psychic dangers of inflation and alienation, under different
names, have always been recognized in the religious practice and

[*] Vaughn, Thomas, *Anthroposophia Theomagica*, in *The Works of Thomas
Vaughn*, Waite, A. E., (ed.), reprinted by University Books, New Hyde Park,
N.Y., p. 5.

folk wisdom of all races and ages. There are many collective and personal rituals which exist for the purpose of avoiding any inflated tendency to tempt God's envy. For instance, we have the age-old practice of knocking on wood when one says things are going well. Behind this is the unconscious or conscious realization that pride and complacency are dangerous. Hence, some procedure must be used to keep one in a humble state. The use of the phrase "God willing" has the same purpose. The taboos encountered in primitive society in the majority of cases have the same basis— protecting the individual from the inflated state, from contact with powers that would be too big for the limited ego consciousness and that might explode it disastrously. The primitive procedure of isolating victorious warriors when they return from battle serves the same protective function. Victorious warriors may be inflated by victory and might turn their strength against the village itself if they were permitted in. Hence there is a few days' cooling off period before reintegration into the community takes place.

There is an interesting ancient Mithraic ritual called "The Rite of the Crown" designed to protect against inflation. The following procedure was enacted during the initiation of a Roman soldier into Mithraism. At sword's point a crown was offered the candidate; but the initiate was taught to push it aside with his hand and affirm "Mithra is my crown." Thereafter he never wore a crown or garland, not even at banquets or at military triumphs, and whenever a crown was offered him he refused it saying, "It belongs to my god." [1]

In Zen Buddhism subtle techniques have been developed for undermining intellectual inflation, the illusion that one *knows*. One such technique is the use of koans or enigmatic sayings. An example would be: A pupil asks his master "Do dogs have a Buddha-nature?" The master replies, "Bow Wow."

In the Christian tradition there is great effort to protect against the inflated state. The seven deadly sins; pride, wrath, envy, lust, gluttony, avarice, and sloth, are all symptoms of inflation. By being labelled sins, which require confession and penance, the individual is protected against them. The basic message of the beatitudes of Jesus is that blessing will come to the non-inflated personality.

There are also many traditional procedures to protect the individual from the alienated state. Understood psychologically, the

[1] Willoughby, Harold R., *Pagan Regeneration*, Chicago, University of Chicago Press, 1929, p. 156.

central aim of all religious practices is to keep the individual (ego) related to the deity (Self). All religions are repositories of transpersonal experience and archetypal images. The innate purpose of religious ceremonies of all kinds seems to be to provide the individual with the experience of being related meaningfully to these transpersonal categories. That is true of the Mass, and of the Catholic confessional in a more personal way, where the individual has an opportunity to unburden himself of whatever circumstances have brought about a sense of alienation from God. Through the acceptance of the priest as God's agent, some sense of return to and reconnection with God is established.

All religious practices hold up to view the transpersonal categories of existence and attempt to relate them to the individual. Religion is the best collective protection available against both inflation and alienation. So far as we know, every society has had such suprapersonal categories in its collective ritual of life. It is quite doubtful if collective human life can survive for any period without some common, shared sense of awareness of these transpersonal categories.

However, although collective methods protect man from the dangers of the psychic depths, they also deprive him of the individual experience of these depths and the possibility of development which such experience promotes. As long as a living religion can contain the Self and mediate its dynamism for its members, there will be little need for the individual to have a personal encounter with the Self. He will have no need to find his individual relation to the transpersonal dimension. That task will be done for him by the Church.

This raises a serious question, i.e., whether modern Western society still has a functioning container for suprapersonal categories or archetypes. Or, as Eliot puts it, do we have no more than "a heap of broken images?" The fact is that large numbers of individuals do not have living, functioning, suprapersonal categories by which they can understand life experience, supplied either by the church or otherwise. This is a dangerous state of affairs because, when such categories do not exist, the ego is likely to think of itself as everything or as nothing. Furthermore, when the archetypes have no adequate container such as an established religious structure, they have to go somewhere else because the archetypes are facts of psychic life. One possibility is that they will be projected into banal or secular matters. The transpersonal value can then become how high one's standard of living is, or personal power, or some social reform movement, or any one of a number of political activities. This happens in Nazism, the radical right, and in Communism, the radical left. The same sort of dynamism can be projected into the race problem, either as racism or antiracism. Personal, secular, or political actions become charged with unconscious religious meaning. This is particularly dangerous because whenever a religious motivation is acting unconsciously it causes fanaticism with all its destructive consequences.

When the collective psyche is in a stable state, the vast majority of individuals share a common living myth or deity. Each individual projects his inner God-image (the Self) to the religion of the community. The collective religion then serves as the container of the Self for a multitude of individuals. The reality of the transpersonal life-forces is mirrored in the external imagery that the church embodies in its symbolism, mythology, rites and dogma. As long as it is functioning adequately, the church protects the society against any widespread inflation or alienation. Such a stable state of affairs is represented diagrammatically in Figure 6. Although this situation is stable it has its defects. The Self or god-image is still unconscious, i.e., not recognized as an inner, psychic entity. Although the community of believers will be in relative harmony with one another because of their shared projection, the harmony is illusory and to some extent spurious. In relation to the church the individuals will be in a state of collective identification or *participation mystique* and will not have made any unique, individual relation to the Self.

If now the outer church loses its capacity to carry the projection of the Self, we have the condition which Nietzsche announced for the modern world, "God is dead!" All the psychic energy and values that had been contained in the church now flow back to the individual, activating his psyche and causing serious problems. What will happen now? There are several possibilities and we see examples of each in contemporary life (See Fig. 7). 1. The first possibility is that with the loss of the god-projection into the church, the individual will at the same time lose his inner connection with the Self (Case 1, Fig. 7). The individual then succumbs to alienation and all the symptoms of the empty meaningless life that are so common today. 2. The second possibility is that the individual may take on himself, on his own ego and personal capacities, all the energy previously attached to deity (Case 2, Fig. 7). Such a person succumbs to inflation. Examples of this are seen in the hybris that over-values man's rational and

66

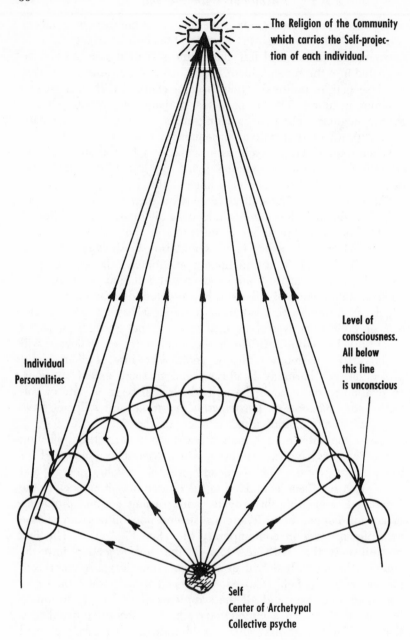

Figure 6. Stable State of a community of Religious believers.

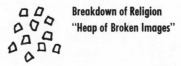

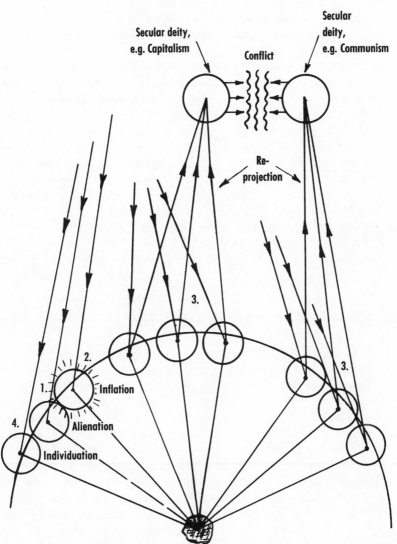

Figure 7. Breakdown of a Religious Projection

manipulative powers and denies the sacred mystery inherent in life and nature. 3. The third possibility is that the projected suprapersonal value which has been withdrawn from its religious container will be reprojected onto some secular or political movement (Case 3, Fig. 7). But secular purposes are never an adequate container for religious meaning. When religious energy is applied to a secular object we have what can be described as idolization—which is spurious, unconscious religion. The outstanding current example of reprojection is the conflict between communism and capitalism. Communism in particular is clearly a secular religion which actively attempts to channel religious energies to secular and social ends.

When the value of the Self is projected by opposing groups onto conflicting political ideologies, it is as though the original wholeness of the Self were split into antithetical fragments which war on each other. In such a case the antinomies of the Self or God are acted out in history. Both sides of the partisan conflict derive their energy from the same source, the shared Self; but being unconscious of this they are condemned to live out the tragic conflict in their lives. God himself is caught in the coils of the dark conflict. In every war within Western Civilization, both sides have prayed to the same God. As Matthew Arnold put it:

> And we are here as on a darkling plain
> Swept with confused alarms of struggle and flight
> Where ignorant armies clash by night.
>
> (DOVER BEACH)

4. The fourth possible way of dealing with the loss of a religious projection is shown in Case 4, (Fig. 7). If when the individual is thrown back on himself through the loss of a projected religious value, he is able to confront the ultimate questions of life that are posed for him, he may be able to use this opportunity for a decisive development in consciousness. If he is able to work consciously and responsibly with the activation of the unconscious he may discover the lost value, the god-image, within the psyche. This possibility is represented in the diagram by the circle that now has a larger section of itself outside the arc of unconsciousness. The connection between ego and Self is now consciously realized. In this case the loss of a religious projection has served a salutary purpose; it has been the stimulus which leads to the development of an individuated personality.

A prominent feature of the collective loss of the suprapersonal categories has been an increased pre-occupation with the sub-

Plate 2
DANAE by Titian

jectivity of the individual. This is really a modern phenomenon, and indeed could not exist as long as the transpersonal values were satisfactorily contained in a traditional collective religion. But once the traditional symbol system breaks down, it is as if a great surge of energy were returned to the individual psyche, and much greater interest and attention then becomes focused on the subjectivity of the individual. It is out of this phenomenon that depth psychology was discovered. The very existence of depth psychology is a symptom of our time. Other evidences are in all the arts. In plays and novels the most banal and commonplace individuals are described exhaustively in their most petty and personal aspects. A degree of value and attention is being given to inner subjectivity that never before happened. Actually this tendency is a pointer toward things to come. If it is pursued to its inevitable conclusion, it cannot help but lead more and more people to a rediscovery of the lost suprapersonal categories within themselves.

2. THE BREAKTHROUGH

At a certain point in psychological development, usually after an intense alienation experience, the ego-Self axis suddenly breaks into conscious view. The condition represented by Fig. 3 is realized. The ego becomes aware, experientially, of a transpersonal center to which the ego is subordinate.

Jung describes this happening as follows:
When a summit of life is reached, when the bud unfolds and from the lesser the greater emerges, then, as Nietzsche says, "One becomes Two," and the greater figure, which one always was but which remained invisible, appears to the lesser personality with the force of a revelation. He who is truly and hopelessly little will always drag the revelation of the greater down to the level of his littleness, and will never understand that the day of judgement for his littleness has dawned. But the man who is inwardly great will know that the long expected friend of his soul, the immortal one, has now really come, "to lead captivity captive" (Ephesians 4:8), that is, to seize hold of him by whom this immortal had always been confined and held prisoner, and to make his life flow into that greater life—a moment of deadliest peril! [2]

Myth and religion provide many images which symbolize this

[2] Jung, C. G., *The Archetypes and the Collective Unconscious*, C. W., Vol. 9, i, par. 217.

moment of breakthrough. Whenever man consciously encounters a divine agency which assists, commands or directs, we can understand it as an encounter of the ego with the Self.

The encounter generally occurs in the wilderness or in a fugitive state, i.e., alienation. Moses was a fugitive from the law, pasturing his father-in-law's sheep in the wilderness when Yahweh spoke to him from the burning bush and gave him his life-assignment (Exodus 3). Jacob, obliged to run away from home because of Esau's wrath, dreams of the heavenly ladder in the wilderness *(Picture 13)* and makes his covenant with God (Genesis 28:10-22). Francis Thompson, in his poem *The Kingdom of God is Within You,* uses this image:

> The angels keep their ancient places;—
> Turn but a stone, and start a wing!
> 'Tis ye, 'tis your estranged faces,
> That miss the many-splendored thing.
>
> But (when so sad thou canst not sadder)
> Cry—and upon thy so sore loss
> Shall shine the traffic of Jacob's ladder
> Pitched betwixt Heaven and Charing Cross.[3]

Jonah provides another example. His initial encounter with Yahweh occurred in the midst of normal life but could not be accepted, i.e., the ego was still too inflated to acknowledge the authority of the Self. Only after futile efforts to escape which lead him to ultimate despair in the belly of the whale could Jonah acknowledge and accept the transpersonal authority of Yahweh.

When a woman (or the anima in a man's psychology) encounters the Self it is often expressed as celestial impregnating power. Danae while imprisoned by her father is impregnated by Zeus through a golden shower and conceives Perseus *(Plate 2)*. Similarly, the annunciation to Mary is commonly depicted with impregnating rays from heaven *(Picture 14)*. A more psychological version of the same image is used by Bernini in his sculpture, *The Ecstasy of St. Theresa (Picture 15)*.

A modern example of this theme is the striking dream of a woman which was preceded by a long process of psychological effort: *I see a young man, naked, glistening with sweat who catches my attention first by his physical attitude—a combination of the falling motion of a Pieta figure and the energetic release position*

[3] Thompson, Francis, *Poetical Works,* London, Oxford University Press, 1965, p. 349 f.

Picture 13. JACOB'S DREAM by Gustave Doré.

Picture 14. THE ANNUNCIATION by Botticelli.

of the famous Greek Discobolus. He's in a group of other men who in an ambiguous way seem to be supporting him. He stands out from them partly by the color of his skin (bronze) and its texture (anointed, as it were, with sweat) but mainly by the fact that he had an enormous phallus in the form of a third, extended, leg (Picture 16).

The man is in agony with the burden of his erection. This shows not only in the athletic expense of effort (musculature and sweat), but also in the contortion of his facial expression. My sympathy for his plight, and my astonishment (admiration, intrigue) at his male member, draws me to him. We then join in intercourse. Just his entry is enough to cause in me an orgasm so deep and widespread that I can feel it in my ribs and lungs . . . even when I wake up. It's full of pain and pleasure in an indistinguishable sensation. My entire insides are, literally, "up-set," and my womb, specifically, feels as though it has made an entire revolution— inside-out or 180 degrees, I'm not sure which.

In addition to *The Discus Thrower (Picture 17)* and Michaelangelo's *Pieta (Picture 18),* the three-legged man also reminded the dreamer of an alchemical engraving *(Picture 19)* and a picture of a three-footed sun-wheel *(Picture 20)* she had once seen. Thus the dream figure is a rich condensation of multiple images

Opposite: Picture 15. THE ECSTASY OF ST. THERESA by Bernini.

74

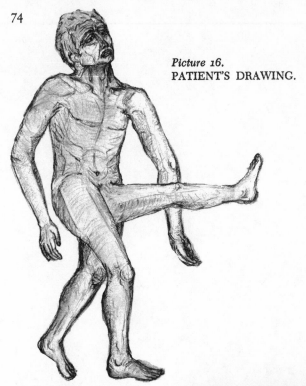

Picture 16.
PATIENT'S DRAWING.

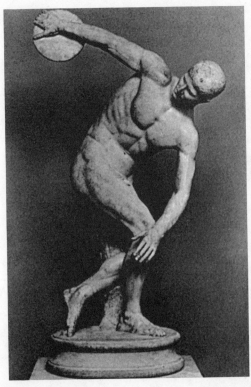

Picture 17.
DISKOBOLOS by Myron,
c. 460-450 B.C., Roman Copy.

Picture 18.
PIETA by Michelangelo.

Picture 19.
ALCHEMICAL DRAWING.

Picture 20. VARIETIES OF THE THREE-FOOTED SUN WHEEL.

and meanings which warrant extensive amplification. Without pursuing that task here, a few observations can be noted. The dreamer has been penetrated and transformed by a masculine entity of creative power. He is an athlete of both body and spirit (St. Paul). He is associated with the ultimate spiritual principle (the sun) and also expresses the whole process of psychic transformation (the alchemical picture).

For the dreamer, this dream initiated a whole new attitude and awareness of life. As its sexual imagery suggests, new levels of physical responsiveness were opened. In addition, the whole sensation function, heretofore largely unconscious, became available. Most important of all was an increase in authentic individual autonomy and the emergence of very sizable creative talents. By the accompanying associations it is evident that this dream expresses a decisive encounter not only with the animus but also with the Self. The triadic symbolism indicates emphasis on the process of concrete, spatio-temporal realization. (See Chapter 7.)

An outstanding example of the breakthrough of the ego-Self axis is the conversion of the apostle Paul (Acts 9:1-9), *(Picture 21).* Jonah tried to escape his vocation by flight; Saul attempted to escape his by persecuting the representatives of his own destiny. The very intensity of his attack against the Christians betrayed his involvement with their cause, for, as Jung says, "The important thing is what (a man) talks about, not whether he agrees with it or not." [4] That which one passionately hates is sure to represent an aspect of his own fate.

3. THE BOOK OF JOB

The Book of Job provides us with a remarkably comprehensive symbolic account of an encounter with the Self. Jung has written about Job in his *Answer to Job*.[5] In this book he treats the Job story as a turning point in the collective development of the

[4] Jung, C. G. *Symbols of Transformation.* C. W., Vol. 5, par. 99.
[5] Jung, C. G. "Answer to Job" in *Psychology and Religion: West and East,* C.W., Vol. 11.

Picture 21. THE CONVERSION OF ST. PAUL, Woodcut 1515.

Hebrew-Christian myth, involving an evolution of the God-image or Self-archetype. Job's encounter with Yahweh is considered to represent a decisive transition in man's awareness of the nature of God, which required in turn a response from God leading to His humanization and eventually to His incarnation as Christ. The story of Job can also be considered in another way, namely, as the description of an individual experience, in which the ego has its first major conscious encounter with the Self. I shall examine *Job* from the latter standpoint.

The present text of *Job* is a composite document and we cannot determine whether, in fact, it derives from an individual's actual experience. However, this is highly likely and in what follows I shall consider it as describing an individual's experience of active imagination. This is a process in which the imagination and the images it throws up are experienced as something separate from the ego—a "thou" or an "other"—to which the ego can relate, and with which the ego can have a dialogue.[6] The fact that *Job* is written in the form of a dialogue, the only book in the Old Testament canon to be so-constructed, supports the hypothesis that it may be based on an experience of active imagination. Even the repetitiousness of the dialogue rings true when we consider it as a record of personal experience. Returning again and again to the same point which the ego refuses to accept is typical behavior for personifications of the unconscious encountered in the process of active imagination.

The story begins with the plot between God and Satan to put Job to the test. The question to be answered is whether or not, through adversity, Job can be made to curse God. The wager in heaven can be understood as portraying the transpersonal or archetypal factors in the unconscious which are setting up Job's ordeal and which ultimately give it meaning. If Job's misfortunes were only fortuitous they would be chance and meaningless happenings without a transpersonal dimension of reference. It is significant that Job never entertains this possibility. The basic assumption that all things come from God, i.e., reflect a transpersonal purpose and meaning, is maintained throughout. This assumption of Job's corresponds to the necessary hypothesis that one must hold if he is to do active imagination at all. If one's moods and affects, which

---

[6] For Jung's description of active imagination see his essay on "The Transcendent Function" in *The Structure and Dynamics of the Psyche*, C. W., Vol. 8, pp. 67 ff.

Picture 22. THE FIRE OF GOD HAS FALLEN FROM HEAVEN.
Etching for the Book of Job by William Blake.

are the starting point for the effort of active imagination, are considered to be fortuitous or to have only external or physiological causes, there will be no ground for seeking their *psychological* meaning. The knowledge that a psychological meaning exists is acquired only by experience. In the beginning one must have at least enough faith to be willing to take the proposition of psychological meaning as an hypothesis to be tested.

Since Yahweh and Satan are working together, they can be considered as two aspects of the same thing, i.e. the Self. Satan provides the initiative and dynamism to set up Job's ordeal and hence represents the urge to individuation which must break up the psychological *status quo* in order to bring about a new level of development. The serpent played the same role for Adam and Eve in the Garden of Eden. Also similar to Eden is the fact that Job's ordeal is designed as a temptation. He is to be tempted to curse God. This would mean psychologically that the ego is being tempted to inflation, to set itself above the purposes of God, i.e., to identify with the Self.

Why should all this be necessary? Evidently Job still has some tendency to inflation. In spite of his blameless reputation, or perhaps because of it, there is some question whether or not he knows decisively the difference between himself and God, between the ego and the Self. Therefore the program is arranged to test the ego in the fire of tribulation and out of that ordeal comes Job's full encounter with the reality of God. If prior purposes can be discerned on the basis of effects we can then say that it was God's purpose to make Job aware of Him. Apparently the Self needs conscious realization and is obliged by the individuation urge to tempt and test the ego in order to bring about full ego-awareness of the Self's existence.

Initially Job is a prosperous, esteemed and happy man, corresponding to a contented "secure" ego blissfully unaware of the unconscious assumptions on which its shaky "security" rests. Abruptly, all that Job values and depends upon are withdrawn —family, possessions and health.

The calamities that precipitously befall Job are represented in an engraving by William Blake *(Picture 22)*. Above the picture Blake printed the caption, "The Fire of God is fallen from Heaven." (Job 1:16). Understood psychologically, the picture represents a break-up of the conscious *status quo* by an influx of fiery energy from the unconscious. Such an image heralds an individuation crisis, a major step in psychological development which requires

Plate 3
PAINTING OF A PATIENT
From C. G. Jung, *The Archetypes of the Collective Unconscious*

that old conditions be destroyed to make room for the new. Destructive or liberating effects may predominate, usually there is
a mixture of both. Emphasis on the latter is seen in a picture published in a case study by Jung *(Plate 3)*.[7] In this picture, which
began a decisive phase of individuation, the lightning from heaven
is blasting a sphere out of its surrounding matrix—the Self is being
born. The tarot card XVI *(Picture 23)* emphasizes the destructive
aspect. When the ego is particularly inflated, as represented by
the tower, the breakthrough of energies from the Self can be
dangerous. The appearance of the Self inaugurates a kind of
"last judgment" *(Picture 24)*. Only that survives which is sound
and based on reality.

With the loss of almost everything to which he attached value,
Job is plunged into an acute state of alienation corresponding
to Tolstoy's state as previously described (page 52). If the Self
is to be recognized as the supreme value, attachments to lesser
values must be destroyed. Job's life meaning was evidently connected to family, property and health. When deprived of these
he fell into despair and entered the dark night of the soul.[8]

> Perish the day when I was born . . .
> Why was I not still-born,
> Why did I not die when I came out of the womb? . . .
> Why should the sufferer be born to see the light?
> Why is life given to men who find it so bitter? . . .
> Why should a man be born to wander blindly,
> hedged in by God on every side? [9]

[7] Jung, C. G. *The Archetypes and the Collective Unconscious*, C.W., Vol.
9 i, par, 525 ff Picture 2.

[8] St. John of the Cross repeatedly uses *Job* as a paradigm of the dark night
of the soul. In speaking of the benefits of the dark night he writes, ". . . the
soul learns to commune with God with more respect and more courtesy, such
as a soul must ever observe in converse with the most high. These it knew
not in its prosperous times of comfort and consolation . . . Even so likewise
the preparation which God granted to Job in order that he might speak with
Him consisted not in those delights and glories which Job himself reports
that he was wont to have in his God, but in leaving him naked upon a dung-
hill, abandoned and even persecuted by his friends, filled with anguish and
bitterness, and the earth covered with worms. And then the Most High God,
He that lifts up the poor man from the dung-hill was pleased to come down
and speak with him there face to face, revealing to him the depths and heights
of His wisdom, in a way that he had never done in the time of his prosperity."
(*Dark Night of the Soul*, I, XII, 3, See also, V, 5; II, VII, 1; II, IX, 7 & 8;
II, XVII, 8; II, XXIII, 6.)

[9] Job 3:3-23, New English Bible.

Picture 23.
THE TOWER, Tarot Card,
Marseilles Deck.

THE TOWER OF DESTRUCTION

With these words Job gives vent to his suicidal despair and his utter alienation from life and its meaning. The repeated questions "Why?" indicate that Job is searching desperately for *meaning;* meaning lost and regained can be considered the ultimate theme if Job is viewed as an individual document.

In states of depression and despair, much of the libido which normally maintains conscious interest and vitality has sunk into the unconscious. This in turn activates the unconscious, causing an increase in dream and fantasy imagery. We can assume that such an occurrence happened to Job. Personified images from the unconscious come to Job in the form of friends or advisers and speak to him in active imagination.

These figures confront him with another viewpoint and gradually draw him closer to the encounter with the numinosum—Yahweh himself. One of the evidences that the speeches by Job's counsellors

Picture 24. FIRE RAINS FROM HEAVEN by Albrecht Dürer. Engraving for "The Revelation of St. John."

are authentic active imagination is that they are contaminated mixtures of several elements. They are partly elaborations of the conventional religious viewpoint that Job has discarded, but they are also partly genuine autonomous expressions of the deeper layers of the unconscious. This kind of contaminated mixture of different things is common in active imagination. Hence the process, to be productive, requires the alert, active participation of consciousness which leads to real dialogue and not just a passive acceptance of whatever the unconscious says. For instance, in the first speech of Eliphaz, Job is told:

> Think how once you encouraged those who faltered,
> how you braced feeble arms,
> how a word from you upheld the stumblers
> and put strength into weak knees.
> But now that adversity comes upon you, you lose patience;
> it touches you, and you are unmanned.[10]

This can be considered as Job's own self-criticism speaking. He is realizing how easy it had been for him to give advice and help to others, but now he can't take his own advice. This self-criticism can only depress him still further and make him even more miserable. Eliphaz continues with superficial reassurance and conventional expressions which perhaps Job had given to others in distress:

> Does your blameless life give you no hope?
> For consider, what innocent man has ever perished?
> Where have you seen the upright destroyed? [11]

These shallow and unrealistic thoughts are of no help. They are a whistling in the dark against the reality of life which is pressing against Job so heavily. Perhaps the very expression of such a superficial, wish-fulfilling view was enough to dissolve it, at least temporarily, because Eliphaz immediately shifts to a deeper chain of associations. Eliphaz tells Job of a numinous dream. Considering the entire dialogue as Job's active imagination, it will be Job's dream that he is being given or being reminded of.

> A word stole into my ears,
> and they caught the whisper of it;
> in the anxious visions of the night,
> when a man sinks into deepest sleep,

[10] Ibid., 4:3-5.
[11] Ibid., 4:6-7.

> terror seized me and shuddering;
> the trembling of my body frightened me.
> A wind brushed my face
> and made the hairs bristle on my flesh;
> and a figure stood there whose shape I could not discern,
> an apparition loomed before me,
> and I heard the sound of a low voice:
> "Can mortal man be more righteous than God,
> or the creature purer than his Maker?" [12]

Shortly later, Job himself mentions frightening dreams.

> When I think that my bed will comfort me,
> that sleep will relieve my complaining,
> thou dost terrify me with dreams
> and affright me with visions.[13]

Blake has done a striking illustration of Job's dreams *(Picture 25)*. In the picture Yahweh is entwined by a serpent, his Satanic side, presumably. He is pointing to hell which has opened up beneath Job and threatens to engulf him by flames and ominous clutching figures. The depths of the unconscious have opened and Job is faced with the primordial power of nature. Obviously this is nothing with which to argue, any more than one would dispute with a tiger he chanced to meet. But Job does not learn from his dreams; he must have a more powerful lesson.

Job is convinced of his innocence and righteousness and hence unconscious of the shadow. For this reason his companions must speak repeatedly about wickedness and evil ones as a compensation for Job's one-sided conscious attitude of purity and goodness. Job is dimly aware that his experience is making him feel bestial and dirty. At once point he exclaims:

> Am I the monster of the deep, am I the
> sea-serpent, that thou settest a watch over me? [14]

and later:

> Though I wash myself with soap
> or cleanse my hands with lye,
> thou wilt thrust me into the mud
> and my clothes will make me loathsome.[15]

[12] Ibid., 4:12-17.
[13] Ibid., 7:13-14.
[14] Ibid., 7:12.
[15] Ibid., 9:30-31.

Picture 25. YAHWEH FRIGHTENS JOB WITH A GLIMPSE OF HELL, William Blake.

At one point he does acknowledge past sins;

> Wilt thou chase a driven leaf,
> Wilt thou pursue dry chaff,
> prescribing punishment for me
> and making me heir to the iniquities
>   of my youth . . . ? [16]

He does not say what the iniquities of his youth were and obviously does not consider himself responsible for them now. Those past sins will be repressed contents which he does not want to make conscious since they would contradict his self-righteous image of himself. Job's self-righteousness is revealed most clearly in Chapters 29 and 30:

[16] Ibid., 13:25-26.

If I could only go back to the old days . . .
If I went through the gate out of the town
to take my seat in the public square,
young men saw me and kept out of sight;
old men rose to their feet,
men in authority broke off their talk
and put their hands to their lips;
the voices of the nobles died away,
and every man held his tongue.
They listened to me expectantly
and waited in silence for my opinion . . .
I presided over them, planning their course,
like a king encamped with his troops.[17]
. . .
"But now I am laughed to scorn
by men of younger generation,
men whose fathers I would have disdained
to put with the dogs who kept my flock." [18]

Job's scornful attitude towards his intellectual inferiors is per-haps one of the "iniquities of his youth" and indicates an inflated ego which projects the weak, shadow side on others. The process of individuation requires that he consciously accept and assimilate his dark, inferior side.

The over-all effect of Job's ordeal is to bring about a death and rebirth experience. However, in the midst of his complaints he is still the once-born man. He reveals his ignorance of the twice-born state in the following passage:

If a tree is cut down,
there is hope that it will sprout again
and fresh shoots will not fail.
Though its roots grow old in the earth,
and its stump is dying in the ground,
if it scents water it may break into bud
and make new growth like a young plant.
But a man dies, and he disappears;
man comes to his end, and where is he?
As the waters of a lake dwindle,
or as a river shrinks and runs dry,
so mortal man lies down, never to rise
until the very sky splits open.
If a man dies, can he live again? [19]

[17] Ibid., 29:1-25.
[18] Ibid., 30:1.
[19] Ibid., 14:7-12.

As the dialogue continues between Job and his companions a mixture of profound truths and conventional, banal opinions are expressed. Generally he is advised to return to the traditional and orthodox views. He is told to accept God's chastening humbly without questioning or trying to understand. In other words, he is advised to sacrifice the intellect, to behave as though he were less conscious than he is. Such behavior would be a regression and he quite properly rejects it. Instead he remonstrates against God, and says in effect, "If you are a loving and good father, why don't you behave like one?" In daring to contend with God, there can be no question that from one standpoint Job is acting in an inflated way; but the whole context makes it clear that this is a necessary and controlled inflation; it is essential for the encounter with God. Fatal inflation would have occurred if he had taken his wife's advice to curse God and die. But Job avoids both extremes. He does not sacrifice the measure of consciousness he has already achieved, but also he does not curse God. He continues to question the meaning of his ordeal and will not relent until he knows for what he is being punished.

Of course the very fact that he thinks in terms of punishment means he is relating to God in an immature way, in terms of a parent-child relationship. This is one of the attitudes from which the encounter with deity releases him. But most important is Job's insistence that he discover the *meaning* of his experience. He challenges God boldly, saying:

> . . . take thy heavy hand clean away from me and
> let not the fear of thee strike me with dread.
> Then summon me, and I will answer;
> or I will speak first, and do thou answer me.[20]

In chapter 32 a change takes place. Job's three companions have finished and now we are introduced to a fourth man, previously unmentioned, named Elihu. He claims he had refrained from entering the discussion previously because of his youth. This brings up the theme of "3 and 4" to which Jung has drawn attention. If Elihu can be considered as the previously missing fourth function, Job's totality has finally been constellated. This interpretation also fits the nature of Elihu's discourse which is largely a prelude to Yahweh's appearance and presents many of the same ideas Yahweh is to express even more forcefully. Particularly noteworthy are Elihu's remarks about dreams:

[20] Ibid., 13:21-22.

In dreams, in visions of the night,
when deepest sleep falls upon men,
while they sleep in their beds, God makes them listen,
and his correction strikes them with terror.
To turn a man from reckless conduct,
to check the pride of mortal man,
at the edge of the pit he holds him back alive
and stops him from crossing the river of death.[21]

This reference to dreams and their function has an astonishing psychological accuracy. It is further proof that *Job* is the report of an individual's actual experience. Evidently Job's unconscious tried to correct his conscious attitude through dreams without success. The dreams can thus be seen as an anticipation of Job's later conscious encounter with Yahweh. It is amazing to find in this ancient text a description of the compensatory function of dreams which Jung has only recently demonstrated.[22]

Following Elihu's speech Yahweh himself appears. The numinous, transpersonal Self manifests out of the whirlwind *(Picture 26)*. Yahweh delivers a magnificent speech which must have been the product of a great deal of conscious effort in trying to assimilate the raw numinosity that surely accompanied the original experience. Yahweh's reply is a review of the attributes of deity and a majestic description of the difference between God and man, i.e., between Self and ego:

Where were you when I laid the earth's foundations?
Tell me, if you know and understand,
Who settled its dimensions? Surely you should know.
Who stretched his measuring-line over it?
On what do its supporting pillars rest?
Who set its corner-stone in place,
When the morning stars sang together
And all the sons of God shouted aloud? [23]

The ego did not make the psyche and knows nothing about the profound foundations on which its (the ego's) existence rests:

Have you descended to the springs of the sea
Or walked in the unfathomable deep?
Have the gates of death been revealed to you?
Have you ever seen the door-keepers of the place of darkness?
Have you comprehended the vast expanse of the world? [24]

[21] Ibid., 33:15-18.
[22] Cf. e.g., Jung, C. G., *The Structure and Dynamics of the Psyche*, C.W., Vol. 8, par. 477 ff.
[23] Ibid., 38:4-7.
[24] Ibid., 38:16-18.

Picture 26. YAHWEH ANSWERS JOB OUT OF THE WHIRLWIND, William Blake.

The ego is being reminded that it knows nothing about the psyche in its totality. The part cannot encompass the whole:

> Can you bind the cluster of the Pleiades
> or loose Orion's belt?
> Can you bring out the signs of the Zodiac in their season
> or guide Aldebaron and its train?
> Did you proclaim the rules that govern the heavens,
> or determine the laws of nature on earth? [25]

The ego is here being contrasted with the size and power of the archetypes which determine psychic existence.

Then Yahweh turns to the animal kingdom and passes in review the uncanny powers of the beasts, especially the most monstrous ones of all:

---

[25] Ibid., 38:31-33.

Behold Behemoth which I made as I made you.[26]

. . . .

Can you draw out Leviathan with a fish hook,
or press down his tongue with a cord? [27]

Now Job is being shown the abysmal aspect of God and the depths
of his own psyche which contains devouring monsters remote from
human values. This aspect of the theophany as pictured by Blake
is shown in *Picture 27*. Behemoth and Leviathan represent the
primordial concupiscence of being. God reveals his own shadow
side and since man participates in God as the ground of his being,
he must likewise share his darkness. The ego's self-righteousness
here receives the *coup de grace*.

By the conclusion of Yahweh's self-revelation Job has undergone
a decisive change. A repentance or metanoia has occurred:

I had heard of thee by the hearing of the ear,
but now my eye sees thee;
therefore I despise myself,
and repent in dust and ashes.[28]

Job's questions have been answered, not rationally but by living
experience. What he has been seeking, the meaning of his suffering,
has been found. It is nothing less than the conscious realization of
the autonomous archetypal psyche; and this realization could come
to birth only through an ordeal. The Book of Job is really a record
of a divine initiation process, a testing by ordeal, which when successful leads to a new state of being. It is analogous to all initiation rituals which attempt to bring about a transition from one state
of consciousness to another.

The cause of Job's ordeal is Yahweh, through his dynamic agency,
Satan. Satan's psychological role in the Job story is described co-
gently by Rivkah Schärf Kluger:

He (Satan) appears here in full light, as the metaphysical foe of a
peaceful life and worldly comfort. He intervenes as a disturbance
and hindrance to the natural order of living and steps in man's way
like the *mal'ah Yahweh* as *Satan* in the path of Balaam. However,
while the Balaam story concerns the experience of a clash of wills
and blind obedience—a first realization, so to speak, that God's will,
not one's own, must be fulfilled—in Job's case it is a matter of con-

---

[26] Job 4:15, RSV.
[27] Ibid., 41:1.
[28] Ibid., 42:5-6.

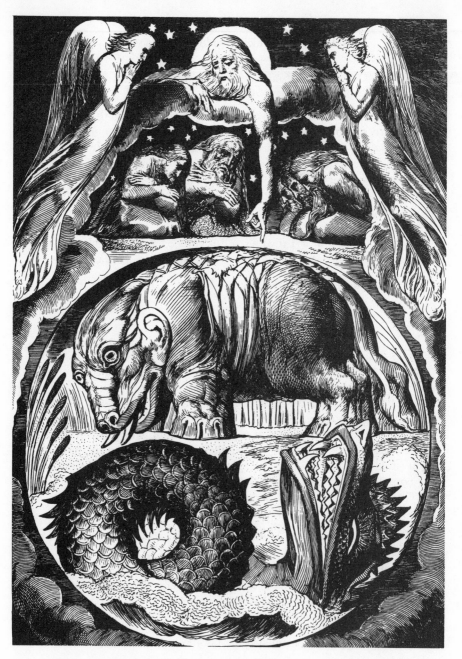

Picture 27. YAHWEH SHOWS JOB THE DEPTHS (BEHEMOTH),
William Blake.

scious submission to God's will, born of inner insight. Satan is here truly Lucifer, the bringer of light. He brings man the knowledge of God, but through the suffering he inflicts on him, Satan is the misery of the world which alone drives man inward, into the "other world." [29]

This description of Satan, which must be acknowledged as psychologically accurate, brings him in close proximity to the fiigure of Wisdom. In *Ecclesiasticus*, the feminine personification, Wisdom, is described in these terms:

> Wisdom brings up her own sons,
> and cares for those who seek her.
>
> . . .
>
> for though she takes him at first through winding ways,
> bringing fear and faintness on him,
> plaguing him with her discipline until she can trust him,
> and testing him with her ordeals,
> in the end she will lead him back to the straight road,
> and reveal her secrets to him.[30]

According to this passage, Wisdom puts her sons to the test just as Yahweh did Job, through the agency of Satan. The favorites of God receive the severest ordeals, i.e., it is one's potential for individuation that causes the test. John Donne makes this observation:

> . . . the best men have had most laid upon them. As soone as I heare God say, that he hath found *an upright man, that feares God, and eschews evill,* (Job I.1) in the next lines I finde a Commission to Satan, to bring in Sabeans and Chaldeans upon his cattell, and servants, and fire and tempest upon his children, and loathsome diseases upon himselfe. As soone as I heare God say, That he hath found *a man according to his own heart,* (I Sam. 13:14) I see his sonnes ravish his daughters, and then murder one another, and then rebell against the Father, and put him into straites for his life. As soone as I hear God testifie of Christ at his Baptisme, *This is my beloved Sonne in whom I am well pleased,* (Mat. 3:17) I finde that Sonne of his *led up by the Spirit, to be tempted of the Devill.* (Matt. 4:1) And after I heare God ratifie the same testimony againe, at his Transfiguration, *(This is my beloved Sonne, in whom I am well pleased)* (Matt. 17:5) I finde that beloved Sonne of his, deserted, abandoned, and given over to Scribes, and Pharisees, and Publicans, and Herodians, and Priests, and Souldiers, and people, and Judges,

[29] Kluger, Rivkah Schärf, *Satan in the Old Testament,* Evanston, Northwestern University Press, 1967, p. 132.
[30] Ecclus., 4:11-21, Jerusalem Bible.

and witnesses, and executioners, and he that was called the beloved Sonne of God, and made partaker of the glory of heaven, in this world, in his Transfiguration, is made now the Sewer of all the corruption, of all the sinnes of this world, as no Sonne of God, but a meere man, as no man, but a contemptible worme.[31]

Although the testing may bring wisdom it is a fearful thing and hence the Lord's prayer requests that we be spared it: "and do not bring us to the test, but save us from the evil one." [32]

Jung considers that Job was released from his despair through a process of increasing consciousness on the part of deity. Kluger reports the following remark of Jung in paraphrase:

> In his great final speech God reveals himself to Job in all his frightfulness. It is as if he said to Job: "Look, that's what I am like. That is why I treated you like this." Through the suffering which he inflicted upon Job out of his own nature, God has come to this self-knowledge and admits, as it were, this knowledge of his frightfulness to Job. *And that is what redeems the man Job.* This is really the solution to the enigma of Job, that is, a true justification for Job's fate, which, without this background, would, in its cruelty and injustice, remain an open problem. Job appears here clearly as a sacrifice, but also as the carrier of the divine fate, and that gives meaning to his suffering and liberation of his soul.[33]

Rudolf Otto, the man who gave the experience of the *numinosium* its first clear formulation, has used Job's encounter with Yahweh as an example of the numinous experience. I quote him at some length because the passage conveys so well his understanding of the numinous *mysterium:*

> And then Elohim Himself appears to conduct His own defence in person. And He conducts it to such effect that Job avows himself to be overpowered, truly and rightly overpowered, not merely silenced by superior strength. Then he confesses: "Therefore I abhor myself and *repent* in dust and ashes." That is an admission of inward *convincement* and conviction, not of impotent collapse and submission to merely superior power, Nor is there here at all the frame of mind to which St. Paul now and then gives utterance; e.g., Rom. ix. 20: "Shall the thing formed say to him that formed it, Why has thou made me thus? Hath not the potter power over the clay, of the same lump to make one vessel unto honour, and another unto dishonour?"

[31] Simpson, E. M., (Ed.), *John Donne's Sermons on the Psalms and Gospels,* University of California Press, Berkeley and Los Angeles, 1967, p. 97 f.
[32] Matt. 6:9 NEB.
[33] Kluger, *Satan,* p. 129.

To interpret the passage in Job thus would be a misunderstanding of it. This chapter does not proclaim, as Paul does, the renunciation of, the realization of the impossibility of, a "theodicy"; rather, it aims at putting forward a real theodicy of its own, and a better one than that of Job's friends; a theodicy able to convict even a Job, and not only to convict him, but utterly to still every inward doubt that assailed his soul. For latent in the weird experience that Job underwent in the revelation of Elohim is at once an inward relaxing of his soul's anguish and an appeasement, an appeasement which would alone and in itself perfectly suffice as the solution of the problem of the Book of Job, even without Job's rehabilitation in Chapter xlii, where recovered prosperity comes as an extra payment thrown in after quittance has been already rendered. But what is this strange "moment" of experience that here operates at once as a vindication of God to Job and a reconciliation of Job to God? [34]

After reviewing the examples of his mighty works as presented by Yahweh—Leviathan, Behemoth, etc.,—Otto continues:

Assuredly these beasts would be the most unfortunate examples that one could hit upon if searching for evidences of the purposefulness of the divine "wisdom." But they, no less than all the previous examples and the whole context, tenor, and sense of the entire passage, do express in masterly fashion the downright stupendousness, the wellnigh daemonic and wholly incomprehensible character of the eternal creative power; how, incalculable and "wholly other," it mocks at all conceiving but can yet stir the mind to its depths, fascinate and overbrim the heart. What is meant is the *mysterium* not as mysterious simply, but at the same time also as "fascinating" and "august"; and here, too, these latter meanings live, not in any explicit concepts, but in the tone, the enthusiasm, in the very rhythm of the entire exposition. And here is indeed the point of the whole passage, comprising alike the theodicy and the appeasement and calming of Job's soul. The *mysterium*, simply as such, would merely (as discussed above) be a part of the "absolute inconceivability" of the numen, and that, though it might strike Job utterly dumb, could not convict him inwardly. That of which we are conscious is rather an *intrinsic value* in the incomprehensible—a value inexpressible, positive, and "fascinating." This is incommensurable with thoughts of rational human teleology and is not assimilated to them: it remains in all its mystery. But it is as it becomes felt in consciousness that Elohim is justified and at the same time Job's soul brought to peace.[35]

[34] Otto, Rudolf, *The Idea of the Holy*, London, Oxford University Press, 1910, p. 78.
[35] Ibid., p. 80.

Job drama is personally applicable to all. It speaks immedi-
to the almost universal question, "Why must this happen to
We all have an underlying resentment against fate and reality
h is a residue of inflation. Such resentment takes many forms:
nly I had had a better childhood;" "If only I were married;"
"If only I were not married;" "If only I had a better husband or
wife," etc., etc. All of these "if onlys" are the means by which one
excuses himself from relating productively to reality as it is. They
are symptoms of inflation which will not grant the existence of a
greater reality than one's personal desires. Job asked why his misery
should happen to him. The answer that emerges from the Book
of Job is so that he may see God.

Blake has captured the essential feature of the individuated ego
in his picture of the repentant and rejuvenated Job *(Picture 28)*.
What is pictured is the *sacrificial attitude*. Having experienced the
transpersonal center of the psyche, the ego recognizes its subordinate position and is prepared to serve the totality and its ends
rather than make personal demands. Job has become an individuated ego.

4. THE INDIVIDUATED EGO

Individuation is a process, not a realized goal. Each new level of
integration must submit to further transformation if development
is to proceed. However, we do have some indications concerning
what to expect as a result of the ego's conscious encounter with the
Self. Speaking generally, the individuation urge promotes a state
in which the ego is related to the Self without being identified
with it. Out of this state there emerges a more or less continuous
dialogue between the conscious ego and the unconscious, and also
between outer and inner experience. A twofold split is healed to the
extent individuation is achieved; first the split between conscious
and unconscious which began at the birth of consciousness, and
second the split between subject and object. The dichotomy between outer and inner reality is replaced by a sense of unitary
reality.[36-37] It is as though original unconscious wholeness and

[36] Neumann, Erich, "The Psyche and the Transformation of the Reality
Planes" *Eranos-Jahrbuch* XXI. Zurich, Rhein-Verlag 1953. Translated in *Spring*,
Analytical Psychology Club of New York, 1956. I am in debt to this paper of
Neumann's which is the clearest presentation we have of this most difficult
subject.

[37] Jung discusses unitary reality under the term *unus mundus* in *Mysterium
Coniunctionis*, C.W., Vol. 14, par. 759 ff.

Picture 28. JOB SACRIFICES TO YAHWEH, William Blake.

oneness with life, in which we began and out of which we had to
emerge, can now be recovered in part on a conscious level. Ideas
and images representing infantilism at one stage of development
represent wisdom at another stage. Images and attributes of the
Self are now experienced as separate from and supraordinate to
the ego. This experience brings with it the realization that one is
not master in his own house. He comes to realize that there is an
autonomous inner directiveness, separate from the ego and often
antagonistic to it. Such an awareness is sometimes releasing and

sometimes exceedingly burdensome. One may indeed feel suddenly cast in the role of St. Christopher (*Picture 29*).

The dawning realization of something living in the same house with oneself is often presaged by certain types of dreams, presenting the dreamer with happenings paradoxical or miraculous. Such dreams open up a transpersonal category of experience alien and strange to consciousness. An example of such a dream is the following. The patient was a woman who was a scientist with a very rational matter-of-fact mind. This was her dream: *A man (a scientist of her acquaintance) was having a heart attack. He picked up a Canna plant and clutched it to his breast. Immediately his heart attack was healed. Then he turned to the dreamer and said, "My fellow scientists may laugh at me for using this treatment, but it works and my children are too young to be left fatherless."*

This dream was followed a short while later by a singular experience of synchronicity that finally penetrated the dreamer's rational, mechanistic world view and was experienced as something impressive. Like the super-order in the earlier dream, it is as if the plant were able to drain off the effects of the heart attack and restore the heart to its previous state. The plant symbolizes the vegetative state of life; it is analogous to the autonomic or vegetative nervous system. On the psychological level it represents a primordial, vegetative state or mode of life experience that has a reservoir which can take up destructive excesses of energy that may accumulate in the conscious personality. This happening is experienced by the conscious mind as miraculous, i.e., transcending the categories of conscious understanding.

Another example of the same theme is a dream of a man in the late thirties who had a very alienating childhood. Both parents were alcoholics, so the patient was obliged to assume precociously adult responsibilities and attitudes if the family was to function at all. Hence he grew up into an extremely rational man, functioning well in a responsible position. But then he began to lose his bearings. He didn't like his work; he didn't know what he wanted. Progressively, everything he was doing lost all meaning. He was very difficult in therapy because we couldn't get beyond rational discussion. Then he had this dream: *He met a strange and unusual woman whom he felt he had heard of before. She was an exponent of homeopathic medicine. After talking with her awhile he exclaimed, "How can you believe in such a thing as homeopathy? The latest scientific medical advice is always the best. Homeopathy is only a relic of primitive magic." In response, the woman smiled mysteri-*

Picture 29. ST. CHRISTOPHER CARRYING CHRIST AS A SPHERE,
Oil painting by the Master of Messkirch (?).

ously and said, "Yes, exactly." At this the dreamer was flabbergasted and awoke.

In his associations to this dream the patient said he knew nothing about homeopathy except that it used the principle of similarity. He was reminded of Frazer's account of homeopathic magic in *The Golden Bough* and he also thought of my method of dream interpretation, the method of amplification which brings similar images from mythology to amplify and clarify dreams. He had no associations to the woman, but she is obviously the anima who possesses the secret knowledge of the unconscious and is serving as a bridge between the ego and the collective unconscious.

The dream indicates that the unconscious is being activated and is presenting him with a whole new mode of experience, something similar to primitive magic. According to this mode of experience, analogies are taken as realities. It is the method of associative analogical thinking. This is the way the unconscious works, by symbolical analogy. It is the principle on which our method of dream interpretation is based—amplification by analogy. It is completely erroneous to apply such a primitive mode in dealing with outer reality; that would involve us in magical and superstitious practices of all kinds. But it is precisely the right approach to deal with the unconscious and to make contact with the archetypal psyche.

Modern man urgently needs to re-establish meaningful contact with the primitive layer of the psyche. I do not mean by this the compulsive expression of unconscious primitive affects which is a symptom of dissociation. I mean rather the primitive mode of experience that sees life as an organic whole. In dreams the image of an animal, a primitive, or a child is commonly a symbolic expression for the source of help and healing. Often in fairy tales it is an animal that shows the hero a way out of the difficulty. The images of the primitive and the child serve a healing function because they symbolize our birthright to wholeness, that original state in which we are in rapport with nature and its transpersonal energies which guide and support. It is through the child or primitive in ourselves that we make connection with the Self and heal the state of alienation. In order to relate to the mentality of the child and primitive consciously, rather than unconsciously and inflatedly, we must learn how to incorporate primitive categories of experience into our world view without denying or damaging our conscious, scientific categories of space, time and causality. We must learn how to apply primitive modes of experience psychologically, to the inner world, rather than physically in relation to the outer world. To be primitive in our relation to the outer world is to be superstitious; but to be primitive in relation to the inner world of the psyche is to be wise.

Jung achieved such an attitude of sophisticated primitivity and that is why all who knew him could not fail to be impressed by his wisdom. Only a few days before his death he was asked by an interviewer about his notion of God. He replied in these words: "To this day God is the name by which I designate all things which cross my willful path violently and recklessly, all things which upset my subjective views, plans and intentions and change the course of my life for better or worse." [38]

The view Jung is here expressing is essentially a primitive view, albeit a conscious and sophisticated one. Jung is calling "God" what most people call chance or accident. He experiences apparently arbitrary happenings as meaningful rather than meaningless. This is precisely how the primitive experiences life. For the primitive everything is saturated with psychic meaning and has hidden connections with transpersonal powers. The primitive, like the child, lives in a world that is continuous with himself. He is in rapport with the cosmos. The more one attempts to relate consciously to the depths of the psyche, the more he is led to the same attitude expressed by Jung, namely, that all the vicissitudes of the outer and inner life have a meaning and are expressions of transpersonal patterns and powers. Chance as a category of experience is a symptom of the alienated life. For the Self-connected man, as for the child and the primitive, chance does not exist. Perhaps this is the meaning of Jesus' saying, "Unless you turn and become like children you will never enter the Kingdom of Heaven." [39]

Emerson expressed the same idea, namely that law lies behind all apparent chance:

> The secret of the world is the tie between person and event . . . the soul contains the event that shall befall it . . . the event is the print of your form.[40]
>
> Events grow on the same stem with persons.[41]

[38] Interview published in *Good Housekeeping Magazine*, Dec. 1961.
[39] Matt. 18:13.
[40] Emerson, Ralph Waldo, *The Conduct of Life*, New York, Dolphin Books, Doubleday & Co., p. 29.
[41] *Ibid.*, p. 30.

> Each creature puts forth from itself its own condition and sphere, as the slug sweats out its slimy house on the pear leaf.[42]
>
> A man will see his character emitted in the events that seem to meet, but which exude from and accompany him.[43]
>
> . . . there are no contingencies . . . Law rules throughout existence . . .[44]

In the early stages of psychological development, God is hidden—in the cleverest hiding place of all—in identification with oneself, one's own ego. This idea of the hidden God corresponds to the Gnostic myth of Sophia, a personification of the Wisdom of God. In the process of creation, Sophia, the divine wisdom, descended into matter; and then in the course of that descent she became lost and imprisoned in matter, thus becoming the hidden God which is in need of release and redemption. This notion of the divine spirit imprisoned in matter, hidden in the darkness of the mind, represents the Self hidden in identification with the ego. Matter, which is hiding Sophia, symbolizes the concrete, temporal, earthy reality of the individual ego. If God is imprisoned in matter, in the immature personality, the task of psychological development is no less than the redemption of God by human consciousness.

The redemption of God was a theme basic to alchemy. The alchemical opus was a work of redemption. The whole process of transmutation attempted to release and redeem a supreme value from its bondage in base matter. The base matter was the *prima materia*, the stuff that one started with, corresponding to the inflated immaturities of one's own psyche. This was to be transformed into the philosopher's stone, a divine essence. The *prima materia* is our ego-Self identity, the residue of original inflation. To submit this material to the alchemical process means to apply conscious effort and attention to the task of refining and separating this composite mixture to the end that the Self or archetypal psyche will be freed from its contamination with the ego.

There is a contrast between the conventional Christian attitude which has the theme of passive redemption of man through faith in Christ, and the alchemical attitude which is an active effort by man to redeem God. About this contrast, Jung writes:

> . . . (In the Christian attitude) man attributes to himself the need of redemption and leaves the work of redemption, the actual *athlon*, or

[42] *Ibid.*, p. 30.
[43] *Ibid.*, p. 31.
[44] *Ibid.*, p. 35.

opus, to the autonomous divine figure; . . . (in the alchemical attitude) man takes upon himself the duty of carrying out the redeeming *opus*, and attributes the state of suffering and consequent need of redemption to the *anima mundi* imprisoned in matter.[45]

and again:

. . . the alchemical opus is the labor of Man the Redeemer in the cause of the divine world-soul slumbering and awaiting redemption in matter. The Christian earns the fruits of grace from the work performed by Christ, but the alchemist creates for himself by his own effort a "panacea of life." (Paraphrased slightly.)[46]

Modern man is obliged to proceed in much the same way as the alchemist. If he has no recourse to passive redemption by the mediation of sacred images, he must rely on his own active efforts to work on his own *prima materia*, the unconscious, in hopes of releasing and bringing to awareness the suprapersonal nature of the psyche itself. This is the central theme: *Psychological development in all its phases is a redemptive process. The goal is to redeem by conscious realization, the hidden Self, hidden in unconscious identification with the ego.*

The repetitive cycle of inflation and alienation is superseded by the conscious process of individuation when awareness of the reality of the ego-Self axis occurs. Once the reality of the transpersonal center has been experienced a dialectic process between ego and Self can, to some extent, replace the previous pendulum swing between inflation and alienation. But the dialogue of individuation is not possible as long as the ego thinks that everything in the psyche is of its own making. About this mistaken attitude Jung says:

. . . all modern people feel alone in the world of the psyche because they assume that there is nothing that they have not made up. This is the very best demonstration of our God-almightiness, which simply comes from the fact that we think we have invented everything psychical—that nothing would be done if we did not do it; for that is our basic idea and it is an extraordinary assumption . . . Then one is all alone in one's psyche, exactly like the creator before the creation.[47]

[45] Jung, C. G., *Psychology and Alchemy*, C.W., Vol. 12, par. 414.
[46] *Ibid.*, par. 557.
[47] From excerpts of a seminar given by Jung on the *Interpretation of Visions*, published in *Spring*, Analytical Psychology Club of New York, 1962, p. 110.

For the modern man, a conscious encounter with the autonomous archetypal psyche is equivalent to the discovery of God. After such an experience he is no longer alone in his psyche and his whole world view is altered. He is freed to a large extent from projections of the Self onto secular aims and objects. He is released from the tendency to identify with any particular partisan faction which might lead him to live out the conflict of opposites in the outer world. Such a person is consciously committed to the process of individuation.

The *I Ching* describes the effect an individuated person can have:

> . . . in nature a holy seriousness is to be seen in the fact that natural occurrences are uniformly subject to law. Contemplation of the divine meaning underlying the workings of the universe gives to the man who is called upon to influence others the means of producing like effects. This requires that power of inner concentration which religious contemplation develops in great men strong in faith. It enables them to apprehend the mysterious and divine laws of life, and by means of profoundest inner concentration they give expression to these laws in their own persons. Thus a hidden spiritual power emanates from them, influencing and dominating others without their being aware of how it happens.[48]

Stated in the broadest possible terms, individuation seems to be the innate urge of life to realize itself consciously. The transpersonal life energy, in the process of self-unfolding, uses human consciousness, a product of itself, as an instrument for its own self-realization. A glimpse of this process gives one a new perspective on the vicissitudes of human life and makes one realize that:

> Though the mills of God grind slowly,
> Yet they grind exceeding fine.

---

[48] Wilhelm, Richard (Trans.) *The I Ching or Book of Changes,* Bollingen Series XIX, Princeton University Press, 1950. Commentary on Hexagram #20, Contemplation, p. 88.

Part II

INDIVIDUATION AS A WAY OF LIFE

. . . the work of human works . . . (is) to establish, in and by means of each one of us, an absolutely original center in which the universe reflects itself in a unique and inimitable way.

—PIERRE TEILHARD DE CHARDIN °

° *The Phenomenon of Man*, New York, Harper Torch Books, 1961, p. 261.

CHAPTER FOUR

The Search for Meaning

Every man's condition is a solution in hieroglyphic to those inquiries he would put. He acts it as life, before he apprehends it as truth.

RALPH WALDO EMERSON

1. THE FUNCTION OF THE SYMBOL

One of the symptoms of alienation in the modern age is the widespread sense of meaninglessness. Many patients seek psychotherapy not for any clearly defined disorder but because they feel that life has no meaning. The thoughtful psychotherapist can scarcely avoid the impression that these people are experiencing the disrupting effects not only of an unsatisfactory childhood experience, but also of an upheaval occasioned by a major cultural transition. We seem to be passing through a collective psychological reorientation equivalent in magnitude to the emergence of Christianity from the ruins of the Roman Empire. Accompanying the decline of traditional religion there is increasing evidence of a general psychic disorientation. We have lost our bearings. Our relation to life has become ambiguous. The great symbol system which is organized Christianity seems no longer able to command the full commitment of men or to fulfill their ultimate needs. The result is a pervasive feeling of meaninglessness and alienation from life. Whether or not a new collective religious symbol will emerge remains to be seen. For the present those aware of the problem are obliged to make their own individual search for a meaningful life. Individuation becomes their way of life.

I use the word "meaning" here in a special sense. In general we can distinguish two different usages of the word. Most commonly the term refers to abstract, objective knowledge conveyed by a sign or representation. Thus, for example, the word horse means a particular species of four-legged animals; or a red traffic light means stop. These are abstract, objective meanings conveyed by signs. However, there is another kind of meaning, namely, subjective, living meaning which does not refer to abstract knowledge but rather to a psychological state which can affirm life. It is this sense of the word we use when we describe a deeply moving experience as something meaningful. Such an experience does not convey abstract meaning, at least not primarily, but rather living meaning which, laden with affect, relates us organically to life as a whole. Dreams, myths, and works of art can convey this sense of subjective, living meaning which is quite different from objective, abstract meaning. It is the failure to separate these two different usages of the word "meaning" which leads one to ask the unanswerable question, "What is the meaning of life?" The question cannot be answered in this form because it confuses objective, abstract meaning with subjective, living meaning. If we rephrase the question to make it more subjective and ask, "What is the meaning of *my* life," it then begins to have the possibility of an answer.

The problem of life meaning is closely related to the sense of personal identity. The question, "What is the meaning of my life?" is almost the same as the question, "Who am I?" The latter question is clearly a subjective one. An adequate answer can come only from within. Thus we can say: Meaning is found in subjectivity. But who values subjectivity? When we use the word subjective, we usually say or imply *only* subjective, as though the subjective element were of no consequence. Since the decline of religion, we have had no adequate collective sanction for the introverted, subjective life. All trends are in the opposite direction. The various pressures of Western society all subtly urge the individual to seek life meaning in externals and in objectivity. Whether the goal be the state, the corporate organization, the good material life, or the acquisition of objective scientific knowledge, in each case human meaning is being sought where it does not exist—in externals, in objectivity. The unique, particular, not-to-be-duplicated subjectivity of the individual which is the real source of human meanings and which is not susceptible to an objective, statistical approch is the despised stone rejected by the builders of our contemporary world view.

Even the majority of psychiatrists, who ought to know better,

contribute to the prevailing attitude which depreciates subj
Some years ago I gave a paper concerning the function of
before a group of psychiatrists. Afterwards the discussar
critique of the paper. One of his chief objections was t...
scribed the symbol as though it were something real, almost alive,
as indeed I had. This criticism reflects a general attitude toward the
psyche and subjectivity. The psyche is thought to have no reality
of its own. Subjective images and symbols are considered to be
nothing but reflections of one's environment and interpersonal relations, or *nothing but* instinctive wish fulfillments. Harry Stack Sullivan has even made the extreme statement that the idea of a unique,
individual personality is a delusion! A famous psychiatrist thus becomes unwittingly another exponent of collectivistic, mass psychology.

Modern man's most urgent need is to discover the reality and
value of the inner subjective world of the psyche, to discover the
symbolic life. As Jung has said:

> Man is in need of a symbolic life . . . But we have no symbolic life . . .
> Have you got a corner somewhere in your houses where you perform
> the rites as you can see in India? Even the very simple houses there
> have at least a curtained corner where the members of the household
> can lead the symbolic life, where they can make their new vows or
> meditation. We don't have it . . . We have no time, no place . . . Only
> the symbolic life can express the need of the soul—the daily need
> of the soul, mind you! And because people have no such thing, they
> can never step out of this mill—this awful, grinding, banal life in
> which they are "nothing but." [1]

Man needs a world of symbols as well as a world of signs. Both
sign and symbol are necessary but they should not be confused with
one another. A sign is a token of meaning that stands for a *known*
entity. By this definition, language is a system of signs, not symbols.
A symbol, on the other hand, is an image or representation which
points to something essentially unknown, a mystery. A sign com-
municates abstract, objective meaning whereas a symbol conveys
living, subjective meaning. A symbol has a subjective dynamism
which exerts a powerful attraction and fascination on the individual.
It is a living, organic entity which acts as a releaser and transformer
of psychic energy. We can thus say a sign is dead, but a symbol is
alive.

[1] Jung, C. G., "The Symbolic Life," Transcript of a lecture given in 1939
from the shorthand notes of Derek Kitchin, London, Guild of Pastoral Psychology, Guild Lecture No. 80, April 1954.

Symbols are spontaneous products of the archetypal psyche. One cannot manufacture a symbol, one can only discover it. Symbols are carriers of psychic energy. This is why it is proper to consider them as something alive. They transmit to the ego, either consciously or unconsciously, life energy which supports, guides, and motivates the individual. The archetypal psyche is constantly creating a steady stream of living symbolic imagery. Ordinarily this stream of images is not consciously perceived except through dreams or through waking fantasy when the conscious level of attention has been lowered. However, there is reason to believe that even in the full waking state this stream of symbols charged with effective energy continues to flow beyond the notice of the ego. Symbols seep into the ego, causing it to identify with them and act them out unconsciously; or they spill out into the external environment via projection, causing the individual to become fascinated and involved with external objects and activities.

2. THE CONCRETISTIC AND REDUCTIVE FALLACIES

The relation between the ego and the symbol is a very important factor. In general there are three possible patterns of relation between ego and symbol or, which means the same thing, between ego and archetypal psyche:

1. The ego may be identified with the symbol. In this case the symbolic image will be lived out concretely. Ego and archetypal psyche will be one.

2. The ego may be alienated from the symbol. Although the symbolic life cannot be destroyed, in this case it will function in a degraded fashion outside consciousness. The symbol will be reduced to a sign. Its mysterious urgencies will be understood only in terms of elementary, abstract factors.

3. The third possibility is the one to be desired. In this instance the ego, while clearly separated from the archetypal psyche, is open and receptive to the effects of symbolic imagery. A kind of conscious dialogue between the ego and emerging symbols becomes possible. The symbol is then able to perform its proper function as releaser and transformer of psychic energy with full participation of conscious understanding.

These different relationships between ego and symbol give rise to two possible fallacies which I shall call the concretistic fallacy and the reductive fallacy. In the concretistic fallacy, which is the more primitive of the two, the individual is unable to distinguish symbols of the archetypal psyche from concrete, external reality. Inner symbolical images are experienced as being real, external facts. Examples of this fallacy are the animistic beliefs of primitives, hallucinations and delusions of psychotics, and superstitions of all kinds. Confused mixtures of psychic and physical reality such as the practice of alchemy, astrology, and the numerous present-day cults of healing fall into this category. The same fallacy is at work in those religious believers who misunderstand symbolic religious images to refer to literal concrete facts and mistake their own personal or parochial religious convictions for universal and absolute truth. There is danger of succumbing to the concretistic fallacy whenever we are tempted to apply a symbolic image to external physical facts for the purpose of manipulating those facts in our own interest. Symbols have valid and legitimate effects only when they serve to change our psychic state or conscious attitude. Their effects are illegitimate and dangerous when applied in a magical way to physical reality.

The reductive fallacy makes the opposite mistake. In this case, the significance of the symbol is missed by misunderstanding it only as a sign for some other known content. The reductive fallacy is based on the rationalistic attitude which assumes that it can see behind symbols to their "real" meaning. This approach reduces all symbolic imagery to elementary, known factors. It operates on the assumption that no true mystery, no essential unknown transcending the ego's capacity for comprehension, exists. Thus, in this view, there can be no true symbols but only signs. For those of this persuasion, religious symbolism is no more than evidence of ignorance and primitive superstition. The reductive fallacy is also shared by those psychological theorists who consider symbolism to be no more than the primitive, prelogical functioning of the archaic ego. We fall into this error whenever we treat our subjective reactions and images in the abstract, statistical manner appropriate to natural science and physical reality. This mistake is the reverse of the preceding one where a subjective symbolic image was used to manipulate physical facts, thus doing violence to them. Here, the abstract, objective attitude appropriate for an understanding of outer reality is applied to the unconscious psyche in an attempt to manipulate it. This attitude does violence to the autonomous reality of the psyche.

The conflict between the concretistic fallacy and the reductive fallacy is at the core of the contemporary conflict between the traditional religious view of man and the so-called modern scientific view. And since this is a collective problem, we all carry something of the conflict within ourselves. Concerning this problem Jung writes:

> Whoever talks of such matters (as religious symbolism) inevitably runs the risk of being torn to pieces by the two parties who are in mortal conflict about these very things. This conflict is due to the strange supposition that a thing is true only if it presents itself as a *physical* fact. Thus some people believe it to be physically true that Christ was born as the son of a virgin, while others deny this as a physical impossibility. Everyone can see that there is no logical solution to this conflict and that one would do better not to get involved in such sterile disputes. Both are right and both are wrong. Yet they could easily reach agreement if only they dropped the word *physical*. *Physical* is not the only criterion of truth: there are also *psychic* truths which can neither be explained nor proved nor contested in any physical way. If, for instance, a general belief existed that the river Rhine had at one time flowed backwards from its mouth to its source, then this belief would in itself be a fact even though such an assertion, physically understood, would sound utterly incredible. Beliefs of this kind are psychic facts which cannot be contested and need no proof.
> Religious (or symbolic) statements are of this type. They refer without exception to things that cannot be established as physical facts. . . . Taken as referring to anything physical they make no sense whatever. . . . The fact that religious (or symbolic) statements frequently conflict with the observed physical phenomena proves that in contrast to physical perception the (symbolic) spirit is autonomous, and that psychic experience is to a certain extent independent of physical data. The psyche is an autonomous factor, and religious (or symbolic) statements are psychic confessions which in the last resort are based on unconscious . . . processes. These processes are not accessible to physical perception but demonstrate their existence through the confessions of the psyche . . . Whenever we speak of religious (or symbolic) contents we move in a world of images that point to something ineffable. We do not know how clear or unclear these images, metaphors, and concepts are in respect of their transcendental object . . . (However) there is no doubt that there is something behind these images that transcends consciousness and operates in such a way that the statements do not vary limitlessly and chaotically, but clearly all relate to a few basic principles or archetypes. These, like the psyche itself, or like matter, are unknowable as such.[2]

[2] Jung, C. G., "Answer to Job" in *Psychology and Religion: West and East,* C.W., 11, 1958, par. 553-555.

As with all matters pertaining to personality, the concretistic ar reductive fallacies will not be changed by rational exhortatic Actually they can be considered as two successive stages in personality development. The state of identification between ego and unconscious symbols gives rise to the concretistic fallacy. This state is characteristic of an early stage of ego development seen, for instance, in primitives and children. The reductive fallacy stems from a state of alienation between the ego and the symbolism of the unconscious. It seems to be a later stage of development, perhaps a necessary reaction against the previous state of identity between ego and unconscious. At this point ego development may require a depreciation of the unconscious and of the power of its symbolic images. However, this leaves a dissociation between ego and unconscious which sooner or later must be bridged if one is to become whole.

The ultimate goal of Jungian psychotherapy is to make the symbolic process conscious. To become conscious of symbols we first need to know how a symbol behaves when it is unconscious. All the inhuman practices of savage rites and rituals as well as neurotic symptoms and perversions can be understood if we realize how a symbol functions unconsciously. The basic proposition is this: An unconscious symbol is lived but not perceived. The dynamism of the unconscious symbol is experienced only as a wish or an urgency toward some external action. The image behind the urgency is not seen. No purely psychological meaning is discerned behind the motivating force of the symbolic image which has one in its grip. The ego, identified with the symbolic image, becomes its victim, condemned to live out concretely the meaning of the symbol rather than to understand it consciously. To the degree that the ego is identified with the archetypal psyche, the dynamism of the symbol will be seen and experienced only as an urge to lust or power. This explains the distinction between the depth psychology of Jung and all other psychological theories. Only Jung and his school, so far, have been able to recognize the symbol, and therefore the archetypal psyche of which it is a manifestation, as it functions when the ego is not identified with it. In Freudian psychology, for instance, where Jung sees the transpersonal archetypal psyche, Freud sees the Id. The Id is a caricature of the human soul. The archetypal psyche and its symbols are seen only by the way they manifest themselves when the ego is identified with them. The Id is the unconscious seen only as instinct with no consideration of the images that lie behind the instincts. To the extent that images are dealt with at all, they are reductively interpreted back to the instinct. The symbolic image *per se* is granted no substantive reality. This Freudian attitude toward the unconscious is important to understand because it is shared in one form or another by practically all the schools of modern psychotherapy. No psychiatrist will deny that the urgencies of the instincts are alive and effective but they almost all join in denying the life and reality of symbolic images in and for themselves.

This widespread attitude of modern psychology which sees the unconscious psyche as motivated only by the instincts is basically antispiritual, anticultural, and destructive of the symbolic life. To the extent that such an attitude is held, the cultivation of a meaningful inner life is impossible. Instinctive compulsions do, of course, exist—in abundance. But it is the symbolic image, acting as releaser and transformer of psychic energy, which lifts the instinctive urgency to another level of meaning and humanizes, spiritualizes, and acculturates the raw animal energy. The instinct contains its own hidden meaning which is revealed only by perceiving the image that lies embedded in the instinct.

One way of discovering the hidden image is by the process of analogy. As Jung says, "The creation of . . . analogies frees instinct and the biological sphere as a whole from the pressure of unconscious contents. Absence of symbolism, however, overloads the sphere of instinct." [3] As an example of the analogical method I recall a patient who was in the unconscious grip of a powerful symbolic image which required him to live it out as a symptom until he could understand it consciously. Since it is easier to see large things than small ones, I choose an example that is magnified so to speak by the fact that it is a symptom of psychopathology. I am thinking of a case of transvestism—a young man who had a strong urge to dress in women's clothes. When wearing some piece of feminine clothing, his attitude towards himself underwent a radical change. Ordinarily he felt shy, inferior, and impotent. But when wearing some article of feminine apparel which could be hidden from general view, he felt confident, effective, and sexually potent. Now what does such a symptom mean? This patient was living out an unconscious symbolic image. Since such symptom images have the same origin as dreams, we can approach them in the way we would a dream— by the method of amplification. We then ask ourselves what about dressing in women's clothes? What general and mythological parallels can we find?

[3] Jung, C. G., *The Practice of Psychotherapy*, C.W., Vol. 16, par. 250.

In Book V of the *Odyssey*, Odysseus' journey between Calypso's isle and the land of the Phaeacians is described.[4] During this journey Poseidon stirs up a frightful storm which would have drowned Odysseus except that Ino, a sea goddess, comes to his assistance. She tells him to take off his clothes and swim for it and adds, "Here, take my veil and put it around your chest; it is enchanted and you can come to no harm so long as you wear it. As soon as you touch land take it off, throw it back as far as you can into the sea." Ino's veil is the archetypal image that lies behind the symptom of transvestism. The veil represents the support and containment which the mother archetype can provide the ego during a dangerous activation of the unconscious. It is legitimate to use this support, as Odysseus does, during a time of crisis; but the veil must be returned to the goddess as soon as the crisis is over.

Another parallel is provided by the priests of the Magna Mater in ancient Rome and Asia Minor. After their consecration these priests would wear feminine dress and allow their hair to grow long to represent their commitment to the service of the Great Mother. A remnant of this sacerdotal transvestism exists today in the skirts worn by the Catholic clergy who are in the service of Mother Church. These parallels go to show that the urge of the transvestite is based on the unconscious need for a supporting contact with feminine deity—the mother archetype. This is the way to understand such a symptom symbolically. Of course, whenever we speak of the image of a deity, we are using a symbol because a deity or suprapersonal power cannot be precisely defined. It is not a sign for something known and rationally understood but rather a symbol expressing a mystery. This manner of interpretation, if successful, can lead the patient toward the symbolic life. A paralyzing, guilt-laden symptom can be replaced by a meaningful, life-enriching symbol which is experienced consciously rather than lived out in an unconscious, compulsive, symptomatic way.

This case is an example of how a symptom can be transformed into a symbol through awareness of its archetypal foundations. Every symptom derives from the image of some archetypal situation. For instance, many anxiety symptoms have as their archetypal context the hero's fight with the dragon, or perhaps the rites of initiation. Many symptoms of frustration or resentment are a reenactment of Job's archetypal encounter with God. To be able to

---

[4] I am indebted to Storr for pointing out this amplification. (Storr, A., "The Psychopathology of Fetishism and Transvestism," *Journal of Analytical Psychology*, Vol. 2, No. 2, July 1957, p. 161.)

recognize the archetype, to see the symbolic image behind the symptom, immediately transforms the experience. It may be just as painful, but now it has meaning. Instead of isolating the sufferer from his fellow humans, it unites him with them in a deeper rapport. Now he feels himself a participating partner in the collective human enterprise—the painful evolution of human consciousness— which began in the darkness of the primordial swamp and which will end we know not where.

Intense moods and emotional states will also yield up their meaning if the relevant symbolic image can be found. For example, a man was in the grip of an angry mood. Things were not as he wished but he could neither act out the affect nor repress it. Finally he prayed for understanding of its meaning. Immediately the image came to him of the three men in the fiery furnace as described in the Book of *Daniel*. He read this passage in the Bible and as he re- flected on it, his mood disappeared. The third chapter of *Daniel* describes the decree of Nebuchadnezzar that all people on signal shall fall down and worship his golden idol. Shadrach, Meshach and Abednego refused and Nebuchadnezzar in a state of rage had them thrown into the fiery furnace. But they remained unharmed and a fourth figure was seen walking with them in the fire, "like a son of God."

This image resolved the angry mood because it expresses sym- bolically the *meaning* of the mood. King Nebuchadnezzar represents an arbitrary, tyrannical, power-driven figure who would usurp the prerogatives of God and rages when he is not treated as deity. He is the ego identified with the Self. His rage is synonymous with the fiery furnace. Shadrach, Meshach and Abednego, by declining to give transpersonal value to a personal motivation, expose themselves willingly to the fire of Nebuchadnezzar's frustration. This would correspond to the patient's ability to avoid identification with the affect but instead endure it and finally seek its meaning in active imagination. The fourth figure that appears in the furnace "like the son of God" would represent the transpersonal, archetypal com- ponent that was actualized in the experience. It brings meaning, release and wholeness (as the fourth).

This example illustrates a statement of Jung. About his confronta- tion with the unconscious he writes:

I was living in a constant state of tension . . . To the extent that I managed to translate the emotions into images—that is to say, to find the images which were concealed in the emotions—I was inwardly calmed and reassured.[5]

To the extent that one is unaware of the symbolic dimension of existence, one experiences the vicissitudes of life as symptoms. Symptoms are disturbing states of mind which we are unable to control and which are essentially meaningless—that is, contain no value or significance. Symptoms, in fact, are degraded symbols, degraded by the reductive fallacy of the ego. Symptoms are intolerable precisely because they are meaningless. Almost any difficulty can be borne if we can discern its meaning. It is meaninglessness which is the greatest threat to humanity.

Our waking life is composed of a series of moods, feelings, ideas, and urgencies. These successive psychic states through which we pass are like beads strung on a single string. Depending on our conscious attitude, we experience this rosary of life either as a succession of meaningless symptoms or, through symbolic awareness, as a series of numinous encounters between the ego and the transpersonal psyche. Our pleasures as well as our pains are symptoms if they carry no symbolic import. The sages of India recognize this in their doctrine of Maya. According to this view pain and pleasure, which are the symptoms of life, are indissolubly connected. To gain release from the painful symptoms one must also relinquish the pleasurable symptoms. In terms of analytical psychology, the Indian's striving for release from the urgencies of pain and pleasure is equivalent to the search for the symbolic life. Nirvana is not an escape from the reality of life. It is rather the discovery of the symbolic life which releases man from this "awful, grinding, banal life" which is only a succession of meaningless symptoms.

3. THE SYMBOLIC LIFE

The symbolic life in some form is a prerequisite for psychic health. Without it the ego is alienated from its suprapersonal source and falls victim to a kind of cosmic anxiety. Dreams often attempt to heal the alienated ego by conveying to it some sense of its origin. Here is an example of such a dream. The dreamer was struggling with the problem of ego-Self alienation. She was a prey to profound feelings of depression, unworthiness, and the meaninglessness of her life and capacities. Then she had this dream: *An old man*

[5] Jung, C. G., *Memories, Dreams, Reflections*, New York, Pantheon Books, 1963, p. 177.

*who was both a priest and a rabbi was talking to me. As I listened
to his words I was deeply moved and felt I was being healed. It
seemed as though God spoke through him. I felt the eternal question which is always within me resolve itself. For a moment I knew
why. As he talked he put me back in touch with something I had
known a long time ago—before I was born.*

This dream had a powerful impact on the dreamer. She experienced it as something healing. The eternal question concerning the
meaning of her life was answered. But what was the answer? At
first upon awakening she could not remember what the old man
had said. Then suddenly she thought of an old Jewish legend she
had once read in a book and she realized that it was the essence
of this legend which the priest-rabbi had been telling her. The
story of this legend is as follows:

> Prior to the birth of a child, God calls the seed of the future human
> being before him and decides what its soul shall become: man or
> woman, sage or simpleton, rich or poor. Only one thing He leaves
> undecided, namely, whether he shall be righteous or unrighteous, for,
> as it is written, "All things are in the hand of the Lord except the
> fear of the Lord." The soul, however, pleads with God not to be sent
> from the life beyond this world. But God makes answer: "The world
> to which I send thee, is better than the world in which thou wast;
> and when I formed thee, I formed thee for this earthly fate." There-
> upon God orders the angel in charge of the souls living in the
> Beyond to initiate this soul into all the mysteries of that other world,
> through Paradise and Hell. In such manner the soul experiences all
> the secrets of the Beyond. At the moment of birth, however, when the
> soul comes to earth, the angel extinguishes the light of knowledge
> burning above it, and the soul, enclosed in its earthly envelope, enters
> this world, having forgotten its lofty wisdom, but always seeking to
> regain it.[6]

The dream which brought this beautiful legend to the dreamer's
mind is an excellent example of the operation of the ego-Self axis
which brings into consciousness an awareness of the ego's origin
and meaning and awakens the symbolic life. The figure of the
old man, the rabbi-priest, is a representation of what Jung has called
the archetype of the old wise man. He is a spiritual guide, a
bringer of wisdom and healing. I would consider him to be a personification of the ego-Self axis. In the combination of priest and

[6] Quoted by Gerhard Adler, *Studies in Analytical Psychology*. New York,
C. G. Jung Foundation, 1967, p. 120f.

rabbi he unites two separate religious and symbolic traditions although the tale he has to tell does not belong to any particular religious system. The theme of the prenatal origins of the ego is an archetypal image of which we can find many examples. For instance there is Plato's doctrine of prenatal ideas as elaborated in the *Phaedo*. According to this myth all learning is a recollection of prenatal knowledge which is innate but forgotten. In psychological terms this means that the archetypal forms of human experience are preexistent or *a priori;* they only await incarnation within a particular individual life history. This Platonic theory of reminiscence is sometimes expressly stated in dreams. A person may dream of being involved in a significant happening which he dimly realizes has happened before and is following some predetermined plan. As one dreamer described such a dream:

> It was as though I was experiencing the dream on two levels simultaneously. On the one hand it was unique, spontaneous, and unrehearsed. On the other hand I seemed also to be playing a role and re-enacting a story I had once known but forgotten. The two levels were inextricably connected. I was playing the role perfectly just because I was really living it at the same time. I made up my lines as I went along but I seemed to be helped by the fact that I had once known the story. When each situation came up it struck some chord of memory which came to my assistance.

Another parallel is an old Gnostic tale which has many similarities to the Jewish legend previously quoted but carries it a step further by showing how the soul awakens and remembers its heavenly origin. Modern translators have entitled this text "The Hymn of the Pearl." I quote it, somewhat abridged, from Hans Jonas' book:

> When I was a little child and dwelt in the kingdom of my Father's house and delighted in the wealth and splendor of those who raised me, my parents sent me forth from the East, our homeland, with provisions for the journey. . . . They took off from me the robe of glory which in their love they had made for me, and my purple mantle that was woven to conform exactly to my figure, and made a covenant with me, and wrote it in my heart that I might not forget it: "When thou goest down into Egypt and bringest the One Pearl which lies in the middle of the sea which is encircled by the snorting serpent, thou shalt put on again thy robe of glory and thy mantle over it and with thy brother, our next in rank, be heir to our kingdom."
> I left the East and took my way downwards, accompanied by two royal envoys, since the way was dangerous and hard and I was young

for such a journey. . . . I went down into Egypt, and my companions
parted from me. I went straightway to the serpent and settled down
close by his inn until he should slumber and sleep so that I might
take the Pearl from him. . . . I was a stranger to my fellow-dwellers
in the inn. . . . I clothed myself in their garments, lest they suspect
me as one coming from without to take the Pearl and arouse the
serpent against me. But through some cause they marked that I was
not their countryman, and they ingratiated themselves with me and
mixed me (drink) with their cunning, and gave me to taste of their
meat; and I forgot that I was a king's son and served their king.
I forgot the Pearl for which my parents had sent me. Through the
heaviness of their nourishment I sank into deep slumber.

All this that befell me, my parents marked, and they were grieved
for me. . . . And they wrote a letter to me, and each of the great
ones signed it with his name.

"From thy father the King of Kings, and from thy mother, mistress of
the East, and from thy brother, our next in rank, unto thee our son
in Egypt, greeting. Awake and rise up out of thy sleep, and perceive
the words of our letter. Remember that thou are a king's son: behold
whom thou has served in bondage. Be mindful of the Pearl, for whose
sake thou has departed into Egypt. Remember thy robe of glory, recall thy splendid mantle, that thou mayest put them on and deck
thyself with them and thy name be read in the book of the heroes and
then become with thy brother, our deputy, heir in our kingdom."

Like a messenger was the letter. . . . It rose up in the form of an
eagle, the king of all winged fowl, and flew until it alighted beside
me and became wholly speech. At its voice and sound I awoke and
arose from my sleep, took it up, kissed it, broke its seal, and read.
Just as was written on my heart were the words of my letter to read.
I remembered that I was a son of kings, and that my freeborn soul
desired its own kind. I remembered the Pearl for which I had been
sent down to Egypt, and I began to enchant the terrible and snorting
serpent. I charmed it to sleep by naming over it my Father's name,
the name of our next in rank, and that of my mother, the Queen
of the East. I seized the Pearl, and turned to repair home to my
Father. Their filthy and impure garment I put off, and left it behind
in their land, and directed my way that I might come to the light of
our homeland, the East.

My letter which had awakened me I found before me on my way;
and as it had awakened me with its voice, so it guided me with its
light that shone before me, and with its voice it encouraged my fear,
and with its love it drew me on. . . . (Then, as he approached his
homeland his parents sent out to him his robe of glory and his
mantle.) And I stretched toward it and took it and decked myself
with the beauty of its colors. And I cast the royal mantle about my

entire self. Clothed therein, I ascended to the gate of salutation and adoration. I bowed my head and adored the splendor of my Father who had sent it to me, whose commands I had fulfilled as he too had done what he promised. . . . He received me joyfully, and I was with him in his kingdom. . . .[7]

This charming tale is a beautiful symbolic expression of the theory of analytical psychology concerning the origin and development of the conscious ego. The ego begins as the child of a royal, heavenly family. This corresponds to its original state of identity with the Self or archetypal psyche. It is sent away from this original paradise on a mission. This refers to the necessary process of conscious development which separates the ego from its unconscious matrix. When it reaches the foreign country it forgets its mission and falls asleep. This situation corresponds to ego-Self alienation and the state of meaninglessness. The letter from his parents awakens the sleeper and reminds him of his mission. Meaning has returned to his life. The connecting link between the ego and its suprapersonal origins has been re-established. I would equate this happening with the awakening of symbolic awareness.

There is a particularly interesting parallel between the story and the dream of the priest-rabbi. In the dream, after listening to the words of the wise old man the dreamer remarks, "As he talked he put me back in touch with something I had known a long time ago—before I was born." Similarly, in "The Hymn of the Pearl," after the hero reads the letter, he says, "Just as was written in my heart were the words of my letter." In each case the individual is recalled to something he once knew but had forgotten—his original nature.

In "The Hymn of the Pearl" the awakening is brought about through the agency of a letter. The protean nature of this letter suggests that it is a true symbol whose full meaning cannot be encompassed by a single specific image. It is a letter but it is also an eagle. In addition, it is a voice that became wholly speech. When it was time to make the return trip, the letter underwent still another metamorphosis and became a guiding light. Whenever we encounter in dreams an image which undergoes such numerous transformations, we can be sure we are dealing with a particularly potent and dynamic symbol. Such a symbol is the letter-eagle-voice-light image in this story. A letter is a means of communication from a distance. The eagle, stated in the text to be the king of

[7] Jonas, H., *The Gnostic Religion*, Boston, Beacon Press, 1958, p. 113ff.

birds, reminds one of the fact that birds have always been considered the messengers of God. I once treated a psychotic patient who told me that he was receiving messages from God. When I asked him how he got these messages, he said that the birds brought them. Birds also suggest the dove of the Holy Ghost which is the connecting link between God and man. *(Pictures 30 and 31).* The voice reminds one of the call or the vocation which means literally a calling. This theme has always expressed an experience of awakening which leads the individual out of his personal preoccupations into a more significant destiny. The letter as guiding light is paralleled by the star of Bethlehem which guided men to the birthplace of Christ, the manifestation of deity. All of these amplifications go to show that the letter in its various aspects symbolizes the ego-Self axis, the line of communication between ego and archetypal psyche. Consciousness of this axis has an awakening, transforming effect on the personality. A new dimension of meaning is discovered which conveys value to subjectivity.

Another example of the archetypal theme of the prenatal origin of the soul is found in Wordworth's ode: "Intimations of Immortality." (Quoted here at greater length.)

> Our birth is but a sleep and a forgetting:
> The Soul that rises with us, our life's Star,
>   Hath had elsewhere its setting,
>   And cometh from afar.
>   Not in entire forgetfulness,
>   And not in utter nakedness,
> But trailing clouds of glory do we come
>   From God, who is our home:
> Heaven lies about us in our infancy!
> Shades of the prison-house begin to close
>   Upon the growing boy.
> But he beholds the light, and whence it flows,
>   He sees it in his joy;
> The youth, who daily farther from the east
>   Must travel, still is Nature's Priest,
>   And by the vision splendid
>   Is on his way attended;
> At length the Man perceives it die away,
> And fade into the light of common day.

At this point Wordworth's hero reaches Egypt, forgets his mission, and falls asleep. He never does receive a definite letter of awakening, but he has premonitions of one.

Picture 30. THE ANGEL GABRIEL HANDS MARY A LETTER. The
Annunciation by Dürer.

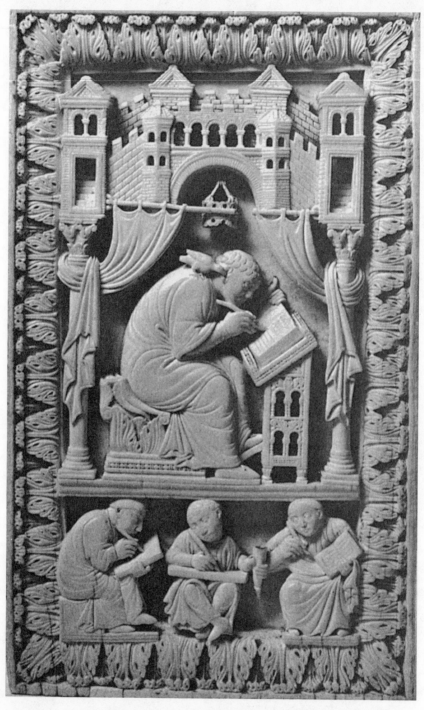

Picture 31. A DOVE TRANSMITS THE DIVINE VOICE TO ST. GREGORY THE GREAT, Ivory Panel, 9-10th Century.

> . . . and in a season of calm weather
> Though inland far we be,
> Our souls have sight of that immortal sea
> Which brought us hither,
> Can in a moment travel thither.
> And see the children sport upon the shore,
> And hear the mighty waters rolling evermore . . .
> Thanks to the human heart by which we live,
> Thanks to its tenderness, its joys, and fears,
> To me the meanest flower that blows can give
> Thoughts that do often lie too deep for tears.

In the last two lines there is a definite allusion to the symbolic life.

Dreams are expressions of the ego-Self axis. Every dream can be considered a letter sent to Egypt to awaken us. We may not be able to read the letter, but at least we should open it and make the effort. I know of a man who had no use for analysis and dream interpretation. He had studied his own dreams and reached the definite conclusion that dreams have no meaning whatever. They are caused only by one's physical sensations while in bed—having one's feet tangled in the covers, lying on one's arm, that sort of thing. It is interesting to note what kind of dreams a man with such a conscious attitude had. He had several frequently recurring nightmares. He dreamt he was in a quagmire up to his knees sinking deeper and deeper, unable to move. At other times he dreamt that he was blind and sometimes that he was a crippled paralytic.

Sometimes dream images refer directly to the functioning of the ego-Self axis. This is true of the dream about the priest-rabbi. I have encountered several dreams which use the image of an island needing a communication system with the mainland. Here is an example of such a dream: *A man dreamt that he was on an island several miles off the mainland. A great pile of telephone cables comes up on the beach. It is connected with the mainland and the dreamer feels he has rescued it from destruction by recognizing what it is. It is an important advance in communications. His neighbors think it is ugly and want it thrown back into the sea but the dreamer is able to persuade them of its value.*

The fact that the neighbors object to the ugliness of the telephone cable is significant. The dreamer has a highly developed aesthetic sense. Indeed, his major value judgments are based on aesthetic considerations. In order to accept the new communication pathway with the mainland, that is the archetypal psyche, the dreamer must depose the tyranny of aestheticism which recognizes no values other than its own. This is an illustration of the fact that the ego-Self axis and the symbolic life are encountered through the inferior function, the weakest portion of the personality. Only by awareness and acceptance of our weakness do we become conscious of something beyond the ego which supports us.

Here is another dream which is a beautiful example of the ego-Self axis and of the numinous impact it can have. The patient had this dream about one year prior to beginning analysis, during a time of considerable distress. Although his psychotherapy was long and arduous, this dream portended eventual success: *I am on the roof of a room completely surrounded by water when I hear wonderful music coming across the water. The music is being brought by four "wise men" standing in small boats and each is coming from one of the four directions. They are magnificently robed and as they proceed across the water through a blue-gray dawn I realize that the music each one brings bears the characteristics of the "direction" from which he comes. These four musical qualities blend and merge into a sound which affects me powerfully in writing about it three years later as it did when it occurred in the dream. The four "wise men" ascend stairs at each corner of the room. I am overcome with a feeling of great reverence and excitement, and as they reach the roof it has grown lighter. The nearness of them is overwhelming. I realize they have come to prepare me for the doing of some work. I then must go downstairs and complete some task which requires prolonged diligence and concentration. When I come back I see the four "wise men" going back across the waters in their small boats. Though there is a sense of disappointment the music seemed more glorious than before, even triumphant. There was definitely a sense of having succeeded or passed the test. Then I saw that in the place where each "wise man" had stood there was now a stone idol which though abstract not only intrinsically represented the "wise man" but indeed all that was implied by the culture and mores of the direction from which he had come. There was a sense of being thankful that I would be able to prove that they had been there.*

Then I turned my attention to the four "wise men" each returning to his own direction in the small boats, and the music became even greater. Once more I heard with special clarity the special personality of each of the four directions blending mysteriously

Picture 32. THE GREAT ZIGGURAT OF UR, Reconstruction.

*into a "supermusical" sound and the day became brighter until
an electric blue surrounded me and a sense of the most intense
well-being I had ever known filled me as the dream ended.*

I do not want to discuss this dream in its personal aspects but
only to the extent that it illustrates the function of the ego-Self
axis. The drama of the dream takes place on the roof of a room
which is a kind of platform raised above the water with steps
at each of its four corners. This reminds one of the early Egyptian
concept of the God Atum. He was represented as the world mound
rising out of the primeval ocean. According to Clark, this primordial
mound symbol "was soon formalized into an eminence with sloping
or battered sides or a platform surrounded by steps on each
side. . . It is probably what the step pyramids represent." [8] Another
analogy is the Babylonian ziggurat, likewise a holy mound with
steps on four sides leading to a platform on top which housed the
shrine of Marduk. *(Picture 32)* The top of the holy mound was
thought of as the navel of the world, the point where divine
creative force is manifested, and the place of meeting between god
and man. The same ideas were associated with the pyramids of
the Mayas *(Picture 33)*.

[8] Clark, R. T. R., *Myth and Symbol in Ancient Egypt*, New York, Grove
Press, 1960, p. 38.

Picture 33. MAYAN PYRAMID. At the top is a Temple of the God.

The image of wise men bringing gifts reminds us of the story of Jesus' nativity and the three wise men. This theme of bringing gifts to the newborn child is part of the myth of the birth of the hero which, we can add, is also the myth of the birth of the ego.[9] But what is the significance of four wise men instead of three? There is a legend that when Jesus was born, not three but four wise men were supposed to have come to him from the four corners of the world, but the fourth was delayed and did not arrive in time. The fact that there are four wise men coming from the four directions alludes to mandala symbolism and indicates that the wise men are a function of the Self, or psychic totality. The wise men thus represent a fourfold ego-Self axis. They are messengers and gift-bringers from the land beyond the sea come to establish communication with the ego. We are reminded of the previous priest-rabbi dream where likewise an old wise man served to connect the dreamer with her suprapersonal origins.

I would draw your attention to the light symbolism in this dream. The dream begins at dawn. It grows lighter as the wise men reach the roof and becomes still brighter at the climax of the dream. Light represents consciousness. All peoples have myths of creation which depict it as the creation of light. Such myths refer to the creation of the ego which is the light of consciousness born out of the darkness of the unconscious. Similarly, dawn is the daily birth of the light of the sun and is an apt image to represent emerging consciousness. Thus we can understand this dream as referring to a growth or increase of consciousness on the part of the dreamer. This interpretation would also correspond to the significance of the wise men whose attribute is wisdom. Wisdom is light in the psychological sense. The wise men are bringers of the light of consciousness.

Another feature of the dream is that each wise man leaves behind an idol or image of himself which epitomizes the direction from which he comes and provides tangible proof of the reality of his visit. This is most interesting. I understand it as a representation of the symbolic process itself. The archetypal forces, represented by the wise men, bring images of themselves as gifts to the ego, symbols that remind the individual of his suprapersonal connections. These images would correspond in their function to

[9] More precisely the hero represents the urge to individuation with which the ego cooperates.

the letter, eagle, and guiding light in "The Hymn of the Pearl." They are connecting links between ego and archetypal psyche which transmit symbolic meaning.

The word symbol derives from the Greek word *symbolon* [10] which combines two rootwords, *sym,* meaning together or with, and *bolon,* meaning that which has been thrown. The basic meaning is thus "that which has been thrown together." In original Greek usage, symbols referred to the two halves of an object such as a stick or a coin which two parties broke between them as a pledge and to prove later the identity of the presenter of one part to the holder of the other. The term corresponded to our word tally concerning which Webster's unabridged dictionary states: "It was customary for traders, after notching a stick to show the number or quantity of goods delivered, to split it lengthwise through the notches so that the parts exactly corresponded, the seller keeping one stick, and the purchaser the other." A symbol was thus originally a tally referring to the missing piece of an object which when restored to, or thrown together with, its partner recreated the original whole object. This corresponds to our understanding of the psychological function of a symbol. The symbol leads us to the missing part of the whole man. It relates us to our original totality. It heals our split, our alienation from life. And since the whole man is a great deal more than the ego, it relates us to the suprapersonal forces which are the source of our being and our meaning. This is the reason for honoring subjectivity and cultivating the symbolic life.

[10] See L. Stein, "What is a Symbol Supposed to be?" *Journal of Analytical Psychology,* Vol. II, No. 1, Jan. 1957, p. 73.

CHAPTER FIVE

Christ as Paradigm
of the Individuating Ego

*I am not . . . addressing myself to the happy possessors
of faith, but to those many people for whom the light
has gone out, the mystery has faded, and God is dead.
For most of them there is no going back, and one does
not know either whether going back is the better way.
To gain an understanding of religious matters, probably all that is left us today is the psychological approach. That is why I take these thought-forms that
have become historically fixed, try to melt them down
again and pour them into moulds of immediate experience.*

—C. G. Jung [1]

1. THE ACCEPTANCE OF SEPARATENESS

The image of Christ, and the rich network of symbolism which
has gathered around Him, provide many parallels to the individuation process. In fact when the Christian myth is examined carefully
in the light of analytical psychology, the conclusion is inescapable
that the underlying meaning of Christianity is the quest for individuation.

The myth of Jesus Christ is unique in its assertion of the paradoxical double aspect of Christ. He is both God and man. As Jesus
he is a human being living a particular, limited, historical existence

[1] Jung, C. G., "Psychology and Religion" in *Psychology and Religion: West
and East.* C.W., 11, par. 148.

131

in space and time. As Christ, he is the "anointed one," the king, the Logos that has existed from the beginning beyond space and time, the eternal deity itself. Understood psychologically, this means that Christ is simultaneously a symbol for both the Self and the ideal ego.

Jung has developed in some detail the idea of Christ as a symbol of the Self.[2] The circumstances of Christ's birth; his performance of miracles; the various images of the "kingdom of heaven;" his cognomen "Son of man" which equates him with the original Anthropos or primordial man; the symbols of totality which surround him such as the four evangelists, the twelve disciples, "alpha and omega," and the symbolism of the cross—all these pertain to the phenomenology of the Self. But although Jung has made interesting suggestions on the subject, he has never really elaborated the idea of Christ as symbol of the ego. In this chapter I shall attempt a brief exploration of this subject. It should be clear, however, that my remarks are only preliminary suggestions toward a future psychology of the Christian myth.

The nature of the historical Jesus has always been a problem for scholars and theologians.[3] In the gospel accounts, personal fact and archetypal image are so closely intermixed that it is almost impossible to distinguish them. However, although details remain uncertain, a definite historical personality with astonishing psychological insight is revealed in the gospels. Jesus was probably an illegitimate child. Certainly he demonstrates some characteristic features of the individual who has had no personal father. When the personal father is missing and, more particularly, when he is completely unknown, as may happen with an illegitimate child, there is no layer of personal experience to mediate between the ego and the numinous image of the archetypal father. A kind of hole is left in the psyche through which emerge the powerful archetypal contents of the collective unconscious. Such a condition is a serious danger. It threatens inundation of the ego by the dynamic forces of the unconscious, causing disorientation and loss of relation to external reality. If, however, the ego can survive this danger, the "hole in the psyche" becomes a window providing insights into the depths of being.

Jesus would appear to fit the above description. He experienced

[2] Jung C. G., *Aion*, C.W., 9 ii, pars. 68-126.
[3] For a detailed historical survey of this problem, see Schweitzer, A., *The Quest of the Historical Jesus*, New York, Macmillan, 1961.

a direct relation to the heavenly (archetypal) father and described in numerous vivid symbolic images the nature of the kingdom of heaven (the archetypal psyche). It is evident from his teachings that he had a profound awareness of the reality of the psyche. Whereas the Mosaic Law recognized only the reality of deeds, Jesus recognized the reality of inner psychic states. For example:

> You have heard that it was said to the men of old, "You shall not kill; and whoever kills shall be liable to judgment." But I say to you that everyone who is angry with his brother shall be liable to judgment . . .[4]

And again:

> You have heard that it was said, "You shall not commit adultery." But I say to you that every one who looks at a woman lustfully has already committed adultery with her in his heart.[5]

These passages have a major psychological import. They represent a transition from a kind of crude behavioristic psychology to one which is aware of the reality of the psyche as such without concrete actions.

The gospel accounts abound in many other major psychological discoveries. Jesus formulated the conception of psychological projection two thousand years before depth psychology:

> Why do you look at the speck of sawdust in your bother's eye with never a thought for the great plank in your own eye? [6]

He recognized the danger of psychic identification with parents and family. Today analysts still encounter references to the Old Testament commandment to honor one's mother and father as justification for a state of unconscious identity with the parents. Jesus expressed himself clearly on this issue:

> . . . I have not come to bring peace, but a sword. For I have come to set a man against his father, and a daughter against her mother, and a daughter-in-law against her mother-in-law; and a man's foes will be those of his own household.[7]

A man's foes are those of his own household because it is those to whom he is closest with whom he is most apt to be identified

---

[4] Matt. 5:21-22, RSV.
[5] Ibid. 5:27-28.
[6] Matt. 7:3, New English Bible.
[7] Ibid. 10:34-36.

unconsciously. Such identifications must be dissolved because an awareness of radical separateness is a prerequisite for individuation.

The divisive aspect of what Jesus represents is made even more explicit in a saying recorded in the Gnostic *Gospel of Thomas*:

> 17. Jesus says: "Men indeed think I have come to bring peace to the world. But they do not know that I have come to bring to the world discord, fire, sword, war. Indeed, if there are five (people) in a house, they will become three against two and two against three—father against son and son against father—and they will be lifted up (to the state of) being solitaries.[8]

The end of this passage makes clear the purpose of inciting discord. It is to achieve the solitary condition, the state of being an autonomous individual. This can be achieved only by a separation from unconscious identification with others. In the early stages, the *separatio* is experienced as painful strife and hostility. Parents and family are the most frequent objects of unconscious identification. Jesus singles out the father for special mention:

> And call no man your father on earth, for you have one Father who is in heaven.[9]

Parents have power over their grown children only because the latter continue to project the images of the archetypal parents to their personal parents. To call no man father means to withdraw all projections of the father archetype and discover it within. Jesus demands a commitment to the Self which transcends loyalty to any personal relationship:

> He who loves father or mother more than me is not worthy of me; and he who loves son or daughter more than me is not worthy of me; and he who does not take his cross and follow me is not worthy of me.[10]

Here we have the origin of the idea of the imitation of Christ, the ideal man (ego) whose life is to be followed as a model. The same idea is in Matt. 16:24-26:

> If anyone wishes to be a follower of mine, he must leave self behind;

[8] Doresse, Jean, *The Secret Books of the Egyptian Gnostics.* New York, Viking Press, 1960. p. 358.
[9] Matt. 23:9.
[10] Matt. 10:37-38.

he must take up his cross and come with me. Whoever cares for his own safety is lost; but if a man let himself (ψυχη) be lost for my sake, he will find his true self. (ψυχη) What will a man gain by winning the whole world, at the cost of his true self? (ψυχη).[11]

To convey the proper meaning, the translators are obliged to translate the same word, ψυχη, by two different terms, self and true self. If psychological terms be permitted, the phrase could read, ". . . if a man will lose his ego for my sake, he will find the Self."

Psychologically understood, the cross can be seen as Christ's destiny, his unique life pattern to be fulfilled. To take up one's own cross would mean to accept and consciously realize one's own particular pattern of wholeness. The attempt to imitate Christ literally and specifically is a concretistic mistake in the understanding of a symbol. Seen symbolically, Christ's life will be a paradigm to be understood in the context of one's own unique reality and not as something to be slavishly imitated. Jung has spoken clearly on this subject:

> We Protestants must sooner or later face this question: Are we to understand the "imitation of Christ" in the sense that we should copy his life and, if I may use the expression, ape his stigmata; or in the deeper sense that we are to live our own proper lives as truly as he lived his in its individual uniqueness? It is no easy matter to live a life that is modelled on Christ's, but it is unspeakably harder to live one's own life, as truly as Christ lived his.[12]

2. THE ETHICAL TEACHING

The ethical teaching of Jesus has always been a problem. It is admittedly a counsel of perfection. If taken literally and applied consistently to the external world, it is inimical to material existence. Jung has suggested another way to understand it, namely on the subjective or inner level. His approach is given its first clear expression in the seminar on "Visions" presented in the autumn of 1930 in Zurich. Jung is discussing a patient and has said that the patient should not look down on her own inferiority but should accept it. He continues:

[11] Matt. 16:24-26, NEB.
[12] Jung, C. G., "Psychotherapists or the Clergy" in *Psychology and Religion: West and East*, C.W., 11, par. 522.

Now this is a Christian attitude: for instance, Jesus said that the least among our brethren is himself, and that we should give him refuge and sanctuary. (Matt. 25:40) And already in the first century after Christ there were philosophers like Carpocrates who held that the least of one's brethern, the inferior man, is oneself; they therefore directly read the Sermon on the Mount on the subjective level. For instance he (Carpocrates) said, ". . . if thou bring thy gift to the altar, and there rememberest that *thou* has aught against *thyself,* leave then thy gift and go thy way; first be reconciled to *thyself* and then come and offer thy gift." (Cf. Matt. 5:22 f.) It is a grand truth and it is most probably the real idea behind the Christian teaching . . .[13, 14]

The subjective method of interpretation when applied consistently to the teachings of Jesus yields a host of insights that are remarkably similar to the discoveries of depth psychology. Seen in this light Jesus' teachings become a kind of manual for promoting the individuation process. By way of example, let us consider the subjective interpretation of the *Beatitudes,* (Matt. 5:3-10).

Blessed are the poor in spirit, for theirs is the kingdom of heaven. In *The New English Bible* we read, ". . . those who know they are poor." The literal meaning of *hoi ptochoi to pneumati* in the Greek text of this passage is "beggars for the spirit."[15] Hence the meaning is, blessed are those who are aware of their spiritual poverty and are humbly seeking what they need. Understood psychologically, the meaning would be: The ego which is aware of its own emptiness of spirit (life meaning) is in a fortunate position because it is now open to the unconscious and has the possibility of experiencing the archetypal psyche (the kingdom of heaven).

Blessed are those who mourn, for they shall be comforted. Mourning is caused by the loss of an object or person who was carrying an important projected value. In order to withdraw projections and assimilate their content into one's own personality it is necessary to experience the loss of the projection as a prelude to rediscovering the content or value within. Therefore, mourners are fortunate because they are involved in a growth process. They will be comforted when the lost projected value has been recovered within the psyche.

---

[13] Jung, C. G., *The Interpretation of Visions,* taken from the privately printed seminar notes of Mary Foote. Vol. I, p. 102. Slightly revised.

[14] For further discussion of Carpocrates and the subjective interpretation of Jesus' sayings, see Jung, C. G., *Psychology and Religion: West and East,* C.W., 11, par. 133.

[15] I am indebted to Dr. Edward Whitmont for drawing my attention to this fact.

Blessed are the meek, for they shall inherit the earth. Subjectivel understood, meekness will refer to an attitude of the ego towar the unconscious. Such an attitude is fortunate because it is teachab.. and open to new considerations which can lead to a rich inheritance. To inherit the earth suggests an awareness of being individually related to or having a personal stake in the whole (the wholeness of life, the total human enterprise).

Blessed are those who hunger and thirst for righteousness, for they shall be satisfied. (In *The Douay Version* we read: "Blessed are those who hunger and thirst after justice, for they shall have their fill.") Right or justice is here represented as something that nourishes. Understood psychologically, it is an objective inner law or guiding principle that brings a sense of fulfillment to the ego which seeks it in hunger, i.e., an empty ego that does not identify its own opinions and judgments with the objective inner law.

Blessed are the merciful, for they shall obtain mercy. It is a basic principle of analytical psychology that the unconscious takes the same attitude toward the ego as the ego takes toward the unconscious. If, for example, the ego has a kind and considerate attitude toward the shadow, the latter will be helpful to the ego. If the ego is merciful, it will receive mercy from within. The contrary corollary is "all who take the sword will perish by the sword."

Blessed are the pure in heart, for they shall see God. Purity or cleanness can signify subjectively a state of the ego which is free from contamination (by identification) with unconscious contents or motivations. That which is conscious is clean or clear. The ego which is conscious of its own dirt is pure, and the way is open to it to experience the Self.

Blessed are the peacemakers, for they shall be called the sons of God. It is the appropriate role of the ego to mediate between the opposing parties of an intrapsychic conflict. If the ego identifies with one side of the conflict, no resolution leading to wholeness is possible. The dissociation becomes permanent. If the ego serves the reconciling function of peacemaker, it is acting in the interests of totality, the Self, and hence as "son of God."

Blessed are they that are persecuted for righteousness' sake ("for justice's sake" in *The Douay Version*) *for theirs is the kingdom of heaven.* The ego needs to endure pain and hurt without succumbing to bitterness and resentment in order to be related to the objective inner law. Such an ego attitude is rewarded by contact with the archetypal psyche and its healing, life-giving images.

The major point of the Beatitudes as understood psychologically is praise of the emptied or non-inflated ego. In Jesus' time, violence and unconscious instinctuality were rampant. The ego easily identified in a primitive fashion with the suprapersonal energies of the archetypal psyche and evidenced its inflation by symptoms of anger, violence and lust. According to Jesus' teaching the ego must be emptied of such inflated identifications before it can perceive the transpersonal psyche as something separate from itself.[16]

In this connection the *kenosis* doctrine of the incarnation is relevant. This doctrine is based chiefly on two Pauline passages. Most important is Philippians 2:5, 6, 7:

> . . . Christ Jesus who, though he was in the form of God, did not count equality with God a thing to be grasped, but emptied himself, taking the form of a servant, being born in the likeness of men.

The second passage is found in II Corinthians 8:9:

> For you know the grace of our Lord Jesus Christ, that though he was rich, yet for your sake he became poor, so that by his poverty you might become rich.

According to the *kenosis* doctrine, the incarnation of Jesus was a voluntary process of emptying, whereby He divested Himself of His eternal and infinite divine attributes in order to take human form. This image of "incarnation by emptying" fits precisely the process of ego development during which the ego progressively relinquishes its original, omnipotent identification with the Self in order to achieve a limited but actual existence in the real world of space and time.

The dream of a patient in analysis indicates how the *kenosis* image is still operating in the modern psyche. The dreamer was a gentle, sensitive, young man who had difficulty in asserting himself and becoming a definite individual. He had this dream: *I dreamed I saw a modern Christ figure. He was travelling in a bus with a group of his disciples. Then I sensed there was danger. He was going to be betrayed. It happened and the bus rocked*

---

[16] Emerson expresses something similar, ". . . whatever lames or paralyzes you, draws in with it the divinity, in some form, to repay." *The Conduct of Life*, Dolphin Books, New York, Doubleday, p. 34.

Picture 34. CRUCIFIXION WITHIN A FIELD OF FORCE. Detail of altar piece.

with violence. He was set upon and subdued. I looked in and saw that they had apparently tied ropes to each of his hands and feet and had pulled him tight, spread-eagled in four directions. I knew they would kill him that way. Then it appeared, when I *looked at him more closely that he was not tied by the hands but was grasping with each hand a wooden bar attached to the rope. He was cooperating in his own death! At the end of the dream came an image of a magnetic field of force which looked like this drawing." (See diagram).*

The nature of this dream indicates that a crucial, nuclear process of transformation is taking place. Such a dream defies adequate rational interpretation, but some amplification is possible. The cross as a field of force has a parallel in a fourteenth century painting *(Picture 34)*. In this picture Christ is being crucified in the lap of God the Father whose garments are represented as lines of force with outward radiations. Thus the human figure is being transfixed on a four-fold structure by a transcendent energy field. Understood psychologically this image would express the experience of the ego as it comes into proximity to the superior energy of the Self.

The dream combines the idea of crucifixion with the image of dismemberment. This same combination is found in a nineteenth century woodcut *(Picture 35)*. Dismembered heads and limbs are hanging from the cross suggesting that the image of the crucifixion is being superimposed on a myth of dismemberment such as that of Osiris. Dismemberment can be understood psychologically as a transformative process which divides up an original unconscious content for purposes of conscious assimilation. Or, put another way, it is original unity submitting to dispersal and multiplicity for the sake of realization in spatio-temporal existence. (Cf. discussion of unity and multiplicity in Chapter 6, pages 172-176).

In the dream, the Christ figure is undergoing a voluntary process of dismemberment or emptying. In terms of the dreamer's psychology this would suggest the breaking up of an ideal or "other-worldly" attitude in order to make a realistic life adaptation. In archetypal terms the dream depicts the willing sacrifice of the Self as an eternal image in order that it can become manifest in consciousness as energy (the magnetic field of force). Unity is split into two pairs of polar opposites which create tension and

Picture 35. CRUCIFIXION AND DISMEMBERMENT. Woodcut made in Rennes, France, c. 1830.

conflict but at the same time generate energy for real life accomplishment.

Numerous other aspects of Jesus' teaching lend themselves to psychological interpretation. I shall review briefly a few of them:

Make friends quickly with your accuser . . . (Matt. 5:25).

Do not resist one who is evil. But if one strikes you on the right cheek, turn to him the other also; and if any one would sue you and take your coat, let him have your cloak as well. (Matt. 5:39-40).

Love your enemies . . . (Matt. 5:44).

These passages all make the same point. To understand them subjectively gives a startling new dimension to the meaning of the Christian myth. We are being instructed to love our inner enemy, to make friends with our inner accuser, and to offer no resistance to that within us which we consider evil (inferior, unacceptable to ego standards). Of course this does not mean to act out crude impulses externally. It refers rather to an internal, psychological acceptance of the rejected, negative side of one's own nature. The inner opponent to our conscious standpoint is to be respected and treated generously. The shadow must be accepted. Only then can wholeness of personality be approached.

The same meaning is attached to the injunction:

Give to him who begs from you, and do not refuse him who would borrow from you. (Matt. 5:42).

The inner beggar is the deprived, neglected aspect of the personality, what Jung calls the inferior function. It needs its place in consciousness and should be given what it asks:

When you give alms, sound no trumpet before you. (Matt. 6:2).
But when you pray . . . pray to your Father who is in secret; . . . (Matt. 6:6).

Here we are told not to be identified with a persona of virtue or piety. To be preoccupied with appearances or the effect one produces on others reveals one's own lack of genuine personality. Form and appearance are empty; the essence comes from the individual's unique inner experience:

Do not lay up for yourselves treasures on earth, where moth and rust consume . . . but lay up for yourselves treasures in heaven . . . (Matt. 6:19-20).

In other words do not project psychic values outside yourself into objects. Projected values are extremely vulnerable to loss (moth and rust). When a value is projected, loss of the object is experienced as loss of the inner value it is carrying. Withdraw such projections and recognize that values originate within:

Do not be anxious about your life, what you shall eat or what you shall drink . . . (Matt. 6:25).

This is a warning against another projection. Psychic life and well-being are not sustained by material objects. They are necessary but are not vessels of ultimate meaning. The source of psychic sustenance is to be found within:

Judge not, that you be not judged. For with the judgment you pronounce you will be judged, and the measure you give will be the measure you get. (Matt. 7:1,2).

Here is an explicit statement of the fact that the unconscious mirrors to the ego the same attitude that the ego takes toward it. Hence it is unwise for the ego to presume to decide by its conscious preconceptions what ought and what ought not exist in the psyche. The judgmental attitude toward the unconscious is an inflation of the ego and will always boomerang against it:

Do not give dogs what is holy; and do not throw your pearls before swine . . . (Matt. 7:6).

This tells us to honor inner values and protect them from our own disparagement and depreciation. But how do we know what is truly valuable? "You will know them by their fruits." (Matt. 7:16). This is the essence of psychological pragmatism. The value of a given concept or attitude is determined by its effects. That which releases constructive energy and promotes psychic well-being is a value to be cherished.

Several gospel passages emphasize the particular importance of that which has been lost, for example, the parables in the fifteenth chapter of Luke, of the lost sheep, the lost coin, and the prodigal son. These parables refer to the special significance of the lost or repressed portion of the personality. The lost part is the most important because it takes with it the possibility of wholeness. The inferior function which has been lost to conscious life needs to be given special value if one's goal is the wholeness of the Self. The last becomes first and the stone that the builders rejected becomes the cornerstone.

Similarly, the image of the child is given special worth:

Truly, I say to you, unless you turn and become like children, you will never enter the kingdom of heaven . . . Whoever receives one such child in my name receives me . . . (Matt. 18:3-5).
Let the children come to me, do not hinder them; for to such belongs the kingdom of God. Truly, I say to you, whoever does not receive the kingdom of God like a child shall not enter it. (Mark 10:14,15).

The child signifies the young, underdeveloped aspect of the personality, that which is fresh, spontaneous, and not yet fixed in rigid patterns. One must become as a child to enter the kingdom of heaven. This means psychologically that the deeper layers of the transpersonal psyche are reached through the undifferentiated, childlike aspect of the personality. These passages caution us against applying the pejorative adjective "childish" to aspects of oneself, because the child image carries a supreme psychic value. A similar idea is expressed in the following parable:

Then the King will say to those at his right hand, "Come, O blessed of my Father, inherit the kingdom prepared for you from the foundation of the world; for I was hungry and you gave me food, I was thirsty and you gave me drink, I was a stranger and you welcomed me, I was naked and you clothed me, I was sick and you visited me, I was in prison and you came to me." Then the righteous will answer him, "Lord, when did we see thee hungry and fed thee (etc.) . . . ?" And the King will answer them, "Truly, I say to you, as you did it to one of the least of these my brethern, you did it to me." (Matt. 25:34-40).

The King is the central authority, a symbol of the Self. He identifies himself with "the least"—that aspect of the personality which is despised and is considered to have no value. "The least" is hungry and thirsty; that is, it is the needy, desirous side of ourselves. It is a stranger, referring to that aspect which is lonely and unaccepted. It is naked, that is, exposed, and unprotected. It is sick, the side of the psyche that is diseased, pathological, neurotic. And finally, it is in prison—confined and punished for some transgression of collective rules and behavior. All these aspects of the rejected shadow are equated with the "King," which means psychologically that acceptance of the shadow and compassion for the inferior inner man are equivalent to acceptance of the Self.

The way of individuation which Christ teaches and exemplifies requires the total efforts and resources of the personality. Nothing may be held back. The parable of the rich young man illustrates this:

Jesus said to him, "If you would be perfect (teleios = complete, full-grown) *go, sell what you possess and give to the poor, and you will have treasure in heaven; and come follow me."* (Matt. 19:21).

The same point is made in the parables of the kingdom of heaven where it is described as a treasure in a field or a pearl of great price; so that when man finds it "he sells all that he has to obtain it." (Matt. 13:44). The treasure is the Self, the suprapersonal center of the psyche. It can be discovered only through a total commitment. It costs all that one has.

There are a few passages in the gospels that raise certain difficulties for psychological interpretation. For instance, in the fifth chapter of Matthew (29,30) we read:

If your right eye causes you to sin, pluck it out and throw it away; it is better that you lose one of your members than that your whole body be thrown into hell. And if your right hand causes you to sin, cut it off and throw it away; it is better that you lose one of your members than that your whole body go into hell.

Similar statements appear in Matt. 18:8 and Mark 9:43-48.

These passages seem to be advising repression, and purposeful dissociation from "bad" or offending psychic contents. Here, I believe a distinction must be made between what is required at one stage of ego development and what at another. From the standpoint of a well-developed ego seeking wholeness and the healing of dissociations, the image of cutting off offending members is not applicable. However, at an earlier phase of development, where the ego is still largely identified with the Self, the image is quite appropriate. In this case the original, unconscious wholeness needs to be broken up, to submit to dismemberment. At this stage, separation of the ego from the shadow is required if the whole personality is not to fall into the unconscious (that is, go to hell).

The passage from Matthew specifies the *right* eye and the *right* hand as the offending members. This detail allows us another interpretation. The right side is characteristically the developed, differentiated side and hence symbolizes consciousness and the will of the ego. To cut off the right hand would thus suggest a sacrifice of the conscious standpoint and the superior function in order to grant more reality to the inferior function and the unconscious. In his discussion of Tertullian and Origen, Jung interprets amputation in this way:

That psychological process of development which we term the *Chris-tian* led him (Tertullian) to the sacrifice, the amputation, of the most valuable function, a mythical idea which is also contained in the great and exemplary symbol of the sacrifice of the Son of God.[17]

In spite of these interpretative suggestions, the fact remains that from the standpoint of psychology Christianity as practiced has encouraged repression, and certain New Testament passages can easily be understood as advising it. How these images are to be interpreted in an individual case must take into account the stage of psychic development of the person concerned.

3. THE SELF-ORIENTED EGO

The image of Christ gives us a vivid picture of the Self-oriented ego, i.e., the individuated ego which is conscious of being directed by the Self. This state of Self-centeredness is expressed for example in John 8:28,29, AV:

> . . . I do nothing of myself; but as my Father hath taught me, I speak of these things. And he that sent me is with me: the Father hath not left me alone; for I do always those things that please him.

The state of Self-acceptance was inaugurated at the time of Christ's baptism: *(Picture 36)* ". . . at that moment heaven opened; he saw the Spirit of God descending like a dove to alight upon him; and a voice from heaven was heard saying, 'This is my Son, my Beloved, on whom my favor rests.'" (Matt. 3:16,17 N.E.B.) Thus a connection with his transpersonal source is realized— a source which loves and supports him.

However, this supreme revelation is immediately followed by a sinister development. The descending "Spirit of God" turns negative and becomes the tempter. "Jesus was then led away by the Spirit into the wilderness, to be tempted by the devil." (Matt. 4:11) This sequence of happenings corresponds psycholog-ically to the almost irresistable temptation to inflation which follows the opening of the archetypal psyche ("heaven opened"). The ego tends to identify with the newly-found wisdom or energy and appropriates it for personal purposes. The inflation motif is indicated by the high mountain to which Jesus is taken. *(Picture 37).*

Three specific temptations are presented. First Jesus is told: "If you are the Son of God, tell these stones to become bread."

---

[17] Jung, C. G., *Psychological Types*, C.W., 6, par. 20.

Picture 36. BAPTISM OF CHRIST, Leonardo de Vinci and Verrocchio.

Picture 37. SATAN TEMPTING CHRIST WITHIN A CIRCLE by Rembrandt.

Jesus answered, 'Scripture says, Man cannot live on bread alone; he lives on every word that God utters.' " (Matt. 4:3, 4). This is a temptation to materialism, the concretistic fallacy which would apply the new energy literally or physically. The danger is to seek one's ultimate security in physical well-being or literal, rigid "truth" rather than from a living contact with the *psychic* center of being.

The second temptation is to throw himself off the parapet: " 'If you are the Son of God,' he said, 'throw yourself down; for scripture says, "He will put his angels in charge of you, and they will support you in their arms, for fear you should strike your foot against a stone." ' Jesus answered him, 'Scripture says again, "you are not to put the Lord your God to the test." ' " (Matt. 4:6, 7). Here the temptation is to transcend human limits for the sake of spectacular effect. The answer indicates that it would be challenging God, i.e., the ego's challenging the totality which is a reversal of prerogatives and hence fatal to the ego.

The third temptation is to power and possessiveness: ". . . . the devil took him to a very high mountain, and showed him all the kingdoms of the world in their glory. 'All these' he said 'I will give you, if you will only fall down and do me homage.' But Jesus said, 'Begone, Satan! Scripture says, "you shall do homage to the Lord your God and worship him alone." ' " (Matt. 4:8-10). One's god is one's highest value. If one seeks personal power above all he is paying homage to a demonic inflation, an homage that belongs to the Self.

The temptation of Christ represents vividly the dangers of encounter with the Self. All degrees of inflation up to overt psychosis may occur. A valuable hint as to how to meet the danger is provided by Christ's answers. In each case he does not respond with a personal opinion but rather quotes the scriptures. This suggests that only transpersonal wisdom is adequate to meet the threat. To rely on one's personal ideas in such a crisis would promote the very inflation which the tempter seeks. This means psychologically that one must seek the myth or archetypal image which expresses his individual situation. The relevant transpersonal image will provide the needed orientation and protect from the danger of inflation.

The drama of the crucifixion and the events leading up to it are a profound expression of the ultimate aspects of individuation. Individual experiences of scorn, disgrace and rejection take on meaning and majesty when related to their archetypal paradigm.

(Picture 38). Exemplary also is Christ's attitude in the Garden of Gethsemane: "My Father, if it be possible, let this cup pass from me; nevertheless, not as I will, but as thou wilt." (Luke 22:42).

This is the classic statement of the ego attitude needed in the face of an individuation crisis. And with such an attitude, support from the archetypal psyche is usually forthcoming. *(Plate 4)*. Likewise, the experience of betrayal, which has its ultimate agonized expression in the words: "My God, my God, why hast thou forsaken me?" (Matt. 27:46) is a characteristic feature of crucial phases of individuation. At such times the ego feels utterly deprived of comfort and support, both from within and from without. Trust, based on projections and unconscious assumptions, is abruptly terminated. This state is a transition period. It is the limbo of despair following the death of an old life orientation and preceding the birth of a new one. Jesus' resurrection symbolizes the birth of a more comprehensive personality which can result from the conscious acceptance of the crucifixion ordeal. St. John of the Cross describes the situation in these words:

> It is meet, then, that the soul be first of all brought into emptiness and poverty of spirit and purged from all help, consolation and natural apprehension with respect to all things, both above and below. In this way, being empty, it is able indeed to be poor in spirit and freed from the old man, in order to live that new and blessed life which is attained by means of this night, (the dark night of the soul) and which is the state of union with God.[18]

The central image of the Christian myth is the crucifixion itself. For close to two thousand years the image of a human being nailed to a cross has been the supreme symbol of Western civilization. Irrespective of religious belief or disbelief, this image is a phenomenological fact of our civilization. Hence it must have something important to tell us about the psychic condition of western man.

The crucifixion was the culmination of Jesus' earthly life. In the course of being crucified, Jesus as ego and Christ as Self merge. The human being (ego) and the cross (mandala) become one. There is a Greek prototype of this union of man and mandala in the image of Ixion bound to the fiery wheel. The implications are far different, however. Ixion was bound to the wheel in punishment

[18] *Dark Night of the Soul*, II, IX, 4.

Picture 38. THE FLAGELLATION OF CHRIST, *The Hours of Catherine of Cleves.*

for his hybris in attempting to seduce Hera. He submitted to the wheel involuntarily, and his union with the wheel was to be eternal. There is no "It is finished." (John 19:30). The myth of Ixion represents what happens to an immature ego which approaches the Self. It succumbs to inflation and identification with the Self-mandala.

The Christian myth applies to a much higher level of ego development. Christ is both man and God. As man he goes to the cross with anguish but willingly, as part of his destiny. As God he willingly sacrifices himself for the benefit of mankind. Psychologically this means that the ego and the Self are simultaneously crucified. The Self suffers nailing and suspension (a kind of dismemberment) in order to achieve temporal realization. In order to appear in the spatio-temporal world it must submit to particularization or incarnation in the finite. The Self's willingness to leave its eternal, unmanifest condition and share the human condition indictates that the archetypal psyche has a spontaneous tendency to nourish and support the ego. Here the passage applies: ". . . though he was rich, yet for your sake he became poor, so that by his poverty you might become rich." (II Cor. 8:9).

For the ego, on the other hand, crucifixion is a paralyzing suspension between opposites. It is accepted reluctantly out of the inner necessity of individuation (the wholeness-making process) which requires a full awareness of the paradoxical nature of the psyche. Speaking of the moral aspect of this image Jung says:

> The reality of evil and its incompatibility with good cleave the opposites asunder and lead inexorably to the crucifixion and suspension of everything that lives. Since "the soul is by nature Christian" this result is bound to come as infallibly as it did in the life of Jesus: we all have to be "crucified with Christ," i.e., suspended in a moral suffering equivalent to veritable crucifixion.[19]

and in another place, speaking more generally,

> All opposites are of God, therefore man must bend to this burden; and in so doing he finds that God in his "oppositeness" has taken possession of him, incarnated himself in him. He has become a vessel filled with divine conflict.[20]

One of the essential features of the Christian myth and the

[19] Jung, C. G., *Psychology and Alchemy*, C.W., 12, par. 24.
[20] Jung, C. G., "Answer to Job" in *Psychology and Religion: West and East*, C.W., 11, par. 659.

Plate 4
CHRIST IN THE GARDEN SUPPORTED BY AN ANGEL,
Paolo Veronese, *Detail*

teaching of Jesus is the attitude taken toward weakness and suffering. A real transvaluation of ordinary values is brought about. Strength, power, fullness, and success, the usual conscious values, are denied. Instead, weakness, suffering, poverty, and failure are given special dignity. This point is developed throughout Jesus' teachings and is given its supreme representation in the crucifixion itself where God is degradingly scourged and dies the shameful death of a criminal on the cross. This is what was beyond the comprehension of the Romans, for whom, honor, strength, and manly virtue were the supreme values. Psychologically understood, we have here, I think, a clash between the goals and values of two different phases of ego development. Preoccupation with personal honor and strength and the despising of weakness is inevitable and necessary in the early stages of ego development. The ego must learn to assert itself in order to come into existence at all. Hence the Christian myth has little place in the psychology of the young.

It is in the later phases of psychic development, when a fairly stable and mature ego has already been achieved, that the psychological implications of the Christian myth are especially applicable. In fact, the Christian myth presents us with images and attitudes pertaining to the individuation process which is specifically a task of the second half of life. At this phase of development, the image of the suffering deity is immensely pertinent. This symbol tells us that the experience of suffering, weakness, and failure belongs to the Self and not just to the ego. It is the almost universal mistake of the ego to assume total personal responsibility for its sufferings and failures. We find it, for instance, in the general attitude people have toward their own weaknesses, an attitude of shame or denial. If one is weak in some respect, as everyone is, and at the same time considers it ignominious to be weak, he is to that extent deprived of self-realization. However, to recognize experiences of weakness and failure as manifestations of the suffering god striving for incarnation gives one a very different viewpoint.

These considerations are particularly applicable to the psychology of depression. To be *depressed* is to be "pushed down" by an excessive weight, a weight of responsibility and self-expectations. The fact that one suffers becomes the basis for self-condemnation that can assume well-nigh total proportions. A patient subject to such depressions had the following dream during a particularly severe depressive episode (I quote only in part): *She sees a "filthy old*

*man" who is sitting on a bench opposite her. He is ragged and en-
crusted with filth . . . He is like the dregs of humanity . . . he
is the disreputable poor, beyond the pale of society, the outsider,
"the least among you."*

*The man says, "They ought to do something about the small ani-
mals." I then really look at him. He is sitting on the right-hand
bench. Strewn on his lap are three dead rats, and one dead grey
rabbit.*

*I then see that his head is veiled by a cloud of gnats. They are
all over his head, and in it, and in his nose and his eyes. At first, it
looks to me like a halo. Rather than being horrified and running,
which is what I would ordinarily do, I feel great compassion for
him. The analyst says: "This is Christ." We decide to call someone to help him.*[21]

This impressive dream shows the relevance of the Christian myth
for the modern psyche. It immediately reminds us of the saying,
"Truly, I say to you, as you did it to one of the least of these my
breathern, you did it to me." (Matt. 25:40). The pitiful figure of
the ragged, filthy beggar with the dead animals on his lap is a
vivid picture of the despised and rejected aspects of the dreamer.
Her conscious attitude toward her own weak, suffering side is mirrored in the condition of the tramp. Most startling is the fact that
the tramp is equated with Christ. This can only mean that what
the dreamer considers most disreputable within herself, beyond the
pale, is in fact the supreme value, God Himself. Properly understood, such a dream can lead to a new attitude toward one's weakness, namely, to an acceptance of the inner inferior man as "the
way" to the Self.

4. MAN AS THE IMAGE OF GOD

A particularly clear expression of the idea of Christ as paradigm
of the ego is found in the apocryphal "Acts of John." In chapter
ninety-five Jesus says to his disciples: "A mirror am I to thee that
perceivest me." [22] Again in chapter ninety-six, he says: "Behold

[21] This dream appeared in an article by Dr. Renée Brand in *Current Trends
in Analytical Psychology*, G. Adler, editor, London, Tavistock Publications,
1961, p. 200 f.
[22] James, M. R., translator, *The Apocryphal New Testament*, London, Oxford
University Press, 1960, p. 253.

thyself in me . . . perceive what I do, for thine is this passion of the manhood, which I am about to suffer." [23]

If the figure of Christ is a mirror for the ego, it is certainly reflecting a paradoxical double image. Is the individual ego then both man and God, ego and Self? Jung touches on this same question in his alchemical studies. He writes: ". . . with their sun symbol they (the alchemists) were establishing an intimate connection between God and the ego." [24] After noting that the alchemists were dealing with unconscious projections which are natural phenomena beyond interference by the conscious mind, he then reaches the conclusion that: ". . . nature herself is expressing an identity of God and ego." [25] And later he adds: "This is understandable when we realize that a world-creating quality attaches to human consciousness as such." [26]

Perhaps the same problem lies at the root of the *homoousia-homoiousia* conflict of the fourth century. Is Christ to be considered of the *same* substance as the Father or only of *similar* substance to the Father? If we equate Christ with the ego and the Father with the Self, the psychological issue is immediately clear. The decision was made in favor of the "same substance" doctrine and this has been the functioning image in the dogma ever since. Hence the implication is that the Western psyche is rooted in a myth which equates man with God, the ego with the Self.

The same issue is expressed in the idea that Christ is an image of God. In Colossians 1:15 Christ is described as "the image of the invisible God . . ." (R.S.V.) Again in Hebrews 1:3 He is called "the express image of his (God's) person." (A.V.) This manner of speaking reminds us of Gen. 1:26 where God says: "Let us make man in our own image." If Christ is an image of God and man likewise has been made in God's image, Christ would be equated with man. Origen resolves the problem by making Christ the second in a three-fold series of God-Christ-Man:

We, therefore, having been made according to the image, have the Son, the original, as the truth of the noble qualities that are within us.

[23] Ibid., p. 254.
[24] Jung, C. G., *Mysterium Coniunctionis*. C.W., 14, par. 131.
[25] Idem.
[26] Jung, C. W., 14, par. 132.

And what we are to the Son, such is the Son to the Father, who is the truth.[27]

If we formulate this idea psychologically, it means that the real ego relates to the Self only via an ideal ego as paradigmatic model (Christ) which bridges the two worlds of consciousness and the archetypal psyche by combining both personal and archetypal factors.

With these rather ambiguous reflections we encounter analytical psychology's most difficult problem, namely, the nature of the relation between the ego and the Self. It is a problem that Christian symbolism has done much to elucidate but which, despite all efforts, remains a paradox for conscious understanding. Once it is realized that "a world-creating quality attaches to human consciousness as such," the terms ego and Self are seen to refer to different experiential levels of the same archetypal psychic process. The ego is the seat of consciousness and if consciousness creates the world, the ego is doing God's creative work in its effort to realize itself through the way of individuation.

[27] Origen, *On First Principles,* edited by G. W. Butterworth, New York, Harper Torchbooks, 1966, p. 20.

CHAPTER SIX

Being an Individual

*The sole and natural carrier of life is the individual, and
that is so throughout nature.*

—C. G. JUNG [1]

1. THE *A PRIORI* EXISTENCE OF THE EGO

The experience of individuality is a mystery of being which
transcends descriptive power. Each person has his own unique
version of this experience which is incommunicable as such. Yet, the
form of the experience is universal and can be recognized by all
men. In fact, it sometimes seems that the goal of the individual's
psychic development is to come ever closer to the realization that
his own personal, unique individuality is identical with the eternal
archetypal *individual.* Uniqueness and universality merge as one
takes upon himself the fate of being an individual.

When we survey the phenomenon of life in all its visible manifestations, what we observe is not a continuum but rather an almost
infinite multitude of discrete units of life in a perpetual state of
collision and competition with one another to feed, beget, and
survive. From the complex molecular particles that are the viruses
to the highest vertebrates, we find that life is carried by indivisible units, each of which has its own autonomous center of being.

[1] Jung C. G., *The Practice of Psychotherapy*, C. W., Vol. 16, 1954, par. 224.

157

It is the same for psychic life; the psyche also manifests itself through a multitude of unique, separate centers of being, each of which is a microcosm . . . "an absolutely original center in which the universe reflects itself in a unique and inimitable way." [2]

Jung puts at the center of his psychology the process of realizing oneself as an individual, the process of individuation. In *Psychological Types* he defines individuation as follows:

> In general, it is the process of forming and specializing the individual nature; in particular, it is the development of the psychological individual as a differentiated being from the general, collective psychology. Individuation, therefore, is a *process of differentiation*, having for its goal the development of the individual personality. [3]

In the same place he also defines the term individual:

> The psychological individual is characterized by its peculiar, and in certain respects, unique psychology. The peculiar character of the individual psyche appears less in its elements than in its complex formations.
> The psychological individual, or individuality, has an *a priori* unconscious existence, but it exists consciously only in so far as a consciousness of its peculiar nature is present, i.e., in so far as there exists a conscious distinctiveness from other individuals. [4]

Note the apparently simple and self-evident statement that "individuality has an *a priori* unconscious existence." On first reading, the full implications of this remark might be missed. A mythological image that says the same thing conveys much more adequately the impact of its meaning. In the Gospel of Luke, when the people rejoiced that they had power over the demons, Jesus replied: "do not rejoice in this, that the spirits are subject to you; but rejoice that *your names are written in heaven*." [5] *(Italics mine)*. Here is the fuller meaning of the abstract statement that individuality has an *a priori* unconscious existence. One's name is written in Heaven! In other words, one's unique individuality has a transpersonal origin and justification for being. Elsewhere Jung puts it another way:

> "The Self, like the unconscious, is an *a priori* existent out of which the

[2] Pierre Teilhard de Chardin, *The Phenomenon of Man*, New York, Harper Torchbooks, 1961, p. 261.
[3] Jung, C. G., *Psychological Types*, C.W., Vol. 6, par. 757.
[4] Jung, C.W., 6, par. 755.
[5] Luke 10:20. RSV.

ego evolves. It is, so to speak, an unconscious prefiguration of the ego." [6]

The notion that one's identity has an *a priori* existence is expressed in the ancient idea that each person has his own individual star, a kind of celestial counterpart, representing his cosmic dimension and destiny. The start of Bethlehem was Jesus' star, having a brightness commensurate with the greatness of his destiny. Wordsworth expresses the same image in his lines:

> The soul that rises with us, our life's star,
> Hath had elsewhere its setting,
> And cometh from afar . . .[7]

The image of the star as a transpersonal center of identity appeared in a woman's dream. Following an important realization that she belonged to herself and not to her husband she dreamed: *I was outside and saw a star fall . . . But it did not disappear. It pulsated a few times, then stayed bright and round. It was much closer than any other star—yellow-orange—like a sun but smaller than our sun. I thought to myself, "I've seen a new star born."*

The "Robe of Glory" in the Gnostic *Hymn of the Pearl* (discussed above, page 119) is another symbol of the transcendental center of individuality. The savior leaves it behind as he descends to the darkness of Egypt. But when his task is completed and he returns to his heavenly home, the Robe of Glory comes to meet him. The text reads: "Its splendor I had forgotten, having left it as a child in my Father's house. As I now beheld the robe, it seemed to me suddenly to become a mirror-image of myself: myself entire I saw in it, and it entire I saw in myself, that we were two in separateness, and yet again one in the sameness of our forms . . ." [8] In Jonas' excellent commentary on this image he says: "It symbolizes the heavenly or eternal self of the person, his original idea, a kind of double or *altar ego* preserved in the upper world while he labors down below." [9]

Another point worth emphasis is the clear distinction Jung makes in his definition between conscious individuality and unconscious

---

[6] Jung, C. G., *Psychology and Religion: West and East.* C.W., vol. 11, 1958, par. 139.

[7] Wordsworth, William, "Ode on Intimations of Immortality from Recollections of Early Childhood."

[8] Jonas, Hans, *The Gnostic Religion,* Boston, Beacon Press, 1958, p. 115.

[9] Ibid., p. 122.

individuality. The process of achieving conscious individuality is the process of individuation which leads to the realization that one's name is written in heaven. Unconscious individuality expresses itself in compulsive drives to pleasure and power and ego defenses of all kinds. These phenomena are generally described by negatively-toned words such as selfish, egocentric, autoerotic, and so forth. Although there is justification for these negative terms, since such behavior can be quite disagreeable to others, the attitude conveyed by these negative words can be quite damaging when the individual applies them to himself. Such pejoratives, if used by the therapist, may only reinforce the patient's own depreciatory attitude toward the unconscious and his own potential wholeness. The fact is that embedded in the manifestations of unconscious individuality lies the supreme value of individuality itself, waiting to be redeemed by consciousness. We will never achieve the *lapis* by throwing away the *prima materia*.

The same idea is expressed in a somewhat different way in the following passage:

> . . . mandala symbolism shows a marked tendency to concentrate all the archetypes in a common center, comparable to the relationship of all conscious contents to the ego. . . . One might perhaps regard the mandala as a reflection of the egocentric nature of consciousness, though this view would be justified only if it could be proved that the unconscious is a secondary phenomenon. But the unconscious is undoubtedly older and more original than consciousness, and for this reason one could just as well call the egocentrism of consciousness a reflection or imitation of the "self"-centrism of the unconscious.[10]

We might add to this statement that if egocentrism is the ego's imitation of the Self, then it will be by conscious acceptance of this tendency that the ego will become aware of that which it is imitating; namely, the transpersonal center and unity of individuality, the Self.

In my experience, the basis of almost all psychological problems is an unsatisfactory relation to one's urge to individuality. And the healing process often involves an acceptance of what is commonly called selfish, power-seeking or autoerotic. The majority of patients in psychotherapy need to learn how to be more effectively selfish and more effective in the use of their own personal power; they need to accept responsibility for the fact of being centers of power

---

[10] Jung, C. G., *Mysterium Coniunctionis*, C.W., Vol. 14, 1963, par. 660.

and effectiveness. So-called selfish or egocentric behavior which
expresses itself in demands made on others is not effective conscious self-centeredness or conscious individuality. We demand from
others only what we fail to give ourselves. If we have insufficient
self-love or self-prestige, our need expresses itself unconsciously
by coercive tactics toward others. And often the coercion occurs
under the guise of virtue, love, or altruism. Such unconscious selfishness is ineffectual and destructive to oneself and others. It fails to
achieve its purpose because it is blind, without awareness of itself.
What is required is not the extirpation of selfishness, which is impossible but rather that it be wedded to consciousness and thus
becomes effective. All the facts of biology and psychology teach
us that every individual unit of life is self-centered to the core. The
only varying factor is the degree of consciousness which accompanies that fact.

The widespread current usage of the Freudian term, narcissism,
is a good example of the general misunderstanding concerning self-
love. The myth of Narcissus implies something quite different from
an excess of indulgent self-love. Narcissus was a youth who rejected
all suitors for his love. In reprisal, Nemesis arranged for him to fall
in love with his own reflected image in a pool and he died in despair
at not being able to possess the object of his love.

Narcissus represents the alienated ego that cannot love, that is,
cannot give interest and libido to life—because it is not yet related
to itself. To fall in love with the reflected image of oneself can
only mean that one does not yet possess oneself. Narcissus yearns
to unite with himself just because he is alienated from his own
being. As Plato expressed it so clearly in the *Symposium,* we love
and yearn for what we lack. Narcissism in its original mythological
implications is thus not a needless excess of self-love but rather just
the opposite, a frustrated state of yearning for a self-possession
which does not yet exist. The solution of the problem of Narcissus
is the fulfillment of self-love rather than its renunciation. We meet
here a common error of the moralizing ego which tries to create a
loving personality by extirpating self-love. This is a profound psychological mistake and only causes a psychic split. Fulfilled self-love
is a prerequisite to the genuine love of any object, and to the flow
of psychic energy in general.

In the case of Narcissus, fulfillment of self-love, or union with the
image in the depths, requires a descent into the unconscious, a
nekyia or symbolic death. That this is the deeper meaning of the
Narcissus myth is indicated by certain other details. After Narcissus

died he turned into the flower narcissus. This is the "death flower" (from *narkao,* to be stiff or dead). The narcissus was sacred to Hades and opened the doors to his realm of the underworld. Persephone had just picked a narcissus when the earth opened up and Hades emerged to abduct her. The inescapable conclusion is that narcissism, at least in its original mythological sense, is the way into the unconscious where one must go in quest of individuality.

Another implication of the Narcissus myth and the theme of falling in love with one's reflection is brought up by a parallel image found in an Orphic interpretation of the Dionysus legend. When the infant Dionysus was torn to pieces by the Titans he was said to be playing with, among other things, a mirror. According to Proclus, the mirror was interpreted as meaning that Dionysus saw his own image in matter and went toward it with desire. He yearned for self-realization (like Narcissus). Thus he became confined in matter (incarnated), and became subject to dismemberment by the Titans.[11] Understood psychologically, this mythologem could refer to an early phase of development during which the primitive ego, still identified with original unconscious totality, begins to function in spatio-temporal reality (embraces matter). But reality is hostile to the inflated state of unconscious totality (ego-Self identity) and dismembers it. Later phases of development then lead to the recollection.

The subjective experience of individuality is a profound mystery that we cannot hope to encompass by rational understanding. However, some of its implications can be approached by examining the symbolic images that refer to this experience. Let us begin by looking at the testimony of etymology. Etymology is the unconscious side of language, hence it is relevant in psychological studies. The word *individual* derives from the two Latin roots, *in* = not, and *dividere* = to divide. Its basic meaning is therefore something that is indivisible. This corresponds to the fact that the experience of individuality is primary; it cannot be analyzed or reduced to simpler elements.

It is interesting to note that such a fundamental concept as the individual must be expressed in terms of what it is not, *i.e.,* not divisible. The same phenomenon occurs with the word *atom,* the basic unit of matter (from the Greek *a* = not, and *tom* from *temnein* = to cut, divide). It appears again in the words *integer* and

[11] Proclus, *Timaeus* iii, 163, cited by G. R. S. Mead in *Orpheus,* reissued London, John Watkins, 1965, p. 160f.

integrate (from the Latin *in* = not, and *tag*, base of *tangere* = to touch). It seems that in attempting to describe such a basic fact as individuality we must resort to the same procedure as used in describing deity; since it is a fact that transcends our categories of conscious understanding, we can do no more than describe it in terms of what it is not, the so-called *via negativa*.

The word *individual* is etymologically related to the word *widow*. According to Skeat,[12] *widow* (Latin, *vidua*) derives from a lost cognate verb *videre*, meaning to part. Jung has demonstrated that the images of widow and orphan are part of the individuation process.[13] In this connection he quotes St. Augustine as saying: "The whole Church is one widow, desolate in this world." and Jung adds: "So too the soul is 'destitute in this world,' " The quotation from Augustine then continues: "But thou are not an orphan, thou are not reckoned as a widow . . . Thou has a friend . . . Thou are God's orphan, God's widow." [14] In a Manichaean text Jesus was called the "son of the widow." [15] Widow means the parted one. Hence, prior to widowhood one is not yet an individual, indivisible, but is still subject to a parting process. The symbolism tells us that widowhood is an experience on the pathway to the realization of individuality, in fact, that individuality is the son of that experience. This can only mean that man must be parted from that on which he is dependent but which he is not, before he can become aware of that which he is, unique and indivisible. A dependent projection must be broken. Similar implications apply to the image of the orphan which was a synonym for the alchemists' philosophers' stone.[16] To be orphaned denotes the loss of parental support and the breaking of parental projections; it is likewise a prerequisite of the conscious experience of individuality. As Augustine puts it, to be a widow or orphan relates one to God (the Self).

2. THE MONAD AND THE MONOGENES

An important body of material referring to the experience of individuality is to be found in the philosophical speculations of the ancients concerning the One or the Monad. The early philosophers

---

[12] Skeat, Walter W., *An Etymological Dictionary of the English Language*, Oxford University Press, 1958, p. 177.
[13] Jung, C. G., *Mysterium Coniunctionis*, C.W., 14, par. 13ff.
[14] Ibid., par. 17.
[15] Ibid., par. 14, n. 69.
[16] Ibid., par. 13.

encountered the mystery of individuality in philosophical, cosmological projections. Their speculations about the Monad or the One that lies behind all phenomena was actually a projection of the inner psychological fact of being an individual. For instance, the Monad was a prominent image in Pythagorean speculation. According to the Pythogoreans, the Monad is the creative principle, imposing order and limitations on the infinite. It was said that, "when the Monad came into existence, it limited the nearest part of the unlimited." [17] The Monad was also identified with the central Creative Fire which was the source of creation and government.[18] This central fire has some interesting appellations. It is called "Tower of Zeus," "Guard-house of Zeus," "Hearth of the World," and "altar, bond and measure of nature." [19]

This passage tells us that the principle of individuality is the creative principle itself and that all order, what the Greeks called *cosmos*, derives from it. The Monad is also identified with fire, which is reminiscent of alchemical symbolism in which the point (a version of the Monad) is equated with the scintilla, a spark of light and fire.[20] Hence, the principle of individuality is the source of both consciousness (light) and energy (fire).

The Monad has a prominent place in Gnostic speculation. Speaking of the Gnostics, Hippolytus writes:

> For them the beginning of all things is the Monad, ingenerable, imperishable, incomprehensible, inconceptible, the creator and cause of all things that are generated. This Monad is called by them the Father.[21]

In the Bruce Codex we have the following description of the Monad:

> This . . . is the Truth which embraces them all (the twelve Depths); . . . this is the Truth of the All; this is the Mother of all Aeons; this it is which surrounds all Depths. This is the Monad which is incomprehensible or unknowable; this it is which has no Seal . . . in which

[17] Freeman, Kathleen, *Companion to the Pre-Socratic Philosophers*, Cambridge, Harvard University Press, 1959, p. 247. Aristotle *Metaphysics* 1091a.

[18] Ibid., p. 250.

[19] Kirk, G. G., and Raven, J. A., *The Pre-Socratic Philosophers*, Cambridge: Cambridge University Press, 1963, p. 260.

[20] Jung, C. G., *Mysterium Coniunctionis*, C.W., 14, par. 42ff.

[21] Mead, G. R. S., *Fragments of a Faith Forgotten*, London, John M. Watkins, 1931. p. 335.

are all Seals; which is blessed for ever and ever. This is the eternal Father; this the ineffable, unthinkable, incomprehensible, untranscendible Father . . .[22]

The image of the Gnostic Monad emphasizes the all-encompassing mystery of individuality. It does not permit much rational exegesis but it does convey forcefully the sense that the individual is the carrier of a profound mystery. Such images are badly needed today since there is very little in our contemporary culture to justify and validate the individual as such.

The same image is taken up in Plato. In the *Parmenides* [23] there is a lengthy discourse on the nature of the One. This dialogue presents great difficulties for rational comprehension; the only conclusions that are reached about the One are paradoxes. Here are some of the conclusions:

> . . . the one is neither at rest nor in motion (139b).
> . . . the one . . . must always be both in motion and at rest (146b).
> . . . the one has nothing to do with time and does not occupy any stretch of time (141d).
> . . . if the one is, it is in time (152a).
> . . . the one both touches, and does not touch, both itself and the others (149d).
> . . . the one both is and is becoming older and younger than itself. (152e).
> . . . the one . . . neither is nor becomes older or younger than itself (152e).
> . . . if there is a one, the one is both all things and nothing whatsoever . . . (160b).

The list of contradictions could be prolonged, but it is sufficient for our purposes. Even the philosophers have difficulty making anything out of this dialogue. I see it as an elaborate philosophical *koan* which confounds the rational faculties in order possibly to open the way for an immediate subjective experience of being an individual. The chief thing that Plato demonstrates is that the One cannot be apprehended by logic or the conscious categories of time, space, and causality. It cannot be apprehended by logic because it involves contradictions. It both participates and does not participate in time, space, and the process of cause and effect. Such

[22] Ibid., p. 549f.
[23] F. M. Cornford's translation in *Plato: The Collected Dialogues,* edited by Hamilton and Cairns, Bollingen Series LXXI, Princeton University Press.

conclusions, of course, make no sense to a rationally oriented philosopher. However, we can understand them as a quite accurate description of an empirical, psychological fact, the fact of individuality. If
we think of the experience of individuality as having two centers,
the ego and the Self, these contradictions fall into place. The ego
is an incarnation, an entity, which participates in the vicissitudes of
time, space and causality. The Self, as the center of the archetypal
psyche, is in another world beyond consciousness and its particular-
izing modes of experience. The ego is the center of subjective
identity; the Self, the center of objective identity. The ego lives on
earth but the name of the Self is written in heaven. This same psychological fact is represented by the myth of the Dioscuri; one son
of Zeus, Castor, is mortal; the other, Pollux is immortal, beyond
space and time.

The image of the Monad is taken up at considerable length by
Plotinus, the neo-Platonic philosopher of the third century A.D. In
the *Enneads* [24] he has many beautiful and profound things to say
about the One that must certainly derive from his own inner experiences:

> It is by the One that all beings are beings . . . for what could exist
> were it not one? If not a one, a thing is not. No army, no choir, no
> flock exists except it can be one. . . . It is the same with plant and
> animal bodies; each of them is a unit. . . . Health is contingent upon
> the body's being coordinated in unity; beauty, upon the mastery of
> parts by the One; the soul's virtue, upon unification into one sole
> coherence.

It would be hard to find a better expression than this for the
primary importance of the principle of individuality. If we understand this passage in a strictly psychological sense, it says that all
authentic being occurs when we live and speak out of our unified
and unique individuality. Of course, this is easy to say in words, but
exceedingly hard to live out in reality.

Another quotation from the *Enneads*:

> As the One begets all things, it cannot be any of them—neither thing,
> nor quality, nor quantity, nor intelligence, nor soul. Not in motion,
> nor at rest, not in space, nor in time, it is "the in itself uniform," or
> rather it is the "without-form" preceding form, movement, and rest,
> which are characteristics of Being and make Being multiple.[25]

[24] This version of the *Enneads* from *The Essential Plotinus*, edited by Elmer
O'Brien, New York, Mentor Books, The New American Library, 1964, VI,, 9, 1.
[25] Ibid., VI, 9, 3.

This passage presents a point the understanding of which is absolutely essential for psychological development and which comes up frequently in psychotherapeutic practice. "As the One begets all things, it cannot be any of them . . ." This means that it is a mistake to identify our individuality with any particular talent, function, or aspect of ourselves. However, very often this is just what we do. If a person feels inferior and depressed in the presence of people who are more intelligent, who have read more books, who have traveled more, who are more famous, or who are more skillful or knowledgeable in art, music, politics, or any other human endeavor, then that person is making the mistake of identifying some particular aspect or function of himself with his essential individuality. Because a particular capacity is inferior to that of another person, he feels himself to be inferior. This feeling then leads either to depressive withdrawal or to defensive, competitive efforts to prove he is not inferior. If such a person can experience the fact that his individuality and personal worth are beyond all particular manifestation his security will no longer be threatened by the accomplishments of others. This sense of innate worth prior to and irrespective of deeds and accomplishments is the precious deposit that is left in the psyche by the experience of genuine parental love. Lacking this experience, one must laboriously seek out from the depths of the unconscious its inner equivalent, the Monad, often symbolized by a mandala. This experience conveys the sense of having a transpersonal basis for being and enables one to feel he has a right to exist as he actually is. The theological equivalent to this experience is justification before God.

Again Plotinus says:

> There must be something that is fully self-sufficient. That is The One; it alone, within and without, is without need. It needs nothing outside itself either to exist, or achieve well-being, or to be sustained in existence.[26]

This passage reminds us of Neumann's description of the uroborus, the image of the tail-eating serpent.[27] His whole discussion is pertinent to our subject although he confines himself largely to the infantile manifestations of the uroborus. But this image is an active and sustaining one throughout all phases of psychic develop-

[26] Ibid., VI, 9, 6.
[27] Neumann, Erich, *The Origins and History of Consciousness*, Bollingen Series, XLII. Princeton University Press, 1954, p. 5 ff.

ment. The psychic fact to which this image points is the antidote to all the frustrations that dependence on outer objects and persons engenders. To be aware of individuality is to realize that one has all that one needs. It also means that one needs all that one has, namely, that every psychic content and happening is meaningful. This idea is expressed in the following quotation from Plotinus:

> Those who believe that the world of being is governed by luck or by chance and that it depends upon material causes are far removed from the divine and from the notion of the One.[28]

To be related to one's individuality means to accept all that is encountered within as meaningful and significant aspects of the single whole. Yet how easily and how frequently we resort to the lazy tactic of evading genuine encounter with some aspect of ourselves by saying, "I didn't really mean that," or "I just forgot," or "It was only a careless slip," and so on. For those who have been initiated into individuality that way out is no longer available. They know that no psychic happening is fortuitous. There is no place for chance in the meaningful world of psyche.

Plotinus sums it up in this passage:

> As the One does not contain any difference, it is always present and we are present to it when we no longer contain difference. The One does not aspire to us, to move around us; we aspire to it, to move around it. Actually we always move around it; but we do not always look. We are like a chorus grouped around a conductor who allow their attention to be distracted by the audience. If, however, they were to turn towards their conductor, they would sing as they should and would really be with him. We are always around the One. If we were not, we would dissolve and cease to exist. Yet our gaze does not remain fixed upon the One. When we look at it, we then attain the end of our desires and find rest. Then it is that, all discord past, we dance an inspired dance around it.
> In this dance the soul looks upon the source of life, the source of The Intelligence, the origin of Being, the cause of the Good, the root of The Soul.
> All these entities emanate from The One without any lessening for it is not a material mass. If it were, the emanations would be perishable. But they are eternal because their originating principle always stays the same; not fragmenting itself in producing them, it remains entire. So they persist as well, just as light persists as long as the sun shines.[29]

[28] Plotinus, VI, 9, 4.
[29] Ibid., VI, 9, 8 and 9.

Before leaving Plotinus, I must mention a speculation of his which is immediately relevant to the subject of this chapter. It is contained in the seventh tractate of the fifth *Ennead* and is entitled, "Is there an Ideal Archetype of Particular Beings?" [30] In other words, does the individual have an eternal form or Platonic Idea as the transcendental basis of his personal identity? Plotinus answers this question in the affirmative and thus, along with other mystical and speculative philosophers, adumbrated Jung's empirical discovery of the Self.

To complete our survey of the Monad image we come to modern times and Leibnitz's *Monadology.* He speaks of windowless Monads, saying: "The Monads have no windows through which anything may come in or go out." (*Monadology,* 7) In our own day F. H. Bradley expresses the same idea. He writes, "My external sensations are no less private to myself than are my thoughts or my feelings. In either case my experience falls within my own circle, a circle closed on the outside; and, with all its elements alike, every sphere is opaque to the others which surround it. . . . In brief, regarded as an existence which appears in a soul, the whole world for each is peculiar and private to that soul." [31]

This idea conveys a basic truth about life as the experience of individuals. We each inhabit our own separate world and have no way of knowing how our world compares with that of others. Of course we have language, but even that, I suspect, is far more of a private and personal experience than we realize. The same applies to art, music, and the external world of objects. I know how I experience these things but how can I know if my experience corresponds to that of another person? For instance, I have a certain image of a room and its contents. How can I know that everyone will have the same image? Of course, we can all agree on a verbal description of the room and the objects it contains. But the words may have different subjective references for each of us. And we cannot see into anybody else's world to make comparisons.

The world does not exist until there is a consciousness to perceive it. It follows then that there will be as many worlds as there are centers of consciousness, and each is separate, complete, and hermetically sealed from all others. This may seem extreme, but I am

[30] Plotinus, *The Enneads,* translated by Stephen MacKenna, London, Faber and Faber Ltd., 1962, p. 419.

[31] Bradley, F. H. *Appearance and Reality.* London, Oxford University Press, 1966. p. 306.

convinced that it is a sober fact that becomes self-evident once certain unconscious assumptions and identifications are dissolved. But what about the undeniable experiences of human solidarity, empathy, understanding, and love? And what about the process of psychotherapy itself which requires that analyst and analysant have a mutual effect on one another? If we are indeed windowless, how can such things happen? First, we must exclude all merely apparent relationship which is actually based on projection and unconscious identification. In such cases one only has the illusion of knowing and relating to the other person. Having discarded projection phenomena which make up the vast majority of what usually goes by the name of love or relationship, we are left with only one experience that we all indubitably share with others, and that can enable us to have objective love and understanding. That experience is the experience of being a windowless Monad, the lone inhabitant of a sealed world. In this respect we are all in the same boat. And since this experience is the primary and essential feature of human existence, what we share with one another is by far the most important thing of all, certainly basic enough for all the love and understanding that is in us. Hence, we are windowless only in regard to the details and particulars of our personal life, our judgments and our perceptions. But to the extent that we are related to our individuality as a whole and in its essence, we come into objective and compassionate relation to others. To put it concisely, we might say that the ego is windowless, but the Self is a window on other worlds of being.

There is another image relevant to our subject which is closely related to that of the Monad but which has some distinctive features of its own. I refer to the *Monogenes*. Whereas the *Monad* is the unbegotten, the *Monogenes* is the *only-begotten*. The most familiar reference to this image is in the Creed which refers to Christ as the *only-begotten*. The same term is used in Plato's description of cosmogony in the "Timaeus." [32] He writes:

> In order then that the world might be solitary, like the perfect Animal, the creator made not two worlds or an infinite number of them, but there is and ever will be the one only-begotten . . . ("Timaeus," 31).

[32] *Plato's Cosmology*, "The Timaeus of Plato," translated with a running commentary by F. M. Cornford, Indianapolis, New York: Library of Liberal Arts, Bobbs Merrill.

According to Valentinian cosmogonic speculation, first there was the Deep, the Father of All called *Bythos;* out of him emanated *Nous* which is also called *Monogenes,* and he "is said to be 'equal and like' to him from whom he had emanated. . . ." [33]

Here are three versions of the same basic image, the Christian version, the Platonic philosophic version and a Gnostic version. In each case an only-begotten one is created, begotten or emanated from the original unbegotten One. If we understand these images as projected psychology, the only-begotten one that emanates from the unbegotten one must refer to the empirical ego that emerges from the original, *a priori* Self. The ego is only-begotten; there is only one and it has no siblings except in the pathological cases of multiple personality. Being an individual is thus related to the experience of being an only child, an experience which has two major aspects; one positive and one negative. The positive aspect is the experience of being the favored one, of having no rivals with whom to compete for the available attention, interest, and love. The negative aspect of being an only child is that it means being lonely.

The same considerations apply to the experience of individuality. To be an individual means to be a special, favored one, and also a lonely one. Alfred Adler was the first to draw attention to the psychology of the only child, emphasizing particularly the only child's demand and expectation to be the center of things, the special one. This is the ego-centrism or unconscious self-centeredness which we have discussed previously. The only child is particularly vulnerable to identification with the *Monogenes* because his early life experiences concretize that image; he is in reality an *only-begotten.* If he is to develop, he must go through the painful experience of learning that he is not at all special in relation to the outer world. However, the image and experience of being special remains valid from the internal psychological standpoint since it is an expression of the nature of individuality as such.

The other aspect of being an only child is loneliness, and this too is a crucial phase in the process of achieving conscious individuality. Loneliness is a precursor of the positive experience of aloneness. We might say that while aloneness is a fact of individual existence, the experience of loneliness is—for an ego which is not yet willing or able to accept it—the first painful emergence of that

[33] Legge, Francis, *Forerunners and Rivals of Christianity,* New Hyde Park, N. Y., University Books, 1964, II, p. 48.

fact into consciousness. Loneliness seeks diversion or togetherness in order to forget the uncomfortable fact of individuality. To be an individual means to be a special favored one, and also a lonely one. If loneliness is faced instead of forgotten, it can lead over to the creative acceptance of the fact of aloneness.

The aloneness of individuality is represented by the hermit, the monk, the solitary one. In a recently discovered Gnostic Gospel called *The Gospel of Thomas* there are several significant sayings of Jesus which speak of the "single ones" or the "solitaries." The Greek word is *monachoi* which could also be translated as the "unified ones":

> 54. Jesus says: "Blessed are the solitary and the elect, for you will find the Kingdom! Because you have issued from it, you will return to it again." [34]
>
> 65. . . . I (Jesus) say this: "When (a person) finds himself solitary, he will be full of light; but when he finds himself divided, he will be full of darkness." [35]
>
> 79. Jesus says: "Many stand outside at the door, but it is only the solitaries who will enter into the bridal chamber." [36]

3. UNITY AND MULTIPLICITY

If unity, singleness, and indivisibility are the hallmarks of individuality, multiplicity and dispersal are its opposites. This opposition is exemplified in the traditional philosophical problem of the one and the many. We have already seen how the myth of Narcissus can be understood as representing a process which breaks up original unconscious unity and submits it to dismemberment and dispersal. This might be called the analytic phase of developing consciousness. But given a state of psychic fragmentation, a unifying or synthetic phase sets in. There are many examples in the Gnostic literature of the image of gathering together that which has been dispersed.[37] For example, in *The Gospel of Eve*, quoted by Epiphanius, is the following passage:

[34] Doresse, Jean. *The Secret Books of Egyptian Gnostics.* New York, Viking Press, 1960, p. 363.
[35] *Ibid.*, p. 365.
[36] *Ibid.*, p. 366.
[37] For a discussion of this theme in Gnosticism, see H. Jonas, *The Gnostic Religion.* 1958, p. 58 ff.

I stood on a lofty mountain and saw a mighty Man, and another, a dwarf, and heard as it were a voice of thunder, and drew nigh for to hear; and it spake unto me and said: "I am thou and thou are I; and wheresoever thou art I am there and I am sown (or scattered) in all; from whencesoever thou willest thou gatherest Me, and gathering Me thou gatherest Thyself." [38]

The mightly man and the dwarf refer to the theme of "the bigger than big and smaller than small" which describes the paradoxical nature of the experience of being an individual. The individual is nothing in collective, statistical terms, but is everything from the inner standpoint. The mighty man who is both great and small is the Anthropos, the original Monad, which has undergone dispersal in the process of the incarnation of the ego. Adaptation to the real world of multiplicity requires attention to and involvement in particulars which fragment the original state of unity. Our text advises that these scattered fragments must now be gathered together.

In another passage from Epiphanius quoting the *Gospel of Philip*, the soul is justifying itself as it ascends to the heavenworld:

I have recognized myself and gathered myself together from all sides. I have sown no children to the Ruler, (the Lord of this world), but have torn up his roots; I have gathered together my limbs that were scattered abroad, and I know thee who thou art. [39]

A theological version of the same image is found in Augustine:

Since through the iniquity of godlessness we have seceded and dissented and fallen away from the one true and highest God and dissipated ourselves into the many split up by the many and cleaving to the many; it was necesary that . . . the many should have joined in clamor for the coming of One (Christ) . . . and, justified in the justice of One, be made One. [40]

Again we have the remarkably psychological expression of the same idea in Origen:

There was one man. We, who are still sinners, cannot obtain this title of praise, for each of us is not one but many . . . See how he who

[38] Mead, G. R. S., *Fragments of a Faith Forgotten*, p. 439.
[39] Mead, p. 439f.
[40] The Trinity IV, 11, as quoted by H. Jones, *op. cit.*, p. 62.

thinks himself one is not one, but seems to have as many personalities as he has moods . . .[41]

Dispersal or multiplicity as a psychological condition can be seen from either the inner or outer standpoint. Seen from within, it is a state of inner fragmentation involving a number of relatively autonomous complexes which, when touched by the ego, cause changes in mood and attitude and make the individual realize that he is not one but many. From the external standpoint, multiplicity is manifested by the exteriorization or projection of parts of the individual psyche into the outer world. In this condition one finds his friends and his enemies, his hopes and his fears, his sources of support and his threats of failure, concretized in outer persons, objects, and events. In such a state of dispersal there can be no experience of essential individuality. One is in thrall to the "ten thousand things." [42]

The inner and outer aspects are only two ways of seeing the same fact. Either way we see it, a process of collecting is needed. This collecting process is what occupies the majority of time in the course of a personal analysis. Over and over again the analysant must be able to say and to know, "I am that," whether he is dealing with a dream image or with an affect-laden projection. The process of self-collection, or better self-recollection, involves accepting as one's own all those aspects of being which have been left out in the course of ego development. Very gradually in the course of this process the realization begins to dawn that there is a unity behind the apparent multiplicity and that indeed it is this pre-existent unity which has motivated the whole arduous task of self-collection in the first place.

A modern dream will illustrate the themes we have been discussing. In fact, this entire chapter can be considered as a commentary on the implications of this dream. It is very brief: *The dreamer saw a one-celled organism, a small mass of pulsating protoplasm like an amoeba. In the center where the nucleus would ordinarily be was a hole. Through this hole he saw another world, a landscape stretching to a horizon.*

---

[41] Quoted by Jung, *Mysterium Coniunctionis*, C.W., Vol. 14, par. 6, n. 26.
[42] Augustine says, ". . . every soul is wretched that is fettered in the friendship of mortal things—it is torn to pieces when it loses them, and then realizes the misery which it had even before it lost them." *Confessions*, Book IV, Chap. VI.

Some of the associations that the dreamer had were these: The one-celled organism reminded the dreamer that life is carried by discrete, individual units, the cells. Here is a definite reference to Monad symbolism. Protoplasm was described as the basic life stuff, the source of all biological urges to survive. We might consider it the seat of concupiscence and desirousness of all kinds. The pulsation brought to mind the ebb and flow of the tide, systole and diastole, and the alternation between day and night. The hole in the center of the cell reminded the dreamer of the rabbit hole which was the entrance to another world in *Alice's Adventures in Wonderland*. The fact that the center of the cell was empty also recalled a passage the dreamer had read in Jung to the effect that traditional religious mandalas have the image of the deity in the center but the center of modern individual mandalas is usually empty. The over-all effect of the hole was described as a window looking into another world.

The dream thus gives us a picture of the Monad in its biological form, the cell. This cell is composed of pulsating protoplasm signifying the psyche's basic hungers, lusts, and urge to live. At the very center of this trembling mass of concupiscent desires is the window or entrance to the other world, the archetypal psyche. The implication is that one gets a glimpse of the other world by piercing to the center of the protoplasmic urges, certainly not by rejecting protoplasm. In other words, the experience of individuality as a transpersonal fact is found at the very center of our personal, selfish urges to power, lust, and self-aggrandisement.

This dream has a parallel in one reported by Jung:

"The dreamer found himself with three younger travelling companions in Liverpool. It was night and raining. The air was full of smoke and soot. They climbed up from the harbour to the 'upper city.' The dreamer said, 'It was terribly dark and disagreeable, and we could not understand how anyone could stick it here. We talked about this, and one of my companions said that, remarkably enough, a friend of his had settled here, which astonished everybody. During this conversation we reached a sort of public garden in the middle of the city. The park was square, and in the center was a lake or large pool . . . On it there was a single tree, a red-flowering magnolia, which miraculously stood in everlasting sunshine. I noticed that my companions had not seen this miracle, whereas I was beginning to understand why the man had settled here.'" [43]

[43] Jung, C. G., *The Archetypes and the Collective Unconscious*, C.W., Vol. 9i, par. 654.

This dream has several similarities to our previous dream. The disagreeable blackness of Liverpool corresponds to the protoplasm. The name Liverpool, referring to the liver, the seat of life, has the same symbolic meaning as protoplasm. In the center of the blackness of Liverpool is a pool of eternal sunshine closely analogous to the view of the other world in the center of the protoplasm. The spot of eternal sunshine is described later by the dreamer as a "Window opening into eternity" just as the other dreamer called the hole a *window* into another world. Here we have empirical proof that the Monad is not windowless after all. The Liverpool dream led to the painting of a mandala which Jung has published.[44] *(Picture 39)*.

The mandala, as Jung has demonstrated, is the major symbolic expression for the experience of being an individual. Such an image emerges spontaneously from the unconscious at times when all the grand and terrible implications of being a unique, indivisible, lonely Monad are beginning to dawn on the individual. Conscious theoretical knowledge of mandala symbolism means very little. In fact it raises the danger that such images may be used deliberately as a substitute for the real experience. As Jung says:

> One cannot be too cautious in these matters, for what with the imitative urge and a positively morbid avidity to possess themselves of outlandish feathers and deck themselves out in this exotic plumage, far too many people are misled into snatching at such "magical" ideas and applying them externally, like an ointment. People will do anything, no matter how absurd in order to avoid facing their own souls.[45]

Leaving aside such aberrations, the experience which the mandala symbolizes is by all evidence the most central and fundamental fact of human existence. It is the condition of being an individual with all the consequences and implications which I have tried to touch upon. This dimly realized fact is the source of our greatest yearnings and our greatest fears. We love it and we hate it. Its imperatives can at one time plunge us into the anguish of separation and dismemberment and at another time convey the profoundest sense of meaning and security. But through all vicissitudes it remains the ultimate fact of our being.

I stated at the beginning that external observation indicates that

44 Ibid., figure 6.
45 Jung, C. G., *Psychology and Alchemy*, C.W., Vol. 12, par. 126.

Picture 39. THE LIVERPOOL MANDALA, C. G. Jung.

life is not a continuum but is made up of discrete units. However, in discussing the windowless nature of the Monad we discovered that the Monad does indeed have a window; that at the center of the experience of individuality is the realization that all other individuals share the same experience as ourselves of living in a single, sealed world, and that this realization connects us meaningfully with all other units of life. The result is that we do experience ourselves as part of a continuum. Internal observation, at sufficient depth, hence contradicts external observation) I am reminded of the problem in physics concerning the nature of light. Is light made up of particles or of waves; that is, is it composed of individual units or is it a continuum? Current data requires that it be considered paradoxically as both particles and waves.[46] And so it is with the psyche; we are *both* unique indivisible units of being and also part of the continuum which is the universal wave of life.

[46] For a discussion of this problem, see Werner Heisenberg, *Physics and Philosophy*. New York: Harper Torchbooks, 1962, p. 44 ff.

CHAPTER SEVEN

The Trinity Archetype and the Dialectic of Development

> There are three sorts of "Wholes"—the first, anterior to
> the parts; the second, composed of the parts; the third,
> knitting into one stuff the parts and the whole.
>
> —PROCLUS °

1. THE THREE AND THE FOUR

One of Jung's major discoveries is the psychological significance of the number four as it relates to the symbolism of psychic wholeness and the four functions. The significance of the quaternity is basic to his whole theory of the psyche, both as regards its structure and its developmental goal, the individuation process. We are thus particularly alert to quaternity symbolism as it appears in dreams and in the imagery of myth and folklore. However, there are other numerical motifs which are commonly encountered. Perhaps the most frequent of these is the theme of three. Because of the predominant value that Jung attached to the quaternity, he tended in most cases to interpret trinitarian images as incomplete or amputated quaternities.[1] This approach calls forth certain objections. Victor White, for instance, writes:

° *Commentary on Timaeus*, 83.265.
[1] Jung, C. G., *Psychology and Alchemy*, C.W., Vol. 12, para. 31 and *Aion*, C.W., Vol. 9 ii, para. 351.

. . . are we *always* compelled to ask, when confronted with the number three, "Where is the fourth?" Are we to suppose that always and everywhere the number three is to be understood only as four minus one?—that every triangle is only a failed square? . . . Or could it possibly be that ternary symbols are, so to speak, archetypal images in their own right, which present a content distinct from that of the quaternity? [2]

The present chapter will examine this question.

Jung's most comprehensive discussion of trinitarian symbolism is in his essay "A Psychological Approach to the Dogma of the Trinity." [3] The essay begins with a review of prechristian trinitarian images, and then proceeds with a description of the numerological symbolism of Plato and the Pythagoreans. Following some psychological commentary on the Christian trinity of father, son and holy spirit, Jung then summarizes the historical development of the dogma of the trinity as part of the creed. This is followed by a detailed discussion of the psychology of the three aspects of the trinity and a comparison with the image of quaternity. The latter is considered as bringing the trinity to completion by the addition of the fourth previously rejected element, namely, matter, devil and the dark side.

Without specifically stating it, Jung seems to be interweaving two different interpretations which are at variance with one another. On the one hand he interprets the trinity as an incomplete representation of deity, perhaps necessary for a certain period of psychic development, but inadequate for the needs of individuation because it leaves out of account the fourth principle of matter and the evil side of God. This interpretation is illustrated by the following quotation. After discussing the reality of the evil power, Jung writes:

> In a monotheistic religion everything that goes against God can only be traced back to God himself. This thought is objectionable to say the least of it and has therefore to be circumvented. That is the deeper reason why a highly influential personage like the devil cannot be accomodated properly in a trinitarian cosmos . . . that would lead straight back to certain Gnostic views according to which the devil, as Satanael, is God's first son, Christ being the second. A further logical inference would be the abolition of the trinity formula and its replacement by the quaternity. [4]

[2] White, V., *Soul and Psyche.* New York, Harper and Brothers, 1960, p. 106.
[3] Jung, C. G., *Psychology and Religion: West and East,* C.W., Vol. 11, par. 169 ff.
[4] Ibid., par. 249.

However, in other places in the essay, Jung speaks of the trinity symbol as referring to three stages of a developmental process which is complete and sufficient in itself, without the need for the addition of a fourth. For instance, he describes the three stages of father, son and holy spirit as follows. About the world of the father:

> The world of the Father typifies an age, which is characterized by a pristine oneness with the whole of nature [5]
> . . . an age far removed from critical judgment and moral conflict [6]
> It is . . . man in his childhood state [7]

About the world of the son:

> A world filled with longing for redemption and for that state of perfection in which man was still one with the Father. Longingly he looked back to the world of the Father, but it was lost forever, because an irreversible increase in man's consciousness had taken place in the meantime and made it independent.[8]
> The stage of the Son is a conflict situation *par excellence* . . . Freedom from the law brings a sharpening of opposites.[9]

Concerning the world of the holy ghost:

> The advance to the third stage (the Holy Ghost) means something like a recognition of the unconscious if not actual subordination to it . . . Just as the transition from the first stage to the second demands the sacrifice of childish dependence, so at the transition to the third stage an exclusive independence has to be relinquished.[10] This third stage means articulating one's ego-consciousness with a supraordinate totality, of which one cannot say that it is "I", but which is best visualized as a more comprehensive being.[11]

In these quotations that describe the three developmental phases of father, son and holy ghost, there is no suggestion that the trinity is an incomplete symbol requiring the addition of a fourth ele-

[5] Ibid., par. 201.
[6] Ibid., par. 199.
[7] Ibid., par. 201.
[8] Ibid., par. 203.
[9] Ibid., par. 272.
[10] Ibid., par. 273.
[11] Ibid., par. 276.

ment. Rather, the trinity seems to symbolize adequately and completely a developmental process in time. In discussing this developmental process Jung says: "The rhythm is built up in three steps but the resultant symbol is a quaternity.[12] This statement clearly implies that the threefold rhythm and the fourfold goal are separate symbolic entities neither of which properly can be interpreted in terms of the other. However, this point is later lost when the trinity is described as an incomplete representation of the deity.

The threefold rhythm of the developmental process deserves greater attention. Let us consider that this ternary symbol is a separate and valid entity within itself. In this case the archetype of the trinity or threefoldness and the archetype of quaternity or fourfoldness would refer to two different aspects of the psyche, each valid, appropriate and complete in its own realm. The quaternity image expresses the totality of the psyche in its structural, static or eternal sense, whereas the trinity image expresses the totality of psychological experience in its dynamic, developmental, temporal aspect.

Quaternity, mandala images emerge in times of psychic turmoil and convey a sense of stability and rest. The image of the fourfold nature of the psyche provides stabilizing orientation. It gives one a glimpse of static eternity. The mandalas of Tibetan Buddhism are used for this purpose. They are instruments of meditation which convey to consciousness a sense of peace and calm as though one were safely grounded in the eternal structural substance and protected from the disrupting dangers of change. Patients in psychotherapy sometimes discover for themselves this method of meditating on their own mandala paintings when their psychic integrity is endangered.

Trinitarian symbols on the other hand imply growth, development and movement in time. They surround themselves with dynamic rather than static associations. Thus Baynes writes, "The triune archetype symbolizes the dynamic or vital aspect." [13] And again, "The number three is specifically associated with the creative process . . . Every function of energy in nature has, indeed, the form of a pair of opposites, united by a third factor, their product. Thus the triangle is the symbol of a pair of opposites joined above or below by a third factor." [14] Jung gives the trinity a dynamic,

[12] Ibid., par. 258.
[13] Baynes, H. G., *Mythology of the Soul,* London, Ryder and Company, 1969, p. 565.
[14] Ibid., p. 405.

developmental interpretation in his description of the three phases of psychological development as the stages of the father, the son and the holy spirit. All events in time naturally fall into a threefold pattern. Every event has a beginning, a middle and an end. The conscious mind thinks of time in the three categories past, present and future. Joachim of Floris 1,000 years ago interpreted the trinity in terms of periods of time. According to his view, before Christ was the age of the father. The first millenium after Christ was the age of the son and the second millenium was to be the age of the holy spirit.

When dealing with temporal or developmental events there seems to be a deep-seated archetypal tendency to organize such events in terms of a threefold pattern. Freud submitted to this pattern when he described psychological development in terms of the three stages oral, anal and genital. Esther Harding made use of this same threefold pattern when she described the three stages of psychological development in the terms autos, ego and Self.[15] Another example of a threefold division in the developmental process is furnished by Alfred North Whitehead. In his essay "The Rhythm of Education" [16] Whitehead distinguishes three stages in the natural learning process. He calls these the stage of romance, the stage of precision and the stage of generalization. The first phase, the stage of romance, is characterized by the emotional excitement of first discovery. There is a total response which does not permit the coolness and discipline of a systematic approach. Rather the child, or man for that matter, is intoxicated by the glimpse of a new world opening. The second phase, the stage of precision, subordinates breadth and totality of approach to exact formulation. Here we have precise accumulation of facts and critical, intellectual analysis. The third phase, the stage of generalization, is called by Whitehead the synthesis of the two previous approaches. It is a return to the total response of the romantic stage with the added advantage of classified ideas and relevant technique.

The process of spiritual development described by the mystics is also a three fold process. According to Inge:

> (The mystic) . . . . loves to figure his path as a ladder reaching from earth to heaven, which must be climbed step by step. This *scala perfectionis* is generally divided into three stages. The first is called

[15] Harding, M. Esther. *Psyhic Energy: Its Source and Its Transformation*, Bollingen Series X, Princeton University Press, 1963, p. 22 f.
[16] Whitehead, A. N. *The Aims of Education*, New York, MacMillan, 1929.

the purgative life, the second the illuminative, while the third, which is really the goal rather than a part of the journey, is called the unitive life, or state of perfect contemplation.[17]

Jung describes Pythagorean number symbolism which is pertinent here. The number one as the first and original number is, strictly speaking, not a number at all. One as unity and totality exists prior to the awareness of numbers which requires a capacity to distinguish between separate, discrete entities. Thus, "one" symbolically corresponds to the uroboric state prior to creation and the separation of things. Two is the first real number since with it is born the possibility of discriminating one thing from another. Two symbolizes the act of creation, the emergence of the ego from the original state of unity. Two implies opposition. Two is the separation of one thing from another and thus represents a state of conflict. Three, however, is the sum of one and two and unites them both within itself. It is the reconciling symbol that resolves the conflict state of two. To three would apply Jung's comment about the symbolic significance of the holy spirit when he says, "The holy ghost is a union of opposites." [18]

Approaching the trinity from this angle there is no room for a fourth element. If we think of it as reflecting a dynamic, developmental process, the third term is the conclusion of the process. The third stage has restored the original unity of the one on a higher level. This new unity can be disturbed only by the emergence of a new opposition which will repeat the trinitarian cycle.

There is an exact parallel to this number symbolism in the formula Hegel proposed for understanding the historical process. According to Hegel, all the movements and happenings in human history fall into a threefold cyclic pattern. First, an original position is conceived and established. This is called the thesis. Next the opposite position is constellated, grows and finally overthrows the first. This is called the antithesis. In the final phase the onesidedness and inadequacy of the antithesis is recognized and replaced by a synthesis of the two opposites. The formula is thus: thesis, antithesis, synthesis. The synthesis can then become a new thesis through which the cycle is repeated. This was an insight of the

[17] Inge, W. R., *Christian Mysticism*, Methuen & Co., 1899, reissued by Meridian Books, pp. 9 f.
[18] Jung, C.W. 11, par. 277.

first magnitude. It is supremely simple and self-evidently true once grasped) Whether or not this can be demonstrated in history, it can certainly be verified empirically in individual psychology. It is one more expression of the archetype of the trinity which gives structure and meaning to the dynamic, temporal events of human life in contrast to the static, eternal aspect.

There is an inveterate tendency for mankind to conceive of deity in a threefold nature. The Christian trinity is only one example of this. In his essay Jung describes Babylonian and Egyptian trinities. In addition, there are the Greek trinities Zeus, Poseidon and Hades and the various embodiments of the triple mother goddess. Destiny, the force directing one's temporal fate, has generally been conceived in a threefold image. For example, in Greece there were the three fates: Clotho who spins the thread of life, Lachesis who measures it and Atropos who cuts it. In Teutonic myth there were the three norns: Urd, Verdandi and Shuld. Urd, the aged one, refers to the past, Verdandi to the present and Shuld to the future. Hermes was most frequently considered as a trinity. Numerous shrines were set up in his honor at the junctions of three roads until they became so commonplace that they provided the origin of the word "trivia." This list of examples, which could be considerably expanded, indicates a widespread tendency to associate deity with a threefold nature. How are we to understand this in the light of our conviction that the psyche has a fourfold structure? These trinitarian images may refer to functional or process deities as opposed to structure deities. In other words, they would be personifications of the psychic dynamism in all its phases. From this standpoint, a trinity could express totality as well as a quaternity, but it would be totality of a different kind. In the one case, it would be a totality of the various dynamic phases of a developmental movement, in the other case a totality of structural elements. Three would symbolize a process, four a goal.

Gerhard Adler makes a distinction between feminine triads and masculine triads. He states: "The feminine triad is always connected with instinctual events in their natural development and growth, whereas the masculine three is based on the dynamic opposition between thesis and antithesis finding its reconciliation in the third step of the synthesis." [19] This is undoubtedly true. The feminine trinities seem to derive from the categories of the natural,

[19] Adler, G. *The Living Symbol.* New York, Pantheon, 1961, p. 260.n.

biological—one could almost say nonpsychic—growth process, such as birth, maturation and death, while the masculine trinities seem to relate specifically to the development of the psyche or consciousness. In the latter case, we have not biological categories but rather spiritual or psychic ones such as thesis and antithesis or God and Satan. However, despite this distinct difference, in the broad sense both masculine and feminine trinities refer to a dynamic, developmental process in time.

In earlier chapters I outlined a scheme of psychological development to explain the relations between ego and Self which we observe at the various levels of conscious development. I likewise made use of a threefold pattern—the three entities being the ego, the Self (or non-ego) and the connecting link between them (ego-Self axis). According to this hypothesis, development of consciousness occurs via a threefold cycle which repeats itself again and again throughout the lifetime of the individual. The three phases of this repetitive cycle are: (1) ego identified with Self, (2) ego alienated from Self and (3) ego reunited with Self through the ego-Self axis. In briefer terms these stages could be called: (1) the stage of the Self, (2) the stage of the ego and (3) the stage of the ego-Self axis. These three stages correspond precisely with the three terms of the Christian trinity: the age of the father (Self), the age of the son (ego) and the age of the holy ghost (ego-Self axis). This is another example of a threefold pattern expressing the totality of a temporal, developmental process.

The medieval idea that man is composed of body, soul and spirit is another trinitarian representation of totality. Similarly, according to alchemical theory, all metals were composed of the three primary principles, Mercury, Sulphur and Salt. Paracelsus combined these two conceptions when he wrote:

> Now, in order that these three distinct substances may be rightly understood, namely, spirit, soul, and body, it should be known that they signify nothing else than the three principles, Mercury, Sulphur, and Salt, from which all the seven metals are generated. For Mercury is the spirit, Sulphur is the soul, and Salt is the body.[20]

A modern dream expresses the same image. A man dreamed, *In order for an enterprise to reach completion three things must come together. There must be chili, a chili-parlor, and R.N. (a*

[20] Waite, A. E. transl., *The Hermetic and Alchemical Writings of Paracelsus*, reprinted by University Books, New Hyde Park, N. Y., 1967, Vol. I, p. 125.

man of initiative and effectiveness) must say the word 'chili.' "
The dream says the enterprise will be consummated only when
body, soul and spirit come together. Chili is the hot "soul stuff;"
the chili parlor is the body, the concrete context for realization; and
the uttering of the word is the spontaneous, creative act of spirit.

2. TRANSFORMATION AND DEVELOPMENT

The theme of transformation, of death and rebirth, which is a dynamic, developmental happening, is also associated with the number
three. Three days is the symbolical duration of the night sea
journey, e.g., Christ, Jonah. Christ was crucified between two
thieves. It was thus a triple crucifixion. Similarly, Mithra was commonly represented between two dadophori or torch bearers, one
with torch raised, the other with torch lowered. The theme of "the
way," in which a third middle course emerges out of the dialectic
of opposites is another expression of triadic symbolism. In this
connection, one thinks of the saying of Lao Tse, "The one engenders the two, the two engenders the three and the three engenders all things." (Tao Teh Ching, 42).

The relation between the image of "the way" and ternary symbolism is illustrated in a very interesting case study published by
Adler. After about three months of analysis, the patient had the
following dream: *I heard a voice saying very clearly: "In three days
time."* [21] Three days after this dream the patient had an intensely
moving fantasy which she described as follows:

> *I can see my own unconscious not as something alien but as some-
> thing made of the same stuff of which I am also made; so that there
> is a* ROAD, *an unbroken connection between me and all other creatures
> and it. I can feel how this goes to the root of my neurotic problem:
> I had had a direct perception of something unrelated to and im-
> possible to relate to the rest of my experience; the world therefore
> did not make sense, and it was therefore almost literally impossible to
> live. Now the world makes sense again.*[22]

Five days after this fantasy she had another visual image of

> *three intersecting circles (seen as three-dimensional) with vertical and
> horizontal poles passing through the points of intersection.*[23]

[21] Adler, G., *op. cit.*, p. 140.
[22] Ibid., p. 144.
[23] Ibid., p. 155.

These three unconscious images, all coming within a period of eight days, demonstrate a clear connection between the number three and the theme of the road or the way. As Adler observes, the phrase "In three days time" refers to the night sea journey. This was verified by subsequent developments. The vision of the three circles again emphasizes the number three. The description of the road fantasy is most interesting. Here the patient is becoming aware of a connecting link between herself, the ego, and the non-ego. (I would understand the road which brings a sense of union and reconciliation as a representation of the ego-Self axis) This discovery is reached through a three-fold process involving the three terms, ego, non-ego and the connecting link between them; hence the emphasis on the number three.

In fairy tales we find a wealth of ternary symbols. Important actions leading to transformation or achievement of the goal must often be repeated three times. In many cases the story makes it clear that action number one is based on one side of a pair of opposites, action number two is based on the other side of the pair of opposites, and action number three is a synthesis or reconciliation of the two opposites. To give a single example, in Grimm's fairy tale "The Water of Life" a princess is waiting to marry the man who will come straight down a golden pavement to her gate. Three brothers try to reach her. The first, not wanting to damage the pavement, rides to the right of it and is refused admittance. The second also not wanting to damage the pavement rides to the left of it and is denied entrance. The third, preoccupied with reaching the princess, does not even see the golden pavement and rides straight down the road. He is the one admitted and allowed to marry the princess.

These examples go to show that in a certain aspect of psychic life, totality is symbolically expressed by three and not by four. This aspect is the developmental, temporal process of realization. Although the goal is fourfold, the process of realizing it is three-fold. Thus the three and the four would represent two separate aspects of life. Four is structural wholeness, completion—something static and eternal. Three on the other hand represents the totality of the cycle of growth and dynamic change—conflict and resolution and renewed conflict again. Thus, in accordance with the trinitarian formula, the thesis three and the antithesis four must be resolved in a new synthesis.

Jung over and over again in his writings returns to the alchemical question: "Three are here but where is the fourth?" This wavering between three and four is well explained by the theory of the four functions and the striving for wholeness. However, the antagonism between the three and the four could have another meaning also. It could refer to the proper and necessary conflict in man between the completeness of the static, eternal quaternity and the dynamic change and vitality of the trinity. Quaternity and mandala symbolism including the temenos and magic circle distinctly emphasize the theme of containment. Add to this the fact that even numbers are traditionally considered feminine while odd numbers are thought of as male. This suggests that the quaternity may be predominantly an expression of the mother archetype or feminine principle with emphasis on static support and containment, whereas the trinity is a manifestation of the father archetype or masculine principle which emphasizes movement, activity, initiative. If this view is valid, we would then need another image of totality to unite the opposites three and four.

If the trinity can carry an equal but different significance to the quaternity, it should emerge in empirical psychological material with about the same frequency and emphasis as does the quaternity. And, indeed this is the case. I turned to a collection of mandalas published by Jung [24] and was surprised to find how frequently there was trinitarian imagery embedded in pictures which had been selected to demonstrate the quaternity. A mandala reproduced by Jung entitled "The Tibetan World Wheel" is interesting in this respect. It is said to represent the world. The wheel is held by the god of death Yama and is based on a trinitarian pattern. *(Picture 7)* [25] At the center are three animals, cock, snake and pig. There are six spokes on the wheel and twelve outer divisions. Jung says about this mandala: "The incomplete state of existence is, remarkably enough, expressed by a triadic system, and the complete (spiritual) state by a tetradic system. The relation between the incomplete and the complete state therefore corresponds to the proportion of 3:4." [26] I would add to this that a complete state is also static, eternal, otherwordly. It would correspond to the image of a god who does not participate in the conflict and flux of history, one who does not undergo development.

[24] Jung, C. G., *The Archetypes and the Collective Unconscious,* C.W., Vol. 9 i.

[25] Jung, C. W., 9, i, Figure 3.

[26] Ibid., par. 644.

When one begins to examine unconscious material with the trinity in mind, he discovers that ternary symbols are not uncommon. For instance, a man who had been in analysis for many years with the problem of persistent containment in the uroborus had the following dream. He dreamt that a circular object was being divided into triangular sectors much as one would cut a pie into pieces. The two geometrical forms, circle and triangle, seemed to stand out in the dream and impress themselves on the dreamer. The dream carried a sense of impact and importance. To the circle was associated Jung's conception of the mandala, wholeness, something to be desired. To the triangle the patient associated the trinitarian image of God. If we are to understand this dream at all, we must resort to some conceptual generalizations such as I am trying to present. In the dream, a circle is being dismembered into triangles following which the image of a circle is contrasted with the image of a triangle. I understand this dream as referring to the break up of an original state of uroboric wholeness, what I have called ego-Self identity, by means of a threefold dynamic process represented by the triangle. The dream contrasts the complete, circular state with the threefold triangular state. I take this to mean that an attitude emphasizing static completeness must be complemented by the trinitarian dynamic principle. The threefold temporal process breaks up the static, eternal state and subjects it to a development of events in time involving recurrent conflicts and resolutions according to the formula thesis, antithesis, synthesis.

Another patient had this dream: *She dreamt she was a student in a classroom. She feels confident about her lesson and when asked to recite the assignment begins to give the multiplication table of four: four times one, four times two, etc. The teacher interrupts saying that this is not the assignment. The assignment is to multiply three-place numbers by four. Her confidence gone, the dreamer realizes she is not yet able to multiply three-place numbers in her head and sits down in confusion.* Her association to four was the quaternity of psychic wholeness, the mandala. About three-place numbers she said that they tripled the difficulty of multiplying and also that three reminded her of the Christian trinity. This dream seems to speak directly to our subject. Simple, one-dimensional fourness is not the assignment. Rather, fourness is to be met in a threefold setting making it much more complex and difficult. Fourness, or psychic totality, must be actualized by submitting it to the threefold process of realization in time. One must submit oneself to the painful dialectic of the developmental process. The quaternity must be complemented by the trinity.

Another example is taken from Adler's case study previously mentioned. This dream occurred several years before the beginning of analysis and is considered to have initiated the individuation process. It carried a powerful impact and was recorded as follows: *I saw on an oval patch of blackness, which shaded off vaguely, a rod made of yellowish-white metal; at one end of it was a monogram of the figures 1, 2 and 4 (superimposed on one another).*[27] The dreamer's associations to the monogram of numbers were particularly significant. The rod reminded her of a key or magic wand, and she associated it with the labarum carried before Roman emperors. She was reminded especially of Constantine's dream on the eve of battle in which he saw the sign of the cross in the sky and heard a voice say: "In hoc signo vinces." Concerning this dream Adler writes:

> So far as the sequence "1, 2, 4" is concerned, it represents the development of the mandala symbol, and of psychic totality. The number 1 represents an original preconscious totality; 2 is the division of this preconscious totality into two polarities, producing two opposites . . . And the further subdivision—corresponding to the synthesis arising out of thesis and antithesis—would produce the four parts of the circle, and with its center, signifying the mandala: ⊙ ① ⊕ . The sequence of the three numbers 1, 2, 4 would thus represent the natural growth, the "formula" of the mandala.[28]

Adler then quotes Jung as saying: "This unspeakable conflict posited by duality . . . resolves itself in a fourth principle, which restores the unity of the first in its full development. The rhythm is built up in three steps, but the resultant symbol is quaternity." [29] Later, Adler confuses this interpretation by finding it necessary to account for what he calls the "striking omission of the number 3." He interprets the omission of the masculine 3 as representing a compensation for the patient's identification with the patriarchal world. In my opinion this second interpretation is dubious and, if true, would invalidate the first. The number three is already in the sequence 1, 2, 4 if it is taken as a totality since it is a threefold sequence. Considering it to be a geometric series rather than

[27] Adler, p. 26.
[28] Adler, p. 29 f.
[29] Ibid.

an arithmetic one, the three is quite properly missing. If I understand the symbolism correctly, substituting the sequence 1, 2, 3,
4 for the dream sequence 1, 2, 4 would destroy the essense of the
symbolic meaning which I understand to be the combination of
a threefold process with a fourfold goal.

Jung provides us with another example of the fusion of
quaternity and ternary images. I refer to the mandala vision published in *Psychology and Alchemy.* [30]

> The dreamer sees a vertical and a horizontal circle having a common
> center. This is the world clock. It is supported by a black bird. The
> vertical circle is a blue disc with a white border divided into thirty-
> two partitions. A pointer rotates upon it. The horizontal circle con-
> sists of four colors. On it stand four little men with pendulums and
> round it is laid a golden ring. The clock has three rhythms or pulses:
> 1) The small pulse: the vertical pointer advances by 1/32;
> 2) The middle pulse: one complete revolution of the vertical pointer.
>   At the same time the horizontal circle advances by 1/32;
> 3) The great pulse: thirty-two middle pulses are equal to one revolu-
>   tion of the golden ring.

This vision is a beautiful mandala image with marked emphasis on the quaternity, e.g., four colors, four little men. However,
it has a threefold pulse or rhythm. In *Psychology and Alchemy*
originally published in 1944, Jung emphasizes the quaternity aspect
of the image and only says about the three rhythms: "I do not
know what the three rythms allude to. But I do not doubt for a
moment that the allusion is amply justified . . . We shall hardly
be mistaken if we assume that our mandala aspires to the most
complete union of opposites that is possible, including that of the
masculine trinity and the feminine quaternity . . ." [31]

In his commentary on the same vision in *Psychology and Religion* published first in English in 1938, Jung has this to say about
the threefold rhythm:

> If we hark back to the old Pythagorean idea that the soul is a square,
> then the mandala would express the Deity through its threefold
> rhythm and the soul through its static quaternity, the circle divided
> into four colors. And thus its innermost meaning would simply be the
> union of the soul with God. [32]

And later he says:

[30] Jung, C. G., *Psychology and Alchemy,* C.W., Vol. 12, par. 307.
[31] Ibid., par. 310 f.
[32] Jung, C. G., *Psychology and Religion: West and East,* C.W., Vol. 11, par.
124.

. . . the quaternity is the *sine qua non* of divine birth and con-
sequently of the inner life of the trinity. Thus circle and quaternity
on one side and the threefold rhythm on the other interpenetrate so
that each is contained in the other.[33]

It is clear from these quotations that Jung does not consider
the quaternity a completely adequate symbol for totality. Rather a
union of the quaternity with the trinity in a more complete synthesis is required.

If, when confronted with three it is proper to ask where is
four, it is equally proper, when confronted with four, to ask where
is three. Because of preoccupation with the quaternity one may
see only the four in imagery that actually combines both four and
three. The theme of twelve, for instance, includes both three
and four as its factors. Likewise, the number seven combines
four and three by being their sum.

The trinity archetype seems to symbolize individuation as a
process, while the quaternity symbolizes its goal or completed
state. Since individuation is never truly complete, each temporary
state of completion or wholeness must be submitted once again
to the dialectic of the trinity in order for life to go on.

[33] Ibid., par. 125.

Part III

SYMBOLS OF THE GOAL

Man has a soul and . . . there is a buried treasure in the field.

C. G. JUNG *

---

* unpublished letter to Eugene Rolfe

CHAPTER EIGHT

Metaphysics and the Unconscious

. . . our labors are witnesses for the living mystery.
—C. G. JUNG [1]

1. EMPIRICAL METAPHYSICS

The process of individuation often expresses itself in symbolic images of a metaphysical nature. Such images can be a problem to the empirical psychotherapist who is reluctant to give credence to grandiose, unprovable ideas about life, especially since such ideas are often associated with obvious inflation, e.g., in psychosis. Also, the common collective misuse of metaphysical images is a cause for caution. For the psychologist, the word metaphysics tends to connote arbitrary assertions on faith about the nature of ultimate reality. It calls to mind dogmatic attitudes which are repugnant to the empirical temperament. To the scientist, metaphysical dogmatism is a demonstration of the fact that one is "most ignorant of what he's most assured." Jung also avoided the term. For instance he wrote:

> I approach psychological matters from a scientific and not from a philosophical standpoint . . . I restrict myself to the observation of phenomena and I eschew any metaphysical or philosophical considerations.[2]

In another place he says:

[1] Jung C. G. Letter to John Trinick, October 15, 1957, published in John Trinick, *The Fire-Tried Stone*, London: Stuart and Watkins, 1967, p. 11.
[2] Jung, C. G., *Psychology and Religion: West and East*, C.W., 11, par. 2.

Psychology as the science of the soul has to confine itself to its subject and guard against overstepping its proper boundaries by metaphysical assertions or other professions of faith . . . The religious-minded man is free to accept whatever metaphysical explanations he pleases about the origin of these images (the archetypes) . . . The scientist is a scrupulous worker; he cannot take heaven by storm. Should he allow himself to be reduced into such an extravagance he would be sawing off the branch on which he sits.[3]

These caveats are certainly in order; however, metaphysics as a subject can be separated from the personal attitude which individuals may take about it. One may take a dogmatic, unempirical attitude toward physics as well as toward metaphysics. Witness, for instance, the refusal to look into Galileo's telescope because it was "known" that Jupiter could not have moons. Metaphysics has been an honored subject of human concern since the beginning of recorded history. Just as man's efforts to adapt to other aspects of reality began with naïve, arbitrary, and concretely mythological viewpoints, so it has been in his relation to metaphysical reality. But this need not discredit the subject itself.

Paul Tillich has made an astute observation concerning the relation between Jung's discoveries and metaphysics. He speaks of "Jung's anxiety about what he calls metaphysics," and continues:

This, it seems to me, does not agree with his actual discoveries, which on many points reach deeply into the dimension of a doctrine of being, that is, an ontology. This fear of metaphysics, which he shares with Freud and other nineteenth-century conquerors of the spirit, is a heritage of this century . . . In taking the biological and, by necessary implication, the physical realm into the genesis of archetypes, he has actually reached the ontological dimension "imprinted upon the biological continuum." And this was unavoidable, given the revelatory power he attributes to the symbols in which the archetypes express themselves. For to be revelatory one must express what needs revelation, namely, the mystery of being.[4]

Of course, Jung was not afraid of metaphysics. He explored that realm with great courage. He was not afraid of metaphysics but of metaphysicians. Although figures don't lie, liars can figure. Likewise, although metaphysical reality can be demonstrated to some extent by the methods of psychological empiricism, those with no

[3] Jung, C. G., *Psychology and Alchemy*, C.W., 12, par. 6.
[4] *Carl Gustav Jung, A Memorial Meeting*, The Analytical Psychology Club of New York, 1962, p. 31.

understanding of these methods can misuse the findings which are reported. Although Tillich is wrong about the nature of Jung's anxiety, he does make an important point, i.e., that the symbolic images of the unconscious, if they are to be revelatory, "must express what needs revelation, namely, the mystery of being." In *Aion*, Jung says something similar. He writes:

> It is possible . . . to relate so-called *metaphysical* concepts, which have lost their root connection with natural experience, to living, universal psychic processes, so that they can recover their true and original meaning. In this way the connection is re-established between the ego and projected contents now formulated as "metaphysical" ideas.[5]

This is a carefully worded psychological statement. It might be added that a projected metaphysical content, when withdrawn from projection, may still retain its metaphysical quality.

We know that occasionally dreams do reveal, to some extent, the "mystery of being." Hence these messages can properly be called metaphysical, i.e., beyond the physical or ordinary conceptions of life. Furthermore, these dreams of individuals, although they use unique imagery and convey an individual revelation to the dreamer, tend also to express a general or common viewpoint, a kind of perennial philosophy of the unconscious which seems to have a more or less universal validity. This general validity can best be understood as being based on the universality of the urge to individuation.

2. A SERIES OF "METAPHYSICAL" DREAMS

Some years ago I had the opportunity to observe a remarkable series of dreams containing many metaphysical images. The dreamer was a man who was standing close to death. He had death on both sides of him, so to speak. Just before the dream series began he had made a sudden, impulsive, unpremeditated suicide attempt by swallowing a bottleful of sleeping pills. He was comatose for thirty-six hours and on the verge of death. Two and a half years later he did die, in his late fifties, of a cerebral vascular accident.

Over a period of about two years, intermittently, this man came to see me once a week and discussed his dreams. Our sessions could hardly be called analysis. The patient lacked the objective

[5] Jung, C. G., *Aion*, C.W., 9 ii, par. 65.

and self-critical capacity to assimilate any interpretation that would lead to an awareness of the shadow. What did happen was that we observed the dreams together and tried to discover the ideas they were trying to express. Repeatedly I had the impression that the unconscious was trying to give the patient lessons in metaphysics—either to help him assimilate the meaning of his very close brush with death or to prepare him to meet death in the near future. I must emphasize that this man had in no way gone through an individuation process as we use the term. Nevertheless many of the images associated with the goal of that process were presented to him in the final dreams of his life.

Over a two year period the patient recorded approximately 180 dreams of which about one third had definite metaphysical or transcendental allusions. Some of the dreams seemed to be presented from the standpoint of the ego, in which case there was an atmosphere of doom and tragedy. On awakening from these dreams the dreamer was left in a mood of profound depression. Other dreams seemed to be an expression of a transpersonal standpoint and these brought with them a sense of peace, joy and security. As a single example of the first category I shall quote the following dream which he had six months before his death: *I am at home but it's nowhere I've been before. I go into the pantry to get some food. The shelves are stacked with seasonings and spices, all the same brand, but there is nothing to eat. I feel I am not alone in the house. It is just turning dawn or is it the brilliant moonlight? I turn on the light but it comes from another room. Something creaks. I am not alone. I wonder where my dog is. I need more light. I need more light and more courage. I am afraid.*

This dream probably expresses the fear of the ego in anticipation of meeting the intruder, death. Light is no longer with the ego but in the other room. We are reminded of Goethe's last words, "more light."

There are only a few of this type of dream. Much more frequent are those in the second category, which contained definite transpersonal imagery and which, I felt, attempted to give him lessons in metaphysics. From this group I have selected thirteen dreams to present and discuss. I give them in chronological order.

Dream 1:
I am to learn how to do the exercises of a Japanese Nō play. It was my intention that at the end of the exercises my body would

arrive at a physical position which would be the equivalent of a Zen Koan.

The Nō drama of Japan is a classical, highly formalized art form. The actors wear masks and in other respects too there are similarities to ancient Greek drama. The Nō play expresses universal or archetypal realities; all emphasis is on the transpersonal. Nancy Wilson Ross describes it as follows:

Anyone lending himself to the timeless experience of the Nō never forgets it, though he may be quite incapable of conveying to others an exact sense of its peculiar enchantment. The Nō explores time and space in ways unfamiliar to our Western aesthetic . . . The eerie use of the human voice, in which normal breathing has been artfully suppressed; the occasional long-drawn, sad and solitary notes of a flute; the periodic sharp cues and catlike yowls from the chorus; the abrupt clack of sticks and the varied tonality of three kinds of drum; the gliding ghostly dancers; . . . the sudden summoning stamp on the bare resonant stage where every "property" has been abstracted to a mere symbol; the extravagant and lavish costumes; the unreal reality of the wooden masks worn by the participants; above all, the artful use of emptiness and silence . . .—these are a few of the traditional elements that help to create the special magic of Nō.[6]

The dream says therefore that the patient must practice relating to archetypal realities. He must put aside personal considerations and begin to live "under the aspect of eternity." The consequence of these exercises will be that his body becomes a Zen Koan. A koan is a paradoxical anecdote or statement used by the Zen master in the hope that it will help the pupil break through to a new level of consciousness (illumination, satori). Suzuki gives the following example. A pupil asks the master, what is Zen. He replies, "When your mind is not dwelling in the dualism of good and evil, what is your original face before you were born?" [7]

Such questions are meant to break through the ego-bound state and give one a glimpse of transpersonal reality, in Jungian terms, the Self. One Buddhist scholar after experiencing Satori, burned his previously treasured commentaries on the *Diamond Sutra* and exclaimed: "However deep one's knowledge of abstruse philosophy, it is like a piece of hair flying in the vastness of space; however

[6] Ross, Nancy Wilson, *The World of Zen.* New York, Random House, 1960. pp. 167 f.
[7] Suzuki, D. T., *An Introduction to Zen Buddhism,* New York, Philosophical Library, 1949, p. 104.

important one's experience in things wordly, it is like a drop of water thrown into an unfathomable abyss." [8]

I think we can assume that the dream is trying to convey some such attitude as this—urging the dreamer to relinquish his personal and ego-centered attitude in preparation for quitting this world.

Dream 2:

I was with several companions in a Dali-esque landscape where things seemed either imprisoned or out of control. There were fires all about, coming out of the ground and about to engulf the place. By a group effort we managed to control the fires and restrict them to their proper place. In the same landscape we found a woman lying on her back on a rock. The front side of her body was flesh but the back of her head and body was part of the living rock on which she lay. She had a dazzling smile, almost beatific, that seemed to accept her terrible plight. The controlling of the fires seemed to have caused a metamorphosis of some kind. There began a loosening of the rock at her back so that we were finally able to lift her off of it. Although she was still partly stone she did not seem too heavy and the change was continuing. We knew she would be whole again."

The patient had a specific association to this dream. The fires reminded him of the fire that was said to accompany Hades when he broke out of the earth to capture Persephone. The dreamer had once visited Eleusis and was shown the spot where Hades was supposed to have emerged. He was also reminded of an un-finished statue of Michelangelo's. (*Picture 40*).

A figure coming out of the rock reminds us of the birth of Mithra from the *petra genetrix*. The dream also has another analogy with the Mithra myth. One of Mithra's first tasks was to tame the wild bull. Similarly in the dream, controlling the fires was somehow con-nected with the emergence of the woman from the rock. By limiting the fires, a living woman is being extracted from stone.[9] This cor-

[8] Ibid., p. 94.

[9] The same combination of ideas—self-discipline and emerging life is found in an apocryphal story of Paul. He is said to have spoken "the word of God concerning self-control and the resurrection." (See Acts of Paul II, 1, 5, in James, M. R., *The Apocryphal New Testament*, Oxford, p. 273). Harnack com-ments on this passage. He says that self-control and the resurrection as a "pair of ideas are to be taken as mutually supplementary; the resurrection or eternal life is certain, but it is conditioned by *egkrateia* (self-control), which is therefore put first. Cf., for example, *Vita Polycarpi*, 14 . . . 'he said that purity was the precursor of the incorruptible kingdom to come.'" (Harnack, Adolph, *The Mission and Expansion of Christianity*, New York, Harper Torch-books, Harper & Brothers, 1962, p. 92 n).

Picture 40. THE AWAKENING GIANT by Michelangelo.

responds to the disengagement of Sophia from the embrace of *Physis*, which is accomplished by the quenching of the fires of desirousness. In a later dream the feminine personification of Wisdom or Logos is again encountered. The image also suggests the separation of the soul from matter or the body which is associated with death.

There is a similar image in the ancient Greek alchemical text of Zosimos: "Go to the waters of the Nile and there you will find a stone that has a spirit (*pneuma*). Take this, divide it, thrust in your hand and draw out its heart: for its soul (*psyche*) is in its heart." [10] An added note in the text states that this refers to the expulsion of the quicksilver. It is the alchemical idea of extracting the soul or spirit which is imprisoned in matter and would correspond to the psychological process of extracting the meaning from a concrete experience (a stumbling stone, I Peter 2:9). In the context of the dreamer's situation perhaps what was being extracted was the meaning of his earthly life.

We must also consider the dreamer's association to Hades, Persephone and the presumed site of the latter's abduction at Eleusis. This association allows us to consider the dream as a modern individual version of the Eleusian mysteries. In ancient Greece, initiation into the mysteries was considered most important in determining one's fate in the afterlife. In the Homeric Hymn to Demeter we read:

> Happy is he among men upon earth who has seen these mysteries; but he who is uninitiate and who has no part in them, never has lot of like good things once he is dead, down in the darkness and gloom.[11]

Plato makes the same point:

> . . . those men who established the mysteries were not unenlightened, but in reality had a hidden meaning when they said long ago that whoever goes uninitiated and unsanctified to the other world will lie in the mire, but he who arrives there initiated and purified will dwell with the gods.[12]

[10] Berthelot, M. P. E., *Collection des anciens alchimistes grecs*, Paris, 1887–88, 3 vols., reprinted by Holland Press, London, 1963, III, vi. 5. Quoted by Jung, *Psychology and Alchemy*, C.W., 12, par. 405.
[11] Hesiod, *The Homeric Hymns and Homerica* (Loeb Classical Library), Cambridge, Harvard University Press, 1914, p. 323, lines 480 ff.
[12] Plato, *Phaedo* 69c.

Although little is known about the content of the Eleusinian Mysteries they must have included a death and resurrection ritual since the Demeter-Kore myth is concerned with this theme. The descent of Persephone to the underworld and the subsequent arrangement whereby she spends part of the year above ground and part of the year in the underworld is a definite reference to the green vegetation spirit which dies and is reborn each year. Thus the dream alludes to resurrection. The woman becoming disengaged from the rock will correspond to Persephone returning from the underworld. This line of interpretation is verified by a later dream in the series in which the green vegetation numen symbolizing resurrection is specifically portrayed.

3. RETURN TO THE BEGINNING

Dream 3:

It was a strange scene. I seemed to be in Africa standing at the edge of an endless veldt, stretching as far as I could see. The heads of animals were emerging from the ground, or had emerged. It was very dusty. As I watched some of the animals emerged completely. Some were quite tame, others quite wild. A rhinoceros and a zebra charged around kicking up a lot of dust. I wondered if this was the Garden of Eden.

This dream has some similarity to the preceding one. Again, living creatures are coming out of solid earth. The dreamer commented that he felt he was being permitted to look in on the original creation. It is reminiscent of the remark of an alchemist:

> Neither be anxious to ask whether I actually possess this precious treasure (the philosopher's stone). Ask rather whether I have seen how the world was created; whether I am acquainted with the nature of the Egyptian darkness; . . . what will be the appearance of the glorified bodies at the general resurrection.[13]

This author is demonstrating that he knew that the alchemical secret was not a substance but a state of consciousness, a perception of the archetypal level of reality.

At the end of his personal life the dreamer is being shown the universal beginning of life. Living forms are emerging from the amorphous, inorganic earth. The emphasis on dust reminds us

[13] Waite, A. E., translator, *The Hermetic Museum*, London, John M. Watkins, 1953, Vol. I. p. 8.

of the use of this image in Genesis. "The Lord God formed man of dust from the ground." (Gen. 2:7 RSV). "You are dust and to dust you shall return." (Gen. 3:19 RSV). Dust is powdery, pulverized dried-out earth. It is similar to ashes and the Hebrew word "aphar" here translated as dust also means ashes. Ashes are the result of the alchemical *calcinatio* which was alluded to in the fire of the second dream. But according to the third dream, out of the dusty ashes of burnt out life, new life emerges.

Shortly later there was another veldt dream:

Dream 4:
Again the landscape of the veldt. Several acres of empty ground. Scattered about were loaves of bread of various shapes. They looked sedate and permanent like stones.

We have again the symbol of the stone that came up first in Dream 2. There it was a stone that was not a stone but a woman. In the present dream it is a stone that is not a stone but a loaf of bread. This motif of the stone that is not a stone is well-known in alchemy (*lithos ou lithos*).[14] It is a reference to the Philosopher's Stone which according to Ruland "is a substance which is petrine as regards its efficacy and virtue but not as regards its substance." [15] This statement would be an allusion to the reality of the psyche.

In the fourth chapter of Matthew, the images of bread and stone are connected. During Jesus' temptation in the wilderness the devil said to him, " 'If you are the Son of God, command these stones to become loaves of bread.' But he answered, 'It is written, "Man shall not live by bread alone, but by every word that proceeds from the mouth of God." ' " (Matt. 4:3, 4 RSV). Again in Matthew 7:9 stone and bread are linked: "or what man of you, if his son asks him for a loaf, will give him a stone?" These passages establish that bread is a human requirement, that stone does not satisfy human needs, and that willingness to turn stone to bread (i.e. to unite these opposites) is a prerogative of deity. Thus this dream is providing a glimpse behind the metaphysical barrier or, as Jung calls it, the epistemological curtain, the figures behind which are "impossible unions of opposites, transcendental beings which can only be apperceived by contrasts." [16]

[14] Berthelot, *op. cit.*, I, iii. 1.
[15] Ruland, Martin, *A Lexicon of Alchemy*, translated by Waite, A. E., London, John M. Watkins, 1964, p. 189.
[16] Jung, C. G., Letter to John Trinick, *op. cit.*, p. 10.

Dream 5:
I was invited to a party for Adam and Eve. They had never died. They were the beginning and the end. I realized this and accepted their permanent existence. Both of them were enormous, overscale, like Maillol's sculptures. They had a sculptural and not a human look. Adam's face was veiled or covered and I longed to know what he looked like. I dared to try to uncover his face and I did. The covering was a very heavy layer of peat-mosses, or some sort of vegetable growth. I pulled it away just a little and peeped behind. His face was kind but frightening—it was like a gorilla or giant ape of some sort.

The location of this party is obviously the eternal, archetypal realm. The figures never die, but live in an eternal present. The "kingdom of heaven" is the place where one meets the ancient worthies. Matthew 8:11 says, "I tell you many will come from east and west and sit at table with Abraham, Isaac, and Jacob in the Kingdom of heaven."

The dream figures were said to be both beginning and end. Traditionally, the characteristic of being both beginning and end has never been applied to Adam. However it is applied to Christ who was called the second Adam. As the Logos He existed from the beginning and was the agent of creation. (John 1:1-3). The apostle Paul's whole passage on the resurrection which mentions the second Adam (*deuteros Anthropos*) is relevant to this dream:

> The first man Adam became a living being; the last Adam became a life-giving spirit . . . The first man was from the earth, a man of dust, the second man is from heaven . . . Just as we have borne the image of the man of dust, we shall also bear the image of the man of heaven . . . Lo! I tell you a mystery. We shall not all sleep, but we shall all be changed, in a moment, in the twinkling of an eye, at the last trumpet. For the trumpet will sound, and the dead will be raised imperishable, and we shall be changed. For this perishable nature must put on the imperishable, and this mortal nature must put on immortality." [17]

Adam, as the first man, is an image of the *Anthropos*, the Primal Man of Gnostic speculation. According to the Gnostic Hermetic treatise, *Poimandres,* the eternal Mind gave birth to the *Anthropos* which then fell into the world of spatio-temporal existence because "Nature" loved him:

[17] I Corinthians 15:45-53 RSV.

And Nature took the object of her love and wound herself completely around him, and they were intermingled, for they were lovers. And this is why beyond all creatures on the earth man is two-fold; mortal because of body, but because of the essential Man immortal.[18]

The Anthropos is the pre-existent form of man, the eternal Platonic idea, the divine thought which became incarnated by the embrace of *Physis*. Thus, for the dreamer to be introduced to Adam suggests that he is being shown his "original face" prior to the birth of the ego and implies that a process of disincarnation is coming.

Dream 6:

I am in a garden, a handsome sunken terrace. The place is called "The Thoughts of God." Here it is believed that the twelve Words of God are to conquer the world. Its walls are lined like a nest with ivy and something as soft as down or fur. I, together with others, am walking inside the enclosure. The force of the words come with the force of an explosion or earthquake that knocks us to the ground. The cushioned walls prevent one from being hurt. It is the custom in this enclosure to walk next to the walls around the walk. The point is to complete the circle either clockwise or anti-clockwise. As we walk the area grows smaller and more intimate, more padded and more like a nest. The walking itself seems to have something to do with the process of learning.

This dream further elaborates themes to which previous dreams have alluded. Again the dreamer is taken to the pre-existent beginning, the source of the Logos. I know of no reference to the twelve words of God; however, in the Kabbalah, the divine name is sometimes said to consist of twelve letters.[19] More commonly it is thought of as having four letters, the Tetragrammaton Yod, He, Vau, He. According to Mathers, the tetragrammaton "is capable of twelve transpositions, which all convey the meaning of 'to be;' it is the only word that will bear so many transpositions without its meaning being altered. They are called 'the twelve banners of the mighty name;' and are said by some to rule the twelve signs of the Zodiac." [20]

---

[18] Mead, G. R. S., editor, *Thrice-Greatest Hermes*, London, John M. Watkins, 1964, Vol. II, pp. 6 f.

[19] Waite, A. E. *The Holy Kabbalah*, reprinted by University Books, New Hyde Park, New York, p. 617.

[20] Mathers, S. L. MacGregor, translator, *The Kabbalah Unveiled*, London, Routledge and Kegan Paul, 1962, pp. 30 f.

The dream makes it clear that the garden of the thoughts of God is a circle with twelve words emanating from it. It would thus be analogous to the signs of the Zodiac which are a twelve-fold differentiation of the circle of the year. Other parallels would be the twelve sons of Jacob and the twelve disciples of Christ. The pantheons of many peoples were made up of twelve gods. According to Herodotus, the Egyptians were the first to name the twelve gods.[21]

An unusual feature is that the twelve words of God are said to *conquer* the world. The typical function of the Logos is to create the world, not conquer it. Perhaps this is an allusion to the fact that shortly the conscious ego (world ego) is to be extinguished in death. The same idea is implied by the fact that the circular nest grows smaller as it is circumambulated, becoming more and more of a padded womb. The nest symbol emphasizes the maternal, protective, containing aspect of returning to the metaphysical source, and would surely be reassuring to the ego anxious about death. The nest where eggs are laid and hatched also has rebirth implications. For instance, we are told that in Egypt the New Year's festival was called the "day of the child in the nest." [22]

The nest was lined with ivy. According to Frazer, ivy was sacred to both Attis and Osiris. The priests of Attis were tattoed with a pattern of ivy leaves. Because it is evergreen and non-deciduous Frazer suggests that it may have represented "the seal of a diviner life, of something exempt from the sad vicissitudes of the seasons, constant and eternal as the sky . . ." [23] The evergreen ivy is even more explicitly connected with Osiris as the immortal vegetation spirit. This image is given fuller expression in Dream 9.

4. THE TRANSCENDENT DIMENSION

Dream 7:
Two prize-fighters are involved in a ritual fight. Their fight is beautiful. They are not so much antagonists in the dream as they are collaborators, working out an elaborate, planned design. They are

[21] Herodotus, *Histories*, II, 4.
[22] Erman, Adolf, *The Religion of the Egyptians*, quoted by Neumann, E., *The Great Mother*, Princeton University Press, 1955, p. 243.
[23] Frazer, James G., "Adonis, Attis, Osiris," Part IV of *The Golden Bough*, reprinted by University Books, New Hyde Park, New York, 1961, Vol. I, pp. 277 f.

calm, unruffled and concentrated. At the end of each round they retire to a dressing room. In the dressing room they apply "makeup." I watch one of them dip his finger in some blood and smear it on the face of his opponent and himself. They return to the ring and resume their fast, furious but highly controlled performance.

This dream gives one the eerie feeling that it is a glimpse of how human life appears from beyond the veil of Maya. The strife between the opposites is reconciled by being seen as part of a larger design. There is a fight but no one gets hurt, it is only a beautiful dramatic spectacle. There is blood but it is only "make-up," belonging to the world of appearance and illusion. The lesson of the dream seems to be very similar to that given by Krishna to Arjuna in *The Bhagavadgita*, where also there is the image of the fight, the war which Arjuna is reluctant to engage in:

> O mighty among men, he is fit to attain immortality who is serene and not afflicted by these sensations, but is the same in pleasure and pain. There is no existence for the unreal and the real can never be non-existent. The Seers of Truth know the nature and final ends of both. Know that to be indestructible by which all this is pervaded. No one is ever able to destroy that Immutable. These bodies are perishable; but the dwellers in these bodies are eternal, indestructible and impenetrable. Therefore fight, O descendent of Bharata! He who considers this (Self) as a slayer or he who thinks that this (Self) is slain, neither of these knows the Truth. For It does not slay, nor is It slain. This (Self) is never born, nor does It die, nor after once having been, does It go into non-being. This (Self) is unborn, eternal, changeless, ancient.[24]

Dream 8:
There are three squares, heating units made of metal coil or neon tubing. They represent my sexual problems. Now they have been disconnected and are being cleaned. There is a new world concept of God, a widening of awareness of the vastness of the universe. Against the background of eternity a thing as temporal as a sexual problem is inconsequential. The washing is in a sense a ritual washing, a cleansing of the three squares to let them fall into their natural place in the vast overall.

In the dream, my mind played with the visual image of the three squares. It was only natural to draw a circle first inside each, then outside each.

[24] *Bhagavad Gita*, II, 15-20, translated by Swami Paramandenda, *The Wisdom of China and India*, The Modern Library, New York, Random House, 1942, p. 62.

In the dream the reference to the eternal, divine realm as contrasted with the temporal, personal realm is made explicit. The three squares apparently represent the dreamer's personal, particularized existence in space and time. They are associated with sexuality, the source of heat or energy. The fact that there are *three* squares brings up the symbolic meaning of the triad which is discussed in Chapter 7. Threeness refers to dynamic existence in historical reality. It expresses the painful dialectic of the developmental process which proceeds according to the Hegelian formula of thesis, antithesis, synthesis.

The square, on the other hand, is a four-fold image which expresses totality with emphasis on the static, structural, containing aspects. In Eastern symbolism the square represents the earth in contrast to heaven. According to an ancient idea the human soul is a square.[25] The circle in contrast is a common symbol for God and eternity. Thus when the dreamer draws a circle within the square and another one surrounding the square, he is combining the individual and personal with the eternal and transpersonal. The dream expresses the same idea in its statement that the squares "fall into their natural place in the vast over all."

The image of a square containing a circle and surrounded by a circle has parallels in alchemy. If we move from within outward, the inner circle would correspond to the *prima materia,* the original boundless chaos. The square would represent the separation of the *prima materia* into the four elements, that is, the discrimination that the conscious ego brings out of the original undifferentiated whole. However, as Jung states, the square is an imperfect form because, "In the square the elements are still separate and hostile to one another." [26] Thus they need to be reunited in a higher unity, the quintessence which would correspond to the outer circle surrounding the square. According to the dream this reunification of the square is a process of finding its "natural place in the vast over all."

The psychological condition of the first circle, prior to emergence of squareness is beautifully described by Black Elk, a Sioux holy man. He is deploring the fact that Indians now live in square houses. He says:

[25] Jung, C. G., *Psychology and Religion: West and East,* C.W., 11, par. 124.
[26] Jung, C. G., *The Practice of Psychotherapy,* C.W., 16, par. 402.

. . . we made these little grey houses of logs that you see, and they
are square. It is a bad way to live, for there can be no power in a
square.

"You have noticed that everything an Indian does is in a circle,
and that is because the Power of the World always works in circles,
and everything tries to be round. In the old days when we were a
strong and happy people, all our power came to us from the sacred
hoop of the nation, and so long as the hoop was unbroken, the people
flourished. The flowering tree was the living center of the hoop, and
the circle of the four quarters nourished it. The east gave peace and
light, the south gave warmth, the west gave rain, and the north with
its cold and mighty wind gave strength and endurance. This knowledge came to us from the outer world with our religion. Everything
the Power of the World does is done in a circle. The sky is round,
and I have heard that the earth is round like a ball, and so are all
the stars. The wind, in its greatest power, whirls. Birds make their
nests in circles, for theirs is the same religion as ours. The sun comes
forth and goes down in a circle. The moon does the same, and both
are round. Even the seasons form a great circle in their changing, and
always come back again to where they were. The life of a man is a
circle from childhood to childhood, and so it is in everything where
power moves. Our tepees were round like the nests of birds, and these
were always set in a circle, the nation's hoop, a nest of many nests,
where the Great Spirit meant for us to hatch our children. But the
Wasichus (white men) have put us in these square boxes. Our power
is gone and we are dying, for the power is not in us any more.[27]

Dream 9:
*I am alone in a great formal garden such as one finds in Europe.
The grass is an unusual kind of turf, centuries old. There are great
hedges of boxwood and everything is completely ordered. At the
end of the garden I see a movement. At first it seems to be an
enormous frog made of grass. As I get closer I see it is actually
a green man, herbal, made of grass. He is doing a dance. It is
very beautiful and I think of Hudson's novel,* Green Mansions. *It
gave me a sense of peace, although I could not really understand
what I was beholding.*

In this dream we have a remarkably explicit representation of
the vegetation spirit which played such an important part in ancient
mythology and which has received a comprehensive discussion in
Fraser's *Golden Bough*. The most fully developed image in this
category, is Osiris as corn-spirit, tree spirit, and God of fertility.

[27] Neihardt, John G., *Black Elk Speaks*, Lincoln, University of Nebraska
Press, 1961, pp. 198 ff.

The death and rebirth of vegetation were episodes in *his* drama: "The ivy was sacred to him, and was called his plant because it was always green." [28]

On the symbolism of greenness, Jung says: "In the sphere of Christian psychology, green has a spermatic, procreative quality, and for this reason it is the color attributed to the Holy Ghost as the creative principle." [29] And again, "Green is the color of the Holy Ghost, of life, procreation and resurrection." [30] An example of the greenness of the Holy Ghost is found in Hildegard of Bingen's "Hymn to the Holy Ghost": "From you the clouds rain down, the heavens move, the stones have their moisture, the waters give forth streams, and the earth sweats out greenness." [31] This passage has a close parallel in an ancient Egyptian hymn to Osiris which says, "the world waxes green through him." [32] Another connection between greenness and resurgent life is found in an Egyptian Pyramid text. This passage evokes *Kheprer* (Khoprer, Khopri, "the becoming one")[33] the scarab god who is the rising sun: "Hail thou god . . . who revolvest, Kheprer . . . Hail, Green one. . . ." [34]

Greenness is an important image in alchemy. Some texts refer to it as the *benedicta viriditas*, blessed greenness. According to Mylius, the Soul of the World, or *Anima Mundi*, is green:

> God breathed into created things . . . a certain germination or greenness, by which all things should multiply . . . they called all things green, for to be green means to grow . . . therefore this virtue of generation and the preservation of things might be called the Soul of the world.[35]

In another alchemical text, the feminine personification of the black and rejected *prima materia* says: I am alone among the hidden; nevertheless I rejoice in my heart, because I can live privily, and refresh myself in myself . . . under my blackness I

[28] Frazer, *op. cit.*, Vol. II, p. 112.

[29] Jung, C. G., *Mysterium Coniunctionis*, C.W., 14, par. 137.

[30] Ibid., par. 395.

[31] Jung, C. G., *Psychology and Religion: East and West*, C.W., 11, par. 151.

[32] Frazer, *op. cit.*, Vol. II, p. 113.

[33] Clark, R. T. Rundle, *Myth and Symbol in Ancient Egypt*, New York, Grove Press, 1960, p. 40.

[34] Budge, E. A. Wallis. *Osiris the Egyptian Religion of Resurrection*, reprinted by University Books, New Hyde Park, New York, 1961. Vol. II. p. 355.

[35] Jung, C. G., *Mysterium Coniunctionis*, C.W., 14, par. 623.

have hidden the fairest green." Jung interprets this passage as follows:

> The state of imperfect transformation, merely hoped for and waited for, does not seem to be one of torment only, but of positive, if hidden happiness. It is the state of someone who, in his wanderings among the images of his psychic transformation, comes upon a secret happiness which reconciles him to his apparent loneliness. In communing with himself he finds not deadly boredom and melancholy but an inner partner; more than that, a relationship that seems like the happiness of a secret love, or like a hidden springtime, when the green seed sprouts from the barren earth, holding out the promise of future harvests. It is the alchemical *benedicta viriditas*, the blessed greenness, signifying on the one hand the "leprosy of the meals" (verdigris), but on the other the secret immanence of the divine spirit of life in all things.[36]

What Jung refers to as the secret happiness accompanying the discovery of the green one would correspond, perhaps, to the sense of peace which the dreamer describes. For this man who is shortly to die, the unconscious is presenting a vivid and beautiful image of the eternal nature of life, whose particular manifestations are continually passing away, but which is being continually re-born in new forms. The dream expresses the same idea as the words of Paul in his resurrection passage, "Death is swallowed up in victory. O death where is thy sting? O grave where is thy victory?" (I Corinthians 15:54-55AV).

5. COMPLETION OF THE OPUS

Dream 10:
As in Ginsberg's Legends of the Jews, where God was in personal communication with various individuals, He seemed to have assigned me a test, distasteful in every way, for which I was in no way fitted, technically or emotionally. First I was to search for and find a man who was expecting me, and together we were to follow exactly the instructions. The end result was to become an abstract symbol beyond our comprehension, with religious, or sacred, or tabu connotations. The task involved removing the man's hands at the wrists, trimming them and uniting them to make a hexagonal shape. Two rectangles, one from each hand were to be removed, leaving windows of a sort. The rectangles themselves were also

[36] Ibid., par. 623.

symbols of great value. The results were to be mummified, dried-up, and black. All of it took a long time, was extremely delicate and difficult. He bore it stoically as it was his destiny as well as mine, and the end result, we believed, was what was demanded. When we looked at the symbol that had resulted from our labors, it had an impenetrable aura of mystery about it. We were both exhausted by the ordeal.

The dreamer had browsed in Ginsberg's *Legends of the Jews* at the house of a friend, but had done no extensive reading in this book. Also, his knowledge of the Old Testament was minimal. The dream is reminiscent of tasks imposed on individuals by Yahweh, e.g., Jonah, Hosea, etc. If one's life is governed by the sense of a divine task, this means psychologically that the ego is subordinated to the Self and has been freed of ego-centered pre-occupations. Something of this idea is indicated by the nature of the task imposed in the dream. A man's hands are to be amputated. This rather grisly primitive image expresses a psychological process. The same image occurs in alchemy as the lion with his paws cut off,[37] (*Picture 41*) and in more extreme form as the dismembered man in the *Splendor Solis* treatise (*Picture 42*).[38] The hands

Picture 41.
LION WITH HIS
PAWS CUT OFF,
Alchemical Drawing.

[37] Jung, C. G., *Psychology and Alchemy*, C.W., 12, Fig. 4.
[38] Trismosin, Solomon, *Splendor Solis*, reprinted by Kegan Paul, Trench, Trubner and Company, London, Plate X.

are the agency of the conscious will. Hence to have them cut off would correspond to the experience of the impotence of the ego. In Jung's words, "the experience of the Self is always a defeat for the ego." [39]

The next step in the dream task is to unite the amputated hands into a hexagon. Here we have a reference to the union of the opposites, right and left, conscious and unconscious, good and evil. The product of the union is a six-fold figure. A well-known six-fold symbol which also is made of the union of two similar but contrasting elements is the so-called Solomon's Seal. ✡
It consists of two triangles, one pointing upward and one downward. For the alchemists it represented the union of fire ($\triangle$) and water ($\triangledown$). For others it has signified the interpenetration of the trinity of spirit (upward-pointing) with the chthonic trinity of matter (downward-pointing) and hence symbolized the process of interrelation between the two. The number six is associated with the completion or fulfillment of a creative task. In Genesis the world was created in six days with the final act, the creation of Adam, on the sixth day. Jesus was crucified on the sixth day of the week. According to Joannes Lyndus, quoted by Jung,

> The number 6 is most skilled in begetting, for it is even and uneven, partaking both of the active nature on account of the uneven, and of the hylical nature on account of the even, for which reason the ancients also named it marriage and harmony . . . And they say also that it is both male and female . . . And another says that the number six is soul-producing because it multiplies itself into the world-sphere, and because in it the opposites are mingled.[40]

Summing up the meaning of these amplifications, the dream seems to say that a task must be performed whereby the powers of the individual ego, for both good and evil, are separated or extracted from their union with that ego and reunited in an abstract or suprapersonal image. When the two rectangular windows are added a rather eerie effect is created

 reminding one of a primitive mask. The net result is a geometrical image which I would venture to suggest is a symbolic representation of the face of God.

[39] Jung, C. G., *Mysterium Coniunctionis*, C.W., 14, par. 778.
[40] Jung, C. G., *The Practice of Psychotherapy*, C.W., 16, par. 451, n. 6.

Picture 42. THE DISMEMBERED MAN, Alchemical Drawing.

Dream 11:
There is a darkness, but with a luminosity in it, not describable. A darkness somehow glowing. Standing in it is a beautiful golden woman, with an almost Mona Lisa face. Now I realize that the glow is emanating from a necklace she is wearing. It is of great delicacy: small cabochons of turquoise, each circled in reddish gold. It has a great meaning for me, as if there were a message in the complete image if only I could break through its elusiveness.

The dreamer, who was quite uninformed about philosophy and religion, did not know the opening passage in the Gospel of John concerning the Logos. It is certainly relevant to the dream.

In the begining was the Word and the Word was with God, and the Word was God. He was in the beginning with God; all things were made through him, and without him was not anything made that was made. In him was life, and the life was the light of men. The light shines in the darkness, and the darkness has not overcome it. John 1:1-5.

John's Logos doctrine applied to Christ the Logos theory of
Hellenistic philosophy. Christ became the creative Word or
Thought of God who had been with Him from the beginning. In
Gnostic circles the Logos was equated with Sophia, the feminine
personification of Wisdom. The same image had already appeared
in the Hebrew wisdom literature. For instance she is mentioned
in this prayer to God: "With you is Wisdom, she who knows your
works, she who was present when you made the world; she under-
stands what is pleasing in your eyes and what agrees with your
commandments." (Wisdom 9:9 Jerusalem). M.-L. Von Franz, in
her *Aurora Consurgens*, has discussed at length the figure of
Sophia or *Sapentia Dei*. She writes:

> In patristic literature she was mostly interpreted as Christ, the pre-
> existent Logos, or as the sum of the *rationes Aeternae* (eternal forms),
> of the "self-knowing primordial causes," exemplars, ideas, and proto-
> types in the mind of God. She was also considered the *archetypus
> mundus* "that archetypal world after whose likeness this sensible
> world was made," and through which God becomes conscious of
> himself. *Sapientia Dei* is thus the sum of archetypal images in the
> mind of God.[41]

Thomas Aquinas expresses the same idea:

> . . . divine wisdom devised the order of the universe residing in the
> distinction of things, and therefore we must say that in the divine
> wisdom are the models of all things, which we have called *ideas*—i.e.,
> exemplary forms existing in the divine mind.[42]

The golden woman with the Mona Lisa face in the dream
is thus Sophia or Divine Wisdom. Her luminous necklace of blue
and gold would be a kind of celestrial rosary which unites on a
single circular string various forms and modes of being as the circle
of the year unites the signs of the Zodiac—"the sum of archetypal
images in the mind of God."

Dream 12:
*I have been set a task nearly too difficult for me. A log of hard
and heavy wood lies covered in the forest. I must uncover it, saw
or hew from it a circular piece, and then carve through the piece*

[41] von Franz, Marie-Louise *Aurora Consurgens*, Bollingen Series LXXVII,
Princeton University Press, pp. 155 f.
[42] Aquinas, Thomas. *Summa Theologica* I, q. 44, art. 4.

a design. The result is to be preserved at all cost, as representing
something no longer recurring and in danger of being lost. At the
same time, a tape recording is to be made describing in detail what
it is, what it represents, its whole meaning. At the end, the thing
itself and the tape are to be given to the public library. Someone
says that only the library will know how to prevent the tape
from deteriorating within five years. ✪

Again we have the theme of the difficult, assigned task analogous
to the alchemical opus. The covered log is the hidden, original
material which first must be uncovered or made manifest and then
given a special form which has some uniqueness since it will not
recur again. The carved design is a five-fold image. The number five
occurs again in the remark that there is danger of deterioration in
five years. The symbolism of five comes up in the quintessence
of the alchemists. It is the fifth form and ultimate unity of the
four elements and hence the final goal of the process. Ruland says
the quintessence is "the medicine itself, and the quality of sub-
stances separated by the art from the body." [43] Jung says that the
number five suggests the predominance of the physical man.[44] This
would correspond to the fact that the dream image reminds one
of an abstract human figure with five protuberances—four limbs
and head. Hence it would suggest the goal and completion of
physical existence.

The deposit of the object and a tape recording of its meaning
in the public library raises some very interesting points. In some
respects the object and the tape recording can be considered as
synonymous since the sketch of the object looks much like a reel
of recording tape. By this line of associations the task can be seen
as the transformation of Wood into Word, i.e., matter into spirit.
It is possible that this dream was foreshadowing the fact that I
would publish a series of his dreams in the future. The task would
then be the recording of his dreams which he deposited with me.
However, especially in the context of the other dreams, this simple,
personalistic interpretation is completely inadequate to the data.
Much more likely is the assumption that the dream task refers
to his psychological life task, the results of which are to be deposited as a permanent increment to a collective or transpersonal
library, i.e., a word or spirit treasury.

[43] Ruland, *op. cit.*, p. 272.
[44] Jung, C. G., *Psychology and Alchemy*, C.W., 12, Par. 287, n. 122.

The motif of the treasure-house is found in alchemy as a synonym for the philosopher's stone.[45] The fifth parable of *Aurora Consurgens* is entitled "Of the Treasure-House which Wisdom built upon a Rock." Alphidius says, "This is the treasure-house in which are treasured up all the sublime things of science or wisdom or the glorious things which cannot be possessed." [46] In Alphidius, the treasure-house is a fourfold structure and thus clearly a symbol of the Self.

A similar "treasury" image occurs in Catholic theology concerning the "treasure of merits" accumulated by Christ and the saints.[47] In spite of the concretistic misuse of this image by the Church to justify the sale of indulgences, it is an archetypal idea which expresses some aspect of the objective psyche.

In the examples cited, the treasury, when found, will convey benefits to the finder. In our dream, however, the dreamer is not making a withdrawal for his own use, but rather a deposit which will augment the public treasury. We recall the words of Jesus, "Even as the Son of man came not to be served but to serve." (Matthew 20:28 RSV). The dream seems to imply that the psychological accomplishments of the individual leave some permanent spiritual residue that augments the cumulative collective treasury, a sort of positive collective karma. In that case the words of Milton concerning a good book could apply equally to the fruits of the inner psychological task of individuation. A permanent spiritual deposit is left which "is the precious life-blood of a master spirit, embalmed and treasured up on purpose to a life beyond life." [48]

The dream mentions the need to prevent deterioration. Some preservative or embalming process is required. Dream 10 brought up the same theme in the mummification of the amputated hands. Perhaps the significance of these references corresponds to the archetypal symbolism that lay behind the elaborate embalming procedures of ancient Egypt. This idea seems provocative, although I cannot pursue it further at present.

Dream 13:
I was looking at a curiously unique and beautiful garden. It was a large square with a floor of stone. At intervals of about two

[45] Jung, C. G., *Mysterium Coniunctionis*, C.W., 14, par. 2, n. 9.
[46] Von Franz, *op. cit.*, p. 314.
[47] Hastings, James, editor, *Encyclopaedia of Religion and Ethics*, New York, Charles Scribner's Sons, 1922, Vol. VII, pp. 253 ff.
[48] Milton, John, *Areopagitica*.

feet were placed brass objects, standing upright, and looking very much like Brancusi's "Bird in Space." I stayed a long time. It had a very positive meaning but what that was I was unable to grasp.

Brancusi's "Bird in Space" is a graceful, slightly curved vertical pole of polished metal thicker in its mid-region and tapering to a point at the top (*Picture 43*). It brings up the whole question of the symbolism of the pole or pillar. In simplest terms it represents the phallic, striving, vertical thrust towards the upper spirit realm. It may signify the *axis mundi* which is the connection between the human world and the trans-personal divine world. On such a cosmic pole the gods descend to manifest themselves or the primitive shaman ascends to seek his ecstatic vision.[49] An Egyptian religious ritual gives us some other symbolic implications of a vertical pole or pillar. In the rites which celebrated the death and resurrection of Osiris, the ceremonies culminated when the chief priest set the so-called *Djed* column upright. R. T. Rundle Clark says about this column,

> The idea of the *Djed* Column is that it stands firmly upright—for to be upright is to be alive, to have overcome the inert forces of death and decay. When the *Djed* is upright it implies that life will go on in the world.[50]

The *Pistis Sophia* speaks of A Treasury of Light in which are gathered the particles of light that have been redeemed from their imprisonment in the darkness of matter. This treasury is a kind of intermediate collecting station which then transmits the accumulated light to a higher region, the World of Light, by means of a light stream called the Pillar of Glory.[51] According to Manichaen doctrine the elect perform this redemptive function for the scattered light. Having been reborn through gnosis, the elect become instruments for the gathering and concentration of light particles dispersed in matter. At the time of death each carries his accumulated bundle of light out of the material world and into the eternal realm of light.[52] Brancusi's sculpture plunging sky-

[49] Eliade, Mircea, *Shamanism*, Bollingen Series LXXVI, Princeton University Press, 1964. pp. 259 ff.

[50] Clark, *op. cit.*, p. 236.

[51] *Pistis Sophia*, G. R. S. Mead translator, London, John M. Watkins, 1947, p. 2 *et passim*.

[52] Legge, Francis, *Forerunners and Rivals of Christianity*, 1915, reprinted by University Books, New Hyde Park, New York, 1964, II, 296.

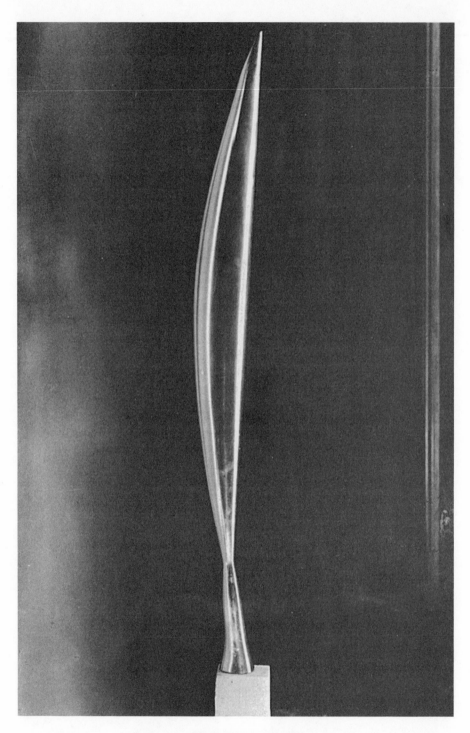

Picture 43. BIRD IN SPACE, Brancusi.

ward might be compared with the Pillar of Glory through which the collected particles of redeemed light stream into the eternal realm. A similar image occurs in the Manichaean eschatology. At the end of time the last "statue" (or pillar) appears:

> All the light that can still be saved is united in the "Great Idea" . . . in the form of the "last statue," which rises up to heaven, while the damned and the demons, matter with its lust and bisexuality, are cast into a pit sealed over with an immense stone.[53]

Jung refers to the Manichaean "statue" and relates it to an alchemical text. He writes:

> It is clear . . . that the statue or pillar is either the perfect Primordial Man . . . or at least his body, both at the beginning of creation and at the end of time." [54]

The dream image which combines a stone square with poles has a parallel in ancient Semitic sanctuaries as described by Fraser. He writes:

> We know that at all the old Canaanite sanctuaries, including the sanctuaries of Jehovah down to the reformations of Hezekiah and Josiah, the two regular objects of worship were a sacred stock and a sacred stone, and that these sanctuaries were the seats of profligate rites performed by sacred men (kedeshim) and sacred women (kedeshoth).[55]

Jeremiah refers to the sacred stock and stone when he criticizes the Israelites for "saying to a stock, thou art my father; and to a stone, thou has brought me forth." (Jeremiah 2:27 A.V.). Stone and pole are therefore representations of the feminine and masculine deities respectively. In psychological terms the dream is thus presenting a *coniunctio* of the masculine and feminine principles. Why there should be a multiplicity of masculine poles contained within one stone square, I do not know. Perhaps it has similar implications to the multiplicity of pearls in the necklace of Sophia. However, as an expression of totality and the union of opposites it is an image of completion. This dream is one of the last I have of this patient. Three months later he died.

---

[53] Peuch, Henri-Charles, "The Concept of Redemption in Manichaeism," in *The Mystic Vision*, Papers from the Eranos Yearbooks 6. Bollingen Series XXX, Princeton University Press, 1968, p. 313.

[54] Jung, C. G., *Mysterium Coniunctionis*, C.W., 14, par. 567.

[55] Frazer, *op. cit.*, vol. I, p. 107.

This dream series demonstrates, I think, that the unconscious under certain circumstances brings up considerations which properly can be called metaphysical. Although the dreamer did not undergo the process of individuation in the usual sense of that term, it can be surmised that the pressure of impending death may have telescoped that process. Certainly these dreams suggest an urgency on the part of the unconscious to convey awareness of a metaphysical reality, as if such an awareness were important to have before one's physical death.

∽

The question will be asked, what effect did these dreams have on the dreamer. This is difficult to answer with certainty; practically all of the dreams reported here had an intense emotional impact on the dreamer, but interestingly he experienced this impact only when recounting the dreams in the analytic session, not beforehand. Somehow the presence of the analyst was needed to release the numinosity of the dream images. Taken as a whole, the dreams conveyed a series of small religious experiences which brought about a gradual and definite change in the dreamer's life attitude. This unreligious, unphilosophical man was given a metaphysical initiation. As a result, he was at least partially released from pre-occupation with personal frustrations and his personality acquired a new level of depth and dignity. After being brought back from near death he voiced the question several times, "Why is my life prolonged?" Perhaps these dreams contain the answer.

CHAPTER NINE

The Blood of Christ

Theology without alchemy is like a noble body without its right hand.*

Our Art, its theory as well as its practice, is altogether a gift of God, Who gives it when and to whom He elects: It is not of him that wills, or of him that runs, but simply through the mercy of God.**

1. INTRODUCTION

The subject of this chapter is an ancient archetypal image laden with the sacred meanings of millenia. Such an image has great power for good or ill and must be treated with care. When it is embedded in the protective substance of orthodoxy it can be handled with safety. But the empirical method of analytical psychology requires that we attempt to strip away the protective, traditional context in order to examine the living symbol itself and to explore its spontaneous function in the individual psyche. It is as if we were visiting powerful wild animals in their natural habitat rather than looking at them confined to cages in a zoo. Although this method is necessary, we should recognize its danger. If we must work with explosives in our laboratory let us treat them respectfully. The naive ego that approaches such an image carelessly can fall

---

* Waite, A. E., trans., *The Hermetic Museum*, London, John M. Watkins, 1953, Vol. I, p. 119.
** Ibid., p. 9.

into hybris and then be blasted by the inevitable recoil of nemesis. With these thoughts in mind I have appended two alchemical quotations as mottoes. The first expresses the attitude of scientific empiricism and practical psychotherapy. It reads: "Theology without alchemy is like a noble body without its right hand." [1] But to guard against the hybris of the human will, the second quotation must immediately follow: "Our Art, its theory as well as its practice, is altogether a gift of God, Who gives it when and to whom He elects: it is not of him that wills, or of him that runs, but simply through the mercy of God." [2]

Jung has demonstrated that the figure of Christ is a symbol of the Self [3] and this discovery has enabled us to go a long way toward relating traditional Christian mythology to modern depth psychology. An important corollary image associated with the symbolism of Christ is the image of the blood of Christ. My attention was first directed to this theme when I encountered several dreams referring to the blood of Christ. Such dreams indicate that the blood of Christ is a living symbol which still functions in the modern psyche. I therefore propose to explore this symbol and some of its ramifications in the light of Jung's psychology.

In order to demonstrate that this image together with its associative connections is a living organism and not a theoretical construct, one must use the empirical, descriptive, phenomenological approach. However, this approach makes great demands on the reader. As the various links are traced out among various parallels and analogies, he is in danger of getting lost in the maze of interconnections. I know of no way to avoid this problem if one is to be true to the empirical method. Misunderstanding critics notwithstanding, Jung's psychology is not a philosophy or a theology but a verifiable science. In order not to obscure this fact we are obliged to use the cumbersome empirical-descriptive method which always keeps in immediate view the actual manifestations of the psyche, despite their confusing complexity. To provide an overall orientation I include a chart showing some of the inter-connected images which we shall see are associated with the image of the blood of Christ. (*Figure 8*).

[1] Waite, A. E., trans., *The Hermetic Museum*, London, John M. Watkins, 1953. Vol. I, p. 119.
[2] Ibid., p. 9.
[3] *E.g. vide* Jung, C. G., "Christ, a Symbol of the Self" in *Aion*, C.W., 9 ii, par. 68 ff.

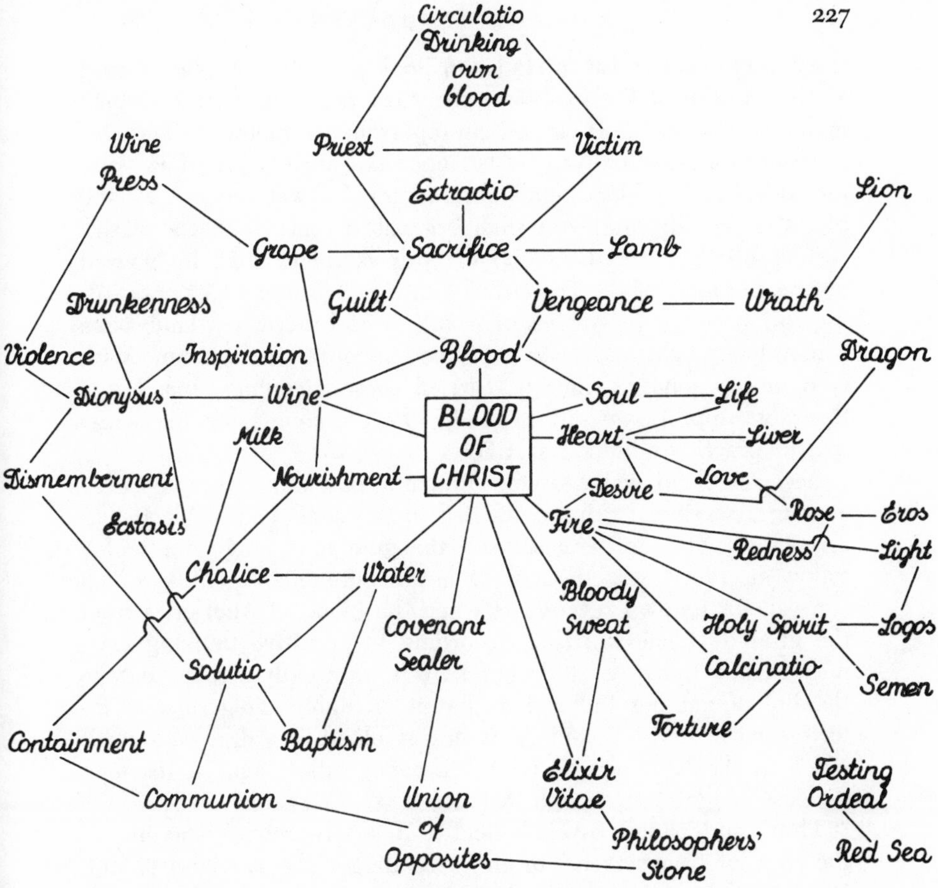

Figure 8.

2. THE MEANING OF BLOOD

The image of the blood of Christ has numerous connections with ancient thought and practices. Since primitive times blood has carried numinous implications. The blood was considered to be the seat of life or soul. Because the liver was thought to be a mass of clotted blood, the soul was located in that organ.[4] Since life ebbed away as one bled to death, the equation of blood and life was natural and inevitable. Likewise, the shades of the dead in Hades could be restored briefly to some semblance of life by giving them blood to drink. The classic example of this practice is the

[4] Yerkes, R. K., *Sacrifice in Greek and Roman Religions and Early Judiasm*, New York, Scribner's, 1952, p. 42 n.1.

story of Odysseus' visit to Hades in Book XI of the *Odyssey*. Blood as the essence of life itself was the most precious thing of which man could conceive. It carried suprapersonal connotations and was thought to belong only to God. Hence the ancient Hebrews were forbidden to eat blood. In Deuteronomy Yahweh says, ". . . the blood is the life, and you shall not eat the life with the flesh." (12:23 RSV). ". . . the blood of your sacrifices shall be poured out on the altar of the Lord your God . . ." (12:27 RSV). According to Pausanias, priestesses of Apollo would sacrifice a lamb once a month at night and taste the blood in order to commune with God and prophesy.[5] Since it carried these meanings, blood was the most appropriate gift to God, which accounts for the widespread practice of blood sacrifice.

Because blood was a divine fluid it was a crime to spill it except in a sacrificial ritual dedicated to the gods. Hence blood was associated with murder and with the guilt and vengeance which follow it. Blood was thought of as an autonomous entity which can call for its own revenge as when the blood of Abel cries from the ground (Genesis 4:10). According to primitive thinking (i.e., unconscious thinking) it is not that it is morally wrong to take the life of another but rather that it is highly dangerous to interfere with such a potent substance as blood. It will avenge itself much as the high tension wire will avenge itself against the man careless or ignorant enough to grasp it.

Thus, understood psychologically, blood represents the life of the soul, of transpersonal origin, exceedingly precious and potent. It is to be reverenced as divine and any effort of the ego to manipulate, appropriate or destroy it for personal purposes provokes vengeance or retribution. Blood spilled requires more blood to pay the debt. The books must be balanced. Such thinking illustrates the law of the conservation of psychic energy. There is so much psychic life to be lived. If it is denied fulfillment in one area, it must be made up elsewhere. There must be blood for blood. Repression, which is internal murder, will out. It is a crime against life for which payment will be extracted. Jung has this fact in mind when he says:[6]

> . . . nature seems to bear us a grudge . . . if we withhold our emotions from our fellow men. . . . To cherish secrets and hold back emotion is a psychic misdemeanour for which nature finally visits us with sickness—that is, when we do these things in private.[6]

[5] Yerkes, p. 43.
[6] Jung, C. G., *The Practice of Psychotherapy*, C.W., 16, par. 132.

Another feature of ancient blood symbolism is the notion that blood establishes a bond or covenant between the divine or demonic powers and man. Pacts with the devil must be signed in blood and blood must flow to bind a contract between God and man. The "blood of the covenant" occurs in the ceremony through which Yahweh binds himself to Israel in the 24th Chapter of Exodus:

> And Moses wrote all the words of the Lord. And he rose early in the morning, and built an altar at the foot of the mountain; and twelve pillars, according to the twelve tribes of Israel. And he sent young men of the people of Israel, who offered burnt offerings and sacrificed peace offerings of oxen to the Lord. And Moses took half of the blood and put it in basins, and half of the blood he threw against the altar. Then he took the book of the covenant, and read it in the hearing of the people and they said, "all that the Lord has spoken we will do, and we will be obedient." And Moses took the blood and threw it upon the people, and said, "Behold the blood of the covenant which the Lord has made with you in accordance with all these words." (Exodus 24:4-8 RSV).

The blood here serves as a kind of glue or binding agent. Half of it is thrown on Yahweh, represented by his altar, and half is thrown on the people. The people are thus united with God "in one blood." God and people have participated in a joint baptism or *solutio*, which unites them in a communion.

The idea of the "blood of the covenant" is picked up again in the New Testament and applied to the blood of Christ. Just as the blood of the sacrificial animals poured out by Moses cemented the old bond between God and Israel, so Christ's blood, willingly poured out by himself, cements the new bond between God and man. This parallel is made explicit in the Ninth Chapter of Hebrews:

> Therefore he (Christ) is the mediator of a new covenant, so that those who are called may receive the promised eternal inheritance . . . even the first covenant was not ratified without blood. For when every commandment of the law had been declared by Moses to all the people, he took the blood of calves and goats with water and scarlet wool and hyssop, and sprinkled both the book itself and all the people saying, "This is the blood of the covenant which God commanded you." And in the same way he sprinkled with the blood both the tent (tabernacle) and all the vessels used in worship. Indeed, under the law almost everything is purified with blood, and without the shedding of blood there is no forgiveness of sins. Thus it was necessary for the copies of the heavenly things to be purified with these rites, but the heavenly things themselves with better sacrifices

than these. For Christ has entered, not into a sanctuary made with hands, a copy of the true one, but into heaven itself, now to appear in the presence of God on our behalf. Nor was it to offer himself repeatedly, as the high priest enters the Holy Place yearly with blood not his own; for then he would have had to suffer repeatedly since the foundation of the world. But as it is, he has appeared once for all at the end of the age to put away sin by the sacrifice of himself. (Heb. 9:15-26 RSV).

This passage demonstrates how Hebrew myth and ritual merges with Platonic thought in evolving the Christian symbolism of the blood of Christ. The Hebrew "blood of the covenant" is considered a "copy" of the genuine article and it is sprinkled on the tabernacle of Yahweh which is a copy of the eternal heaven. This idea, together with the statement that Christ's blood is only once for all time, implies psychologically that a transformation has occurred in the archetypal level of the collective psyche. God himself has undergone a change so that the cementing and redeeming fluid which unites man with God, i.e., the ego with the Self, is now continually available through the initiative of the Self as Christ.

In the new dispensation the "blood of the covenant" becomes the blood of the communion meal. This connection is made in the account of the last supper where it is said: "And he took a cup, and when he had given thanks he gave it to them saying, 'Drink of it, all of you; for this is my blood of the covenant, which is poured out for many for the forgiveness of sins.'" (Matt. 26:27-28 RSV. See also Mark 14:23-24 and I Cor. 11:25). Thus the Old Testament injunction to eat no blood has been superseded, at least for symbolic and ritual purposes. Drinking the blood of Christ becomes a means of cementing the connection between God and man.

Concerning blood as the sealer of a covenant, W. Robertson Smith gives us some important information. He writes:

The notion that, by eating the flesh, or particularly by drinking the blood, of another living being, a man absorbs its nature, or life, into his own, is one which appears among primitive peoples in many forms . . . The most notable application of the idea is in the rite of blood brotherhood, examples of which are found all over the world. In the simplest form of this rite, two men become brothers by opening their veins and sucking one another's blood. Thenceforth their lives are not two but one . . . In ancient Arabic literature there are many references to the blood covenant, but instead of human blood that of a victim slain at the sanctuary is employed.

. . . In later times we find the conception current that any food which two men partake of together, so that the same substance enters into their flesh and blood, is enough to establish some sacred unity of life between them; but in ancient times this significance seems to be always attached to participation in the flesh of a sacrosanct victim, and the solemn mystery of its death is justified by the consideration that only in this way can the sacred cement be procured which creates or keeps alive a living bond of union between the worshippers and their god. This cement is nothing else than the actual life of the sacred and kindred animal, which is conceived as residing in its flesh, but especially in its blood, and so, in the sacred meal, is actually distributed among all the participants, each of whom incorporates a particle of it with his own individual life." [7]

Understood psychologically, it is joint libido investment which generates brotherhood. People engaged in a mutual enterprise, sharing the same goals, the same ordeals and the same value-commitments are those who experience themselves as brothers of one blood. Likewise, in the inner life of the individual, it is from occasions of intense affect faced consciously that the ego discovers the existence of the Self and becomes bound to it. Libido intensity symbolized by blood is necessary to forge the connection between man and man and between man and God.

With these observations in mind, the drinking of Christ's blood in the ritual of the Roman Catholic Mass can be seen symbolically to represent a two-fold cementing process. First, the individual communicant cements his personal relation to God. Secondly, he becomes psychologically identified with all the other communicants as part of the mystical body of Christ. Christ's action of offering his blood as a nourishing drink (like the pelican) is an expression of the positive mother archetype, or rather, that component of the Self. The same meaning must be attached to the cup or chalice symbolism which has gathered round the blood of Christ. Relevant to this line of thought is an interesting and unusual image in the apocryphal *Odes of Solomon*. The first four verses of Ode 19 read as follows:

A cup of milk was offered to me: and I drank it in the sweetness of the delight of the Lord. The Son is the cup, and He who was milked is the Father: and the Holy Spirit milked Him: because His breasts were full, and it was necessary for Him that His milk should be sufficiently released; and the Holy Spirit opened His bosom and

[7] Smith, W. Robertson, *The Religion of the Semites*, 1899, Reprinted by Meridian Books, New York, 1956, pp. 313 f.

mingled the milk from the two breasts of the Father; and gave the mixture to the world without their knowing.[8]

Because of the patriarchal bias of most theologians, the phenomenological fact that the Self is a union of both masculine and feminine principles is generally obscured in canonical material. This passage is thus unusual in giving overtly feminine attributes to the deity. However in empirical psychological material it is the rule that the Self is represented in paradoxical or androgynous images.

The text presents a striking picture of the trinity. In relation to communion symbolism, the milk will equate with the blood of Christ which is the milk or blood of the Father, i.e., the remote or transcendent aspect of the Self which is not accessible to the conscious ego. The Son is the cup, i.e., the human incarnation in personal, temporal life is the vessel which contains and transmits the archetypal life energy. For this life-fluid to be realized in its essential nature the cup, its particular personal container, must be emptied. In other words, archetypal life meaning which connects the individual with his transpersonal source must be extracted from the particular incarnations in which it expresses itself in one's personal, concrete life. According to the text, the Holy Spirit is the one that does the milking. It could also be considered as the milk itself. This would fit with other descriptions of the Holy Spirit and also with a conclusion I reach later that the blood of Christ is synonymous with the Holy Spirit.

Clement of Alexandria uses the same image and equates the milk of the Father with the Logos:

> O amazing mystery! We are commanded to cast off the old and fleshly corruption, as also the old nutriment, and to change to a new and different diet, that of Christ . . . *The food is the milk of the Father*, with which children are alone nursed. The very beloved one, he who gives us nourishment, the Logos, has shed his own blood for us and saved human nature. Believing in God through him we take refuge at the "care-soothing breast" (*Iliad*, XXII, 83) of the Father, that is the Logos. And he alone, as is fitting, supplies us babes with the milk of love (*agape*), and those only are truly blessed who suck this breast.[9]

[8] *The Lost Books of the Bible and The Forgotten Books of Eden*, Cleveland, World Publishing Co., II, 130.
[9] "Paedagogos," 1, 42, 2-43, 4, quoted in Goodenough, Erwin, *Jewish Symbols in the Greco-Roman Period*, Vol. 6, Princeton University Press, p. 119.

The Logos is not only milk but also semen as is indicated by the verses of Ode 19 which immediately follow those previously quoted:

And those who take (it) (the milk of the Father) are in the fulness of the right hand. The womb of the Virgin took (it), and she received conception and brought forth: and the Virgin became a mother with great mercy.[10]

According to ancient physiology, the female could turn blood into milk and the male could turn it into semen. Blood, milk and semen were variations of the same essential substance. Thus we arrive at the Stoic concept of the *Logos Spermatikos*, the creative, impregnating Word corresponding to the creative function of the Word in John 1:3: "All things were made through him, and without him was not anything made that was made."

Another Old Testament prototype of the blood of Christ is the blood of the paschal lamb. On the night that all the first-born of Egypt are to be killed by the avenging angel of Yahweh, the Israelites are instructed to kill a lamb without blemish and put some of its blood on the doorposts and lintels of their houses. Thus, says Yahweh, "The blood shall be a sign for you, upon the houses where you are; and when I see the blood, I will pass over you, and no plague shall fall upon you to destroy you, when I smite the land of Egypt." (Exodus 12:13 RSV). A development of this image of God's marking those who will be spared from his blood bath of vengeance is found in a vision of Ezekiel. A man clothed in white with a scribe's ink horn in his belt is described and God tells this man to "Go all through the city, all through Jerusalem, and mark a cross on the foreheads of all who deplore and disapprove of all the filth practiced in it." (Ezekiel 9:4, JB). All those without the cross on their foreheads, God orders slain.

I mention this passage particularly because the figure of the scribe in white with the ink horn corresponds very closely to a figure in a dream to be presented later in which the "ink" is the blood of Christ. The blood mark on the doorpost and the mark on the forehead in Ezekiel are the mark of God's elect. They will be immune to God's bloody wrath or to immersion in the Red Sea which are symbolically equivalent. There is a third variation on the same theme in Revelation (7:2-3 and 9:4) where the servants of God to the number of 144,000 have a seal set upon

[10] Ibid., p. 121.

their foreheads to indicate that they are to be spared in the general destruction.

The blood sacrifice of Christ has many parallels with the sacrifice of the paschal lamb whose blood protects the Israelites from the vengeance of Yahweh and these parallels help elucidate the psychological meaning of the redemptive power of the blood of Christ. In the Exodus story an involuntary sacrifice of the first-born son was re quired of every Egyptian family. The Jews were spared this happening only by substituting a voluntary sacrifice, the blood of which was then displayed. The state of things was signified by the hardness of Pharaoh's heart. A state of petrification prevailed. To remedy this condition, blood must flow. The soul-stuff must liquify, be extracted from the hard, sterile *status quo* so that life and libido might flow again. When put in such terms we can immediately see how these images apply to the inner life of the individual. The urge to individuation, symbolized by Yahweh, demands transformation, freedom for enslaved and repressed capacities. If our Egyptian heart will not yield, blood must be extracted by force. To the extent that libido is voluntarily transferred to the transpersonal purpose by a sacrificial attitude one avoids the destructive consequences to the personality that occur when the ego sets its will against the requirements of the totality, the Self.

Christ was identified with the paschal lamb and called *Agnus Dei*. Also, according to an objective appraisal of the symbolism, Christ as the first born son of God will be equated with the Egyptians' sacrifice of their own first-born sons. To my knowledge this conclusion is not reached in traditional exegesis; however, it is necessary for a full psychological understanding of the myth. The redeeming sacrifice always occurs with a mixture of moods—lamb-like meekness and pharaonic intransigence. At the very best, the ego is willing but reluctant as was Christ in the garden.

More can be said about the symbolism of lamb sacrifice. As signifying innocence, meekness and purity it represents something we least want to kill. This theme comes up occasionally in dreams. For instance, I recall a patient who had what could be called a Job or Ahab complex—an unquenchable resentment against God for permitting the young and innocent to suffer. She once dreamed that a lamb was to be sacrificed and she couldn't bear to watch. In such a case it is lamb-like childhood innocence which must be sacrificed, namely, the expectation that reality is, or should be, superintended by an all-loving father. The "blood of the lamb" must be extracted from this immature attitude in order that the

spirit of benevolence can live effectively in reality, not as the passive
demand of a childish ego but as an active power motivating the
conscious personality. The sacrifice of innocent purity also implies
the realization of the shadow which releases one from identification
with the role of innocent victim and the tendency to project the
evil executioner on to God or neighbor.

3. CHRIST AND DIONYSUS

Another important line of symbolic connections links the blood of
Christ with the grape and wine of Dionysus. The original reference
is in the Gospel of John where Christ says of himself: "I am the
true vine, and my father is the vinedresser. Every branch of mine
that bears no fruit, he takes away, and every branch that does
bear fruit he prunes, that it may bear more fruit . . . I am the
vine, you are the branches." (John 15:1-5 RSV). From this it is
only a short step to the identification of Christ with the grape which
is crushed to make wine. The seventeenth century poet Henry
Vaughn expressed this connection in his verses on *The Passion*.

> Most blessed Vine!
> Whose juice so good
> I feel as Wine,
> But thy faire branches felt as bloud,
> How wert thou prest
> To be my feast! [11]

The miracle at Cana which transformed water into wine (John
2:1 ff) established Christ as a wine-maker, and wine with its
indwelling spirit is analogous to the "living water" which Christ
offered the woman of Samaria. (John 4:10). Living water or
elixir vitae is a term used much later by the alchemists. The chalice
of Antioch in the Cloisters of the Metropolitan Museum, dating back
probably to the fourth century A.D., shows Christ surrounded by
clusters of grapes (*Pictures 44 and 45*). As Jung says: "The wine
miracle at Cana was the same as the miracle in the temple of
Dionysus, and it is profoundly significant that, on the Damascus
chalice, Christ is enthroned among vine tendrils like Dionysus
himself." [12]

[11] Vaughn, Henry, *Silex Scintillans* in *The Complete Poetry of Henry Vaughn*,
edited by French Fogle, Garden City, New York, Anchor Books, Doubleday,
1964, p. 185.
[12] Jung, C. G., *Psychology and Religion: West and East*, C.W., 11, par. 384.

236

Picture 44.
THE CHALICE OF ANTIOCH.

Dionysus with his wine is an ambivalent symbol. He can bring inspiration, ecstasy and benevolent transformation of consciousness as described by the Persian poet Omar Khayyám:

> The Grape that can with Logic absolute
> The two-and Seventy jarring Sects confute:
> The soverign Alchemist that in a Trice
> Life's leaden metal into Gold transmute.[13]

Plato in the *Republic* (II, 363C) describes an idea, current in his time, of a paradisal after-life reserved for the righteous. The gods "conduct them to the house of Hades . . . and arrange a symposium of the saints, where, reclined on couches and crowned with wreaths, they entertain the time henceforth with wine, as if the fairest meed of virtue were an everlasting drunk." (Paul Shorey trans.).

In Euripides' *Bacchae* there is a striking and beautiful image of the miraculous flow of life-fluids during the revels of Bacchantes:

> And one would raise
> Her wand and smite the rock, and straight a jet
> Of quick bright water came, Another set
> Her thyrsus in the bosomed earth, and there
> Was red wine that the God sent up to her,
> A darkling fountain. And if any lips
> Sought whiter draughts, with dipping finger-tips
> They pressed the sod, and gushing from the ground
> Came springs of milk, And reed-wands ivy-crowned
> Ran with sweet honey, drop by drop.
>
> (ll. 700 ff., Murray trans.).

However the sacred orgies of Dionysus can also be violent and terrifying with mad Maenads dismembering alive whatever crosses their path. Such was the fate of Orpheus and Pentheus. The horrors that can be perpetrated when the ego is inflated by identification with the power of the collective unconscious are awesome. Consider for instance the medieval *autos-da-fe* committed by self-righteous ecclesiastics drunk with the blood of Christ.

The terrible aspect of wine symbolism is further elaborated in the image of God's grapes of wrath. In Revelation we read:

"Put in your sickle, and gather the clusters of the vine of the earth, for its grapes are ripe." So the angel swung his sickle on the earth and gathered the vintage of the earth, and threw it into the great wine press of the wrath of God; and the wine press was trodden outside the city, and blood flowed from the wine press . . .[14]

[13] *Rubaayt of Omar Khayyam*, translated by Edward Fitzgerald, Verse LIX.
[14] Rev. 14:18-20, RSV.

Picture 45. CHRIST AS A CLUSTER OF GRAPES.

God's wrath is the winepress that extracts the wine from the grapes, but it can also be the wine itself as evidenced by the phrase in Revelations 16:19 ". . . the wine of the fierceness of his (God's) wrath." (A.V.).

The same fierce image appears in Isaiah 63:1-3:

"Who is this that comes from Edom, in crimsoned garments from Bozrah, he that is glorious in his apparel, marching in the greatness of his strength? . . . Why is thy apparel red, and thy garments like his that treads in the wine press?" Yahweh answers: "I have trodden the wine press alone, and from the peoples no one was with me; I trod them in my anger and trampled them in my wrath; their life-blood is sprinkled upon my garments, and I have stained all my raiment." (RSV).

Church fathers considered this passage to refer to the suffering Messiah.[14] According to them "he who comes 'red' from the 'wine-press' is none other than Our Lord Jesus Christ, for . . . this is the question which the angels put to him on the day of his triumphal ascension." [15]

The Isaiah text says that the figure in bloody garments is Yahweh drenched in the blood of his enemies. The patristic analogists identified the figure in bloody garments with Christ drenched in his own blood. Thus the paradoxical reversal characteristic of Christian symbolism occurs. The sacrificer becomes the sacrifical victim. For Yahweh, the blood of his enemies becomes his own blood.

The ancient Egyptian priests had identified wine with the blood of God's enemies. According to Plutarch:

. . . they did not drink wine nor use it in libation as something dear to the gods, thinking it to be the blood of those who had once battled against the gods, and from whom, when they had fallen and had become commingled with the earth, they believed vines to have sprung. This is the reason why drunkenness drives men out of their senses and crazes them, inasmuch as they are then filled with the blood of their forbears.[16]

[14] Jerusalem Bible, p. 1243, note b.
[15] Pinedo, Ramiro de, El Simbolismo en la escultura medieval espanola, Madrid, 1930, Quoted by Cirlot J. E., A Dictionary of Symbols, New York, Philosophical Library, 1962, p. 29.
[16] Plutarch, "Isis and Osiris" in Plutarch's Moralia Vol. 5., Loeb Classical Library, Cambridge, Harvard University Press, 1962, p. 17.

This idea is most interesting psychologically as a description of the effects of an influx of the collective unconscious: one is filled with the blood of his forebears. Jung has spoken in similar terms about his own experience of the unconscious. Concerning his imperative urge to understand the psyche he says: "Perhaps it is a question which preoccupied my ancestors, and which they could not answer . . . Or is it the restless Wotan-Hermes of my Alemannic and Frankish ancestors who poses challenging riddles?" [17]

Another Old Testament passage associated with Christ is Genesis 49:10-12:

> The scepter shall not depart from Judah, nor the ruler's staff from between his feet, until he comes to whom it belongs . . . he washes his garments in wine and his vesture in the blood of grapes; his eyes shall be red with wine, and his teeth white with milk. (RSV).

"He to whom it belongs" refers to the Messiah according to Jewish and Christian tradition.[18]

The passage gives us a picture of a ruler filled with wine and redness, a kind of fountain brimming with vital juices. Red eyes and white teeth suggest a union of opposites which is taken up much later in alchemy with the *coniunctio* of the red man and white woman. The association of this passage with Christ is another link between him and Dionysus. Eyes "red with wine" are Dionysian eyes, drunk with an excess of blood or life intensity. It is a magnified version of the sanguine or blood-filled temperament. Such an image appeared for example in a patient's dream prior to the emergence of a new quantity of psychic energy. He dreamed: *There was a woman whose blood was very, very red—so red it could almost be seen under her skin. She was a person who lived life to the fullest, taking enjoyment where she could find it.* This dream figure could be a smaller version of the red-eyed ruler washing in the vital life fluid.

Alchemists also used grape and wine symbolism to represent the vital life essence which is the goal of their process. The alchemical opus was called the "vintage." One text says: "Press the grape." Another says: "Man's blood and the red juice of the grape is our fire." Wine is a synonym for the *aqua permanens*. Hermes, the presiding deity of alchemy is called "the vintager" and the philo-

---

[17] Jung, C. G., *Memories, Dreams, Reflections*, New York, Pantheon Books, 1961, p. 318.
[18] *Jerusalem Bible*, p. 75, note g.

sophical water is called "grape-clusters of Hermes," *Uvae Herme-tis.*[19]

The image of wine in dreams will generally convey similar meanings to the alchemical use of the symbol. In addition it often associates ultimately to the blood of Christ. For example, a young man who was discovering his tendency to spill and dissipate his own individual essence dreamed that he was pouring himself some wine. An acquaintance (a shadow figure) took it and poured it down a sink. The dreamer, thoroughly aroused, told him he had gone too far and that there would be no more of that. With this dream the link was made to the blood of Christ through the dreamer's association that consecrated wine left over after communion must not be disposed of by pouring it down the sink.

4. EXTRACTION BY SACRIFICE

Christ is sometimes represented as a grape being pressed in a wine press. For example a fifteenth century woodcut (*Picture 46*) shows Christ in a press. From his breast blood flows into a chalice and from the chalice a number of streams flow out to various

[19] Jung, C. G., *Alchemical Studies*, C.W., 13, par. 359 n.

Picture 46. CHRIST CRUSHED AS A GRAPE.

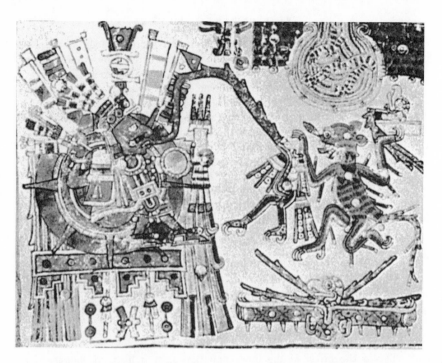

Picture 47. AZTEC SUN GOD FEEDING ON HUMAN BLOOD.

activities of man. In this picture the divine sacrifice is releasing energy to sustain the daily life of man. The Self is supporting the existence of the ego. This idea is the reverse of the ancient view that man must sacrifice in order to nourish the gods, i.e., the ego must support the Self. A striking representation of the latter view is in an Aztec picture (*Picture 47*) showing a stream of blood flowing from a sacrificial victim into the mouth of the sun god.

Understood psychologically, both processes operate at varying times in the psychic life of the individual. At times the transpersonal totality must be fed by the sacrificial blood of the ego. At other times the ego can not survive unless it finds contact with the life-promoting effects of the sacrificial blood of the Self. The reciprocal, two-fold nature of the psychic life-supporting process is expressed in the Christian symbolism itself. According to the myth, Christ is both God and man, i.e., both Self and ego. In terms of the sacrificial rite he is both the sacrificing priest and the sacrificial victim. This point is emphasized in another passage from Hebrews:

But when Christ appeared as a high priest of the good things that have come, then through the greater and more perfect tabernacle (not made with hands, that is, not of this creation) he entered once for all into the Holy Place, taking not the blood of goats and calves but his own blood, thus securing an eternal redemption. For if the sprinkling of defiled persons with the blood of goats and bulls . . . sanctifies for the purification of the flesh, how much more shall the blood of Christ, who through the eternal Spirit offered himself without blemish to God, purifying your conscience from dead works to serve the living God (Hebrews 9:11-14 RSV).

In this passage Christ is simultaneously the sacrificing priest and the sacrificial victim. He is the agent who extracts from himself the redeeming blood. A smiliar image is found in the *Visions of Zosimos*. There we read:

"I am Ion, the priest of the inner sanctuaries, and I submit myself to an unendurable torment . . . till I perceived by the transformation of the body that I had become spirit . . ." and even as he spoke thus, and I held him by force to converse with me, his eyes became as blood.[20]

And later:

This is the priest of the inner sanctuaries. It is he who changes the bodies into blood. makes the eyes clairvoyant, and raises the dead.[21]

Jung says about this vision:

The vision itself indicates that the main purpose of the transformation process is the spiritualization of the sacrificing priest: he is to be changed into *pneuma* . . .
Throughout the visions it is clear that sacrificer and sacrificed are one and the same. This idea of the unity of the *prima* and *ultima materia*, of that which redeems and that which is to be redeemed, pervades the whole of alchemy from beginning to end.[22]

The idea that Christ sacrificed himself in order to extract or make manifest his spiritual essence is expressed in the scriptural passages referring to the coming of the Paraclete. In John 16:7 Christ says to his disciples: "I tell you the truth: it is to your advantage that I go away, for if I do not go away, the Counselor (Paraclete) will not come to you; but if I go, I will send him to you." (RSV). In the

[20] Berthelot, M. P. E., *Collections des Anciens Alchemistes Grecs*, 1888, reprinted by the Holland Press, London, 1963, III, 1, 2. Translated in Jung, C. G., *Alchemical Studies*, C.W., 13, par. 86.
[21] Ibid.
[22] Jung, C. G., *Psychology and Religion: West and East*, C.W., 11, par. 353.

fourteenth chapter of John the Paraclete is referred to in this fashion: "I will pray the Father, and he will give you another Counselor (Paraclete), to be with you forever, even the Spirit of truth, whom the world cannot receive, because it neither sees him nor knows him; you know him, for he dwells with you, and will be in you." (John 14:16, 17 RSV). And again, "These things I have spoken to you, while I am still with you. But the Counselor (Paraclete), the Holy Spirit, whom the Father will send in my name, he will teach you all things . . ." (John 14:25, 26 RSV).

In a certain sense the Paraclete is synonymous with the blood of Christ. Each is the product of Christ's sacrifice. Each is the disembodied effective essence which can come into existence only by the loss of the concrete, particular form of Christ. The Paraclete, as described in John, can only be seen as an individual, inner guide which supercedes the Jesus of history and dogma. It is the "inner Christ" of Meister Eckhart or, in psychological terms, the Way of Individuation.

The connection between Christ and His blood raises questions of importance as demonstrated in a bitter medieval dispute. There was a theological combat between the Dominicans and the Friars Minor concerning the blood of Christ shed during the Passion. The Minors said that it ceased to be united to the divinity of Christ, the Dominicans that the union did not cease. Eventually Pope Pius II forbade both parties to discuss the question further.[23]

Such apparently sterile intellectual disputes are rich with symbolic meaning when viewed psychologically. Here the issue seems to be whether or not it is possible to extract the full archetypal meaning from its particular incarnation in the myth of Christ and the church founded on that myth. In other words, whether it is possible to have a purely psychological approach to the numinous energies of the psyche without benefit of a particular religious faith or church affiliation. For us the answer is obvious; but what a revolutionary question it would have been if consciously formulated in the middle ages.

The method by which the blood of Christ is extracted is the process of sacrifice. The psychological implications of sacrifice are quite complex. For a full discussion of it consult Jung's account in his essay on "Transformation Symbolism in the Mass."[24] For present

[23] Hastings, James, editor, *Encyclopaedia of Religion and Ethics*, New York, Scribner's, 1922, Vol. XII, p. 321.

[24] Jung, C. G., *Psychology and Religion: West and East*, C.W., 11, par. 381 ff.

purposes I would note that at least four different arrangements are possible in the sacrificial situation depending on who is doing the sacrifice, what is being sacrificed, and for whose benefit the sacrifice is done. The four possibilities can be listed as follows:

PRIEST	SACRIFICIAL VICTIM		FOR THE BENEFIT OF
1. God	sacrifices	man	God
2. God	sacrifices	God	man
3. Man	sacrifices	God	man
4. Man	sacrifices	man	man and God

1. *God sacrifices man.* This version corresponds to all ancient sacrificial practice. The priest acting for God sacrifices an animal (originally a human) as representing man. The movement is from human to divine, i.e., it is the divine realm which is to be augmented at the expense of the human. Thus the implication is that the ego is too full and the transpersonal world too empty. The balance must be righted by a sacrifice of the ego to the advantage of the Self.

2. *God sacrifices God.* This procedure corresponds to the symbolism of all totemistic meals to the extent that they are performed as sacred ritual and hence under the auspices of God. The outstanding example is the Roman Catholic Mass in which the celebrating priest stands for God the sacrificer and the elements represent God the sacrificed. In this case the movement is from divine to human, indicating a relative emptiness of the ego (poverty of spirit) which requires a sustaining influx from the transpersonal, collective unconscious.

3. *Man sacrifices God.* This action has no specific religious representation since its essence is apparently secular or personal. It corresponds to a drainage of energy and value from transpersonal categories to serve the interests of the conscious ego. Mythical examples would be Prometheus' theft of fire and the original sin of Adam and Eve. Strictly speaking it would seem that the word sacrifice should not apply here since it is more a matter of desacralizing than of making sacred. However during the empirical vissitudes of psychological development when such a step is required, the experience justifies the term sacrifice to describe the reluctant relinquishing of containment in old modes of being. It is actually the greatest sacrifice of all and as the myths tell us exacts the highest price. In the history of culture, this stage would be represented by atheistic materialism. The movement of energy is from divine to human and thus belongs to a condition requiring an increase in conscious autonomy.

4. *Man sacrifices man.* This fourth type of sacrifice is a hypothetical ideal and has only begun to emerge as a possibility to human understanding. It refers to a sacrifice of the ego by the ego for the double purpose of the ego's own development and the fulfillment of its transpersonal destiny. Since man is both agent and patient it is a conscious procedure, not motivated by unconscious archetypal compulsion, but rather by conscious cooperation with the urge to individuation. It reenacts on the conscious human level what is prefigured on the divine, archetypal level in the sacrifice of Christ by himself. According to Chrysostom, Christ was the first to eat his own flesh and drink his own blood.[25] This action then becomes a model for the ego which has reached a sufficient level of consciousness to understand its meaning. Jung describes this meaning as follows:

> If the projected conflict is to be healed, it must return into the psyche of the individual, where it had its unconscious beginnings. He must celebrate a Last Supper with himself, and eat his own flesh and drink his own blood; which means that he must recognize and accept the other in himself . . . For if you have to endure yourself, how will you be able to rend others also? [26]

The collective effects of self-assimilation are described by Neumann in these words:

> . . . the predigestion of evil which . . . (the individual) carries out as part of the process of assimilating his shadow makes him, at the same time, an agent for the immunization of the collective. An individual's shadow is invariably bound up with the collective shadow of his group, and as he digests his own evil, a fragment of the collective evil is invariably co-digested at the same time.[27]

The same image occurs in the alchemical process of *circulatio* which took place in a pelican or reflux flask. About this Jung says:

> in the age-old image of the uroboros lies the thought of devouring oneself and turning oneself into a circulatory process. . . . This "feed-back" process is at the same time a symbol of immortality. . . . (It) symbolizes the One, who proceeds from the clash of opposites. . . . (These symbols of alchemy were a mystery) whose inner

[25] Jung, C. G., *Mysterium Coniunctonis*, C.W., 14, par. 423.
[26] Ibid., par. 512.
[27] Neumann, Erich *Depth Psychology and a New Ethic*, New York, C. G. Jung Foundation, Putnam's, 1969, p. 130.

kinship with the mystery of faith was sensed by the adepts, so that for them the two were identical.[28]

5. ATTRIBUTES OF THE BLOOD OF CHRIST

The scriptures attribute very definite characteristics to the blood of Christ. We have already noted its cementing, covenant-sealing quality which binds man to God. In addition it cleanses from sin (I John 1:7 RSV and Rev. 1:5 AV), i.e., releases one from unconscious guilt. Also it is said to sanctify (Heb. 13:12 RSV) which, psychologically understood, would suggest the introduction of the sacred or archetypal dimension into personal consciousness. It is called precious (I Peter 1:19) indicating that it carries the highest value. On the Roman Catholic religious calendar July 1 is designated as "The Feast of the Most Precious Blood of our Lord Jesus Christ."

A major attribute of the blood of Christ is its power for the redemption of souls, as evidenced by such passages as:

> In him we have redemption through his blood . . . (Eph. 1:7 RSV).
> . . . his dear Son, In whom we have redemption through his blood, even the forgiveness of sins. (Col. 1:13-14 AV).
> . . . thou was slain, and has redeemed us to God by thy blood . . . (Rev. 5:9 AV).

Popular religious belief has elaborated this theme extensively. For instance, a well-known Catholic missal which includes pictures illustrating certain Christian doctrines, has a most interesting painting representing the redemptive power of the blood of Christ (*Picture 48*).

The upper portion of this picture shows Christ on the cross surrounded by concentric circles of radiating light. On his left is the moon, on his right the sun. An angel holds a chalice which is collecting a stream of blood issuing from his side. The lower part of the picture shows souls tormented in purgatory. An angel is pouring Christ's blood out of a chalice into purgatory. As the blood touches the tortured figures they are released and move out of the flames. Understood psychologically, purgatory is the condition of being identified with the flaming desirousness of concupiscence and the raging wrath which is generated when desire is frustrated. The redeeming blood of Christ can be considered as a consciousness-bringing fluid derived from the Self which conveys a broader viewpoint including the archetypal meaning of existence and which

---

[28] Jung C. G., *Mysterium Coniunctionis*, C.W., 14, par. 512.

Picture 48. CHRIST'S BLOOD SAVING SOULS FROM PURGATORY.

releases the individual from his narrow, personalistic, ego-dimensions. Putting it another way, the picture shows two states of torment, the upper torment of crucifixion and the lower torment of meaningless torture. Both conditions are equally painful but one is voluntary (accepted by consciousness) and hence generates the precious life fluid.

Another important attribute of the blood of Christ is its ability to reconcile and bring peace to warring opposites. Paul says in Colossians:

> . . . through him to reconcile to himself all things, whether on earth or in heaven, making peace by the blood of his cross. (Col. 1:20 RSV).

Again in Ephesians:

> But now in Christ Jesus you who once were far off have been brought near in the blood of Christ. For he is our peace, who has made us both one, and has broken down the dividing wall of hostility, by abolishing in his flesh the law of commandments and ordinances, that he might create in himself one new man in place of the two, so making peace, and might reconcile us both to God in one body through the cross, thereby bringing the hostility to an end. (Eph. 2:13-16 RSV).

Here the aspect of the Self as reconciler of opposites is clearly presented. According to Jung this passage probably influenced the alchemists' conception of *Mercurius* as a peacemaker, a mediator between warring elements and a producer of unity.[29] "Mercurius is conceived as 'spiritual blood' on the analogy of the blood of Christ."[30] Mercurius also corresponds to the Holy Ghost [31] which provides another link between it and the blood of Christ.

The wine of Dionysus shares with the blood of Christ the qualities of reconciliation and communion. The dream of a young minister, which came to my attention, illustrates this point strikingly:

Dream (abbreviated): *I am to celebrate communion. In the sacristy, which looks like a kitchen, the communion wine is to be prepared by mixing two separate wines—a dark blue wine and a red wine. The latter is in a bottle with a yellow label that looks like a Scotch label and is marked "Paul." At a round table, two men*

---

[29] Jung, *Mysterium Coniunctionis*, C.W., 14, par. 10.
[30] Ibid., par. 11.
[31] Ibid., par. 12.

are sitting. One is a political leftist, the other a rightist. Up to now they have maintained a façade of social amenity but now they are becoming hostile to one another. I suggest that they ventilate at the gut level and resolve their feeling relationship. At this point the scene darkens as in a theatre play and a red-yellow spotlight focuses on a small table between and behind the two men. On the table is a bottle of the warm red wine with the Scotch label clearly marked "Paul." Then there is total darkness and the tinkle of glasses, sounding as though they've been clinked and perhaps broken. The sense is obvious in the dream. I think: they've drunk the red wine in their discussion, attained comradeship, became drunk in the process, fallen asleep and dropped their glasses. My response is delight in the aesthetic way this has been portrayed and anxiety about the fact that the service needs to begin and we do not now have the ingredients for the communion wine mixture.

This dream presents the interesting image of two wines—a blue one and a red one—perhaps symbolizing the separate spirits of Logos and of Eros. It shows that the dreamer has achieved a "lesser *coniunctio*," a reconciliation with the shadow, but the "greater *coniunctio*" signified by the full communion service with both wines is not yet ready to take place.

Regressive dissolution and conscious reconciliation of differences are sometimes confused or contaminated with one another. The blood or wine of Christ and Dionysus can cause either. Usually it is experienced as blissful, e.g., the beautiful description by Nietzsche of the Dionysian principle:

Under the charm of the Dionysian not only is the union between man and man reaffirmed, but nature which has become alienated, hostile, or subjugated, celebrates once more her reconciliation with her lost son, man. Freely, earth proffers her gifts, and peacefully the beasts of prey of the rocks and desert approach. The chariot of Dionysus is covered with flowers and garlands; panthers and tigers walk under its yoke. Transform Beethoven's "Hymn to Joy" into a painting; let your imagination conceive the multitudes bowing to the dust, awe-struck—then you will approach the Dionysian. Now the slave is a free man; now all the rigid, hostile barriers that necessity, caprice, or "impudent convention" have fixed between man and man are broken. Now, with the gospel of universal harmony, each one feels himself not only united, reconciled, and fused with his neighbor, but as one with him, as if the veil of *māyā* had been torn aside, and were now merely fluttering in tatters before the mysterious primordial unity.[32]

[32] Nietzsche, Friedrich, "The Birth of Tragedy," in *Basic Writings of Nietzsche*, transl. and edited by Walter Kaufmann, New York, Modern Library, p. 37.

As previously shown, the blood of Christ is synonymous with the Logos. According to the Gospel of John, the Logos is light. "In him was life, and the life was the light of men." (John 1:4 RSV). The blood of Christ as light is presented strikingly in the Gnostic treatise, *Pistis Sophia*. Incidentally, the text also mentions several other related images which we have already considered. Jesus has caused his disciples to ascend with him into heaven and is showing them a vision:

Jesus said to them: "Look up and see what you may see."
And they raised their eyes and saw a great, exceedingly mighty light, which no man in the world can describe.
He said to them anew: "Look away out of the light and see what you may see."
They said: "We see fire, water, wine and blood."
Jesus said unto his disciples: "Amēn, I say to you: I have brought nothing into the world when I came, save this fire, this water, this wine and this blood. I have brought the water and the fire out of the region of the Light of the lights of the Treasury of the Light; and I have brought the wine and the blood out of the region of Barbēlō (the celestial mother or feminine Logos). And after a little while my father sent me the holy spirit in the type of a dove.
"And the fire, the water and the wine are for the purification of all the sins of the world. The blood on the other hand was for a sign unto me because of the human body which I received in the region of Barbēlō, the great power of the invisible god. The breath on the other hand advanceth towards all souls and leadeth them unto the region of the Light."
For this cause I have said unto you: "I am come to cast fire on the earth,—that is: I am come to purify the sins of the whole world with fire."
And for this cause I have said to the Samaritan woman: "If thou knewest of the gift of God, and who it is who saith unto thee: Give me to drink,—thou wouldst ask, and he would give thee living water, and there would be in thee a spring which welleth up for everlasting life."
And for this cause I took also a cup of wine, blessed it and give it unto you and said: "This is the blood of the covenant which will be poured out for you for the forgiveness of your sins."
And for this cause they have also thrust the spear into my side, and there came forth water and blood.
And these are the mysteries of the Light which forgive sins; that is to say, these are the namings and the names of the Light.[33]

[33] Mead, G. R. G., (trans.) *Pistis Sophia*, London, John M. Watkins, 1947. pp. 308 f.

6. RELATIONS TO ALCHEMY

The blood of Christ has many connections with alchemical symbolism. In alchemy, blood is often used to describe the product of
an extraction procedure. For instance one text says: ". . . therefore
pull down the house, destroy the walls, extract therefrom the
purest juice with the blood, and cook . . ."[34] As Jung comments on
this passage: ". . . these instructions are the typical alchemical
procedure for extracting the spirit or soul, and thus for bringing unconscious contents to consciousness."[35] Often mentioned is dragon's
blood or blood of the lion. The dragon and lion are early forms
of Mercurius manifested as passion and concupiscence which must
undergo extraction and transformation. The ancient mythological
parallel is the blood of the Centaur, Nessus, whom Heracles killed
when Nessus attempted to rape Deianeira. This blood was capable
of generating erotic passion and when Deianeira later gave Heracles
a shirt soaked in Nessus' blood in an effort to restore his attraction
to her, it produced a fiery agony that ended only on his funeral
pyre. Thus, like Mercurius who can be either poison or panacea,
the arcane substance symbolized as blood can bring either
passion, wrath and fiery torment or salvation depending on the
attitude and condition of the ego experiencing it.

The symbol of blood links two different operations in the alchemical procedure, *solutio* and *calcinatio*. Water and fluid are parts of
the *solutio* symbol complex. Blood as fluid thus connects with
solutio. However, blood is also associated with heat and fire and
falls into the context of *calcinatio*. Blood as a union of fire and
water is thus a combination of opposites. The double state is alluded
to in Luke 19:34: ". . . one of the soldiers pierced his side with a
spear, and at once there came out blood and water." (RSV). This
is an echo of the water and fire motif in John the Baptist's statement: "I baptize you with water for repentance, but he who is
coming after me is mightier than I . . . he will baptize you with the
Holy Spirit and with fire." (Matt. 3:11 RSV). Water dissolves and
merges separate things in a uniting medium. Fire has different levels
of meaning. It may be the intensity of desirousness, the warmth of
love, or the inspiration of the Holy Spirit. In different contexts it
can refer to either Eros or Logos. The redness of blood connects it
with all the implications of that color and with the foremost red

[34] Jung, C. G., *Mysterium Coniunctionis*, C.W., 14, par. 179.
[35] Ibid., par. 180.

flower, the rose. The poet of the *Rubáiyat* links blood and rose in the lines:

> I sometimes think that never blows so red
> The Rose as where some buried Caesar bled; (Verse XIX)

The term Red Sea was used in alchemy to refer to the tincture or elixir of the Philosopher's Stone. This alludes to the fact that the Church fathers equated the Red Sea with the blood of Christ in which Christians are baptized symbolically. The Red Sea permitted the Israelites to pass through but drowned the Egyptians. Jung notes a Gnostic interpretation of this image as indicating that: "The Red Sea is a water of death for those that are 'unconscious' but for those that are 'conscious' it is a baptismal water of rebirth and transcendence." [36] Thus the effects of immersion in the essence of the Self are liberating or destructive depending on the attitude of the ego. Heracles did not survive his immersion in the Red Sea.

On the other side of the Red Sea the Israelites encountered the wilderness and later the revelations of Yahweh on Sinai. Thus on first encounter with the Self one experiences a certain loneliness and separation from others. Concerning this experience Jung says: "Everyone who becomes conscious of even a fraction of his unconscious gets outside his own time and social stratum into a kind of solitude . . . But only there is it possible to meet the 'god of salvation'. Light is manifest in the darkness, and out of danger the rescue comes." [37]

The blood of Christ parallels very closely the *elixir vitae* or *aqua permanens* of the alchemists which was really a liquid form of the Philosophers' Stone. The texts often state this connection explicitly. From our vantage point we might say that just as the Old Testament "blood of the convenant" was considered by Christians as a prefiguration of the blood of Christ, so the blood of Christ was taken by the alchemists as a prefiguration of the elixir of the Philosophers' Stone.

One text says:

> For as the Philosophers' Stone, which is the Chemical King, has virtue by means of its tincture and its developed perfection to change other imperfect and base metals into pure gold, so our heavenly King and fundamental Corner Stone, Jesus Christ, can alone purify us sinners and imperfect men with His Blessed ruby-coloured Tincture,

[36] Ibid., par. 257.
[37] Ibid., par. 258.

that is to say, His Blood, from all our natural filth and uncleanness, and perfectly heal the malignant disease of our nature . . .[38]

again:

> For, as the Philosophical Stone becomes joined to other metals by means of its tincture and enters into an indissoluble union with them, so Christ, our Head, is in constant vital communion with all His members through the ruby tincture of His Blood, and compacts His whole Body into a perfect spiritual building who after God is created in righteousness and true holiness. Now, that regeneration which is wrought in baptism through the operation of the Holy Spirit is really nothing but an inward spiritual renewal of fallen man, by which we become God's friends, instead of his enemies . . .[39]

Another interesting text of Gerhard Dorn has the following to say:

> (The philosophers) called their stone animate because at the final operations, by virtue of the power of this most noble, fiery mystery, a dark red liquid, like blood sweats out drop by drop from their material and their vessel, and for this reason they have prophesied that in the last days a most pure (genuine) man, through whom the world will be free, will come to earth and will sweat bloody drops of a rosy or red hue, whereby the world will be redeemed from its Fall. In like manner, too, the blood of their stone will free the leprous metals and also men from their diseases . . . and that is the reason why the stone is called animate. For in the blood of this stone is hidden its soul . . . For a like reason they have called it their microcosm, because it contains the similitude of all things of this world, and therefore again they say that it is animate, as Plato calls the macrocosm animate.[40]

The stone that sweats blood is of course a precise parallel to Christ in the garden of Gethsemane: "And being in an agony he prayed more earnestly; and his sweat became like great drops of blood falling down upon the ground." (Luke 22:44 RSV). Psychologically it means that the extraction of the *aqua permanens* inevitably involves psychic pain and conflict. As Jung says: ". . . every psychic advance of man arises from the suffering of the soul . . ." [41] Suffering by itself is of no value. It is only consciously accepted, meaningful suffering which extracts the redeeming fluid. It is the

[38] Waite, A. E., *The Hermetic Museum*, Vol. I, pp. 103 f.

[39] Ibid., pp. 104 f.

[40] Dorn G., "Congeries Paraclesicae Chemicae de transmutatione metallorum" quoted by Jung, C. G., *Alchemical Studies*, C.W., 13, par. 381.

[41] Jung, C. G., *Psychology and Religion: West and East*, C.W., 11, par. 497.

willing endurance of the opposites within onself, the acceptance of one's shadow, rather than indulging in the cheap way out by projecting it onto others, which brings transformation.

Jung gives the following commentary to Dorn's text:

> Since the stone represents the *homo totus,* it is only logical for Dorn to speak of the *"putissimus homo"* (most true man) when discussing the arcane substance and its bloody sweat, for this is what it is all about. *He* is the arcanum, and the stone and its parallel or prefiguration is Christ in the garden of Gethsemane. This "most pure" or "most true" man must be no other than what he is, just as *"argentum putum"* is unalloyed silver; he must be entirely man, a man who knows and possesses everything human and is not adulterated by any influence or admixture from without. This man will appear on earth only "in the last days." He cannot be Christ, for Christ by his blood has already redeemed the world from the consequences of the Fall. . . . On no account is it a question here of a future Christ and *salvator microcosmi,* but rather of the alchemical *servator cosmi* (preserver of the cosmos), representing the still unconscious idea of the whole and complete man, who shall bring about what the sacrificial death of Christ has obviously left unfinished, namely the deliverance of the world from evil. Like Christ he will sweat a redeeming blood, but . . . it is "rose-colored;" not natural or ordinary blood, but symbolic blood, a psychic substance, the manifestation of a certain kind of Eros which unifies the individual as well as the multitude in the sign of the rose and makes them whole . . .[42]

7. MODERN DREAMS

The symbol of the blood of Christ is active in the modern psyche as evidenced by dreams of patients in psychotherapy. For example, the following is a dream of a young housewife whose personal and feminine identity had been very largely submerged by arbitrary and damaging treatment in childhood. She has a considerable creative talent which up to the time of the dream had been completely unrealized. Not long after beginning psychotherapy she had this dream: *A figure, an angel, in a white draped garment on her knee is bent over writing with her right hand on an oval-shaped, sand colored stone which is set in new grass. She is writing with the blood that is contained in a vessel held by a male figure standing on her right side. He holds the vessel with his left hand.*

After the dream, the dreamer painted a picture of it. (*Picture 49*). In the painting the angel has become a large white bird which

[42] Jung, C. G., *Alchemical Studies,* C.W., 13, par. 390.

Picture 49. BIRD WRITING WITH THE BLOOD OF CHRIST, Painting by a patient.

is writing with its bill. The man holding a chalice of blood in his hand is a bearded figure dressed in a robe and is clearly a representation of Christ. The dreamer had essentially no personal associations, saying only that the man reminded her of Christ and the bird of the Holy Ghost.

This dream is obviously of great importance and represents a profound process going on within the dreamer. Concerning the oval slab of stone, a dream occuring about three months later associated to it. In the later dream: *she sees four square concrete slabs with circles on them. They are cracked and broken. A voice says, "These are your erroneous attitudes about femininity which are now destroyed."* Thus the oval stone can be considered a new foundation replacing the old broken slabs, a kind of *tabula rasa* on which her true identity can now be written. That we are witnessing a nuclear process pertaining to the establishment of the central core of her personality is evidenced by the presence of the symbol of the blood of Christ. As previously indicated this symbol belongs to the phenomenology of the Self and its presence indicates that the transpersonal center of individual identity is activated and is pouring an influx of energy and meaning into the conscious personality.

According to the dream picture, Christ provides the blood but the Holy Spirit does the writing. This corresponds very closely to Christ's saying: ". . . it is to your advantage that I go away, for if I do not go away the Paraclete will not come to you." (John 16:7). The going away is the means by which the blood is extracted, leaving individuation energy free to be expressed by the autonomous spirit in its individual manifestation. It is probably significant that this patient had been reared as a Roman Catholic and at the time of the dream was in the process of withdrawing her projection of ultimate authority from the church and its doctrines.

The next dream is that of a young male graduate student. As a child he had been erroneously diagnosed as having heart disease because of a functional heart murmur. This experience caused him considerable anxiety at the time and left him with a phobic reaction to the sight of blood or the prospect of seeing blood. As we explored this symptom, blood was found to represent affect or emotional intensity of all kinds. He was afraid of all reactions that came from his heart. After one particular encounter with his "blood complex" during which he made a special effort to stand his ground and look into his own anxiety rather than run, he had this dream: *I am in the neighborhood of a strange 3-storey house which I begin to explore. I venture down into the basement and there find a fascinating church-sanctuary. Immediately my attention is drawn to a luminous symbol over the altar. It consists of a cross and at the center of the cross a pulsing heart. It holds my attention for some time and seems to carry many hidden meanings. After leaving I decide to return again for another experience of this strange cross. As I enter the sanctuary again, I am startled to find a Catholic sister at the doorway, and the room full of people, all in worship.*
Accompanying the dream he sketched a cross with a superimposed heart (*Picture 50*).

With this dream we have a beautiful example of how a psychic symptom can be resolved when its core of archetypal meaning is penetrated. The dream equates the blood complex (heart) with Christ on the cross. In effect, what this patient is afraid of is the blood of Christ. Put in these religious or archetypal terms the fear of blood loses its irrational nature and hence is no longer a symptom. It becomes rather a reaction to the numinous, a holy, awesome dread of the transpersonal reality of Selfhood. This is not neurosis but rather an awareness of the religious dimension of the psyche. The dream conveys to the dreamer the fact that his affect and emotional intensity is sacred stuff and that, while he may

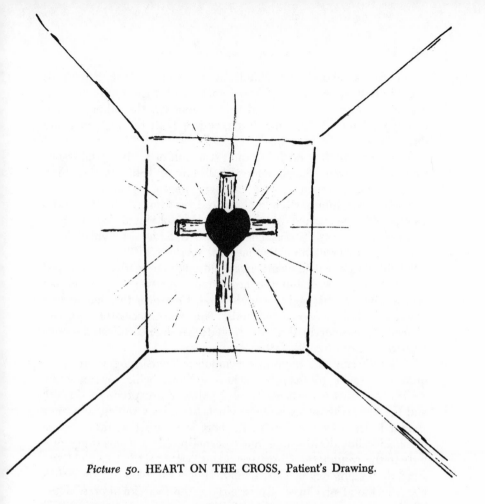

Picture 50. HEART ON THE CROSS, Patient's Drawing.

approach it with fear and trembling, it is in no wise to be despised or rejected as he was previously inclined to do. Or to put it another way, neurotic meaningless suffering has been transformed into conscious, meaningful suffering which is understood as a necessary ingredient of a profound, archetypal life process, i.e., the extraction of the blood of Christ.

The following was the initial dream upon beginning analysis of a man who later became a psychotherapist: *After some difficulty he had caught a golden-colored fish. His task was to extract its blood and heat it until it reached a permanently fluid state. The danger was that the blood might clot during the process. He was in a laboratory boiling the blood of the fish. An older man, a "spokesman for tradition," told him it would never work, the blood was sure to clot. However the heating continued and the dreamer knew it would succeed.*

The fish symbol has a double aspect. On the one hand it is a cold-blooded creature of the depths and thus represents unconscious instinctuality akin to the dragon. On the other hand it is a symbol for Christ. Thus it symbolizes both the redeemer and that which is to be redeemed.

A relevant myth concerning the extraction of a saving substance from a fish is found in the apocryphal book of Tobit. In this story, the hero Tobias was on his way to marry Sarah, a woman who had married seven times. Each time on the wedding night the bridegroom had been killed by a demon who inhabited Sarah's bedroom. On his way Tobias encountered a large fish which leapt out of the water at him. Raphael, his guide, told Tobias to catch this fish and extract its heart, liver and gall. The gall was reserved for another purpose, but the heart and liver were to be burned on the night of his wedding with Sarah to banish the demon that had killed her previous husbands. This was successfully accomplished. Tobias survived his marriage to Sarah and collected money owed him from Sarah's father.

This tale contains important symbolism concerning what is required to relate to the unconscious without being destroyed by it. The *coniunctio* is successful only after the capture of the fish and the extraction of its essence which becomes a saving substance similar to the blood of Christ. In short, it means that the problem of unconscious desirousness must be mastered as a necessary prelude to the *coniunctio*. Christ was identified with the fish (*ichthys*) from the beginnings of Christianity. Hence the blood of the fish is also the blood of Christ. By extension, the fish can represent the whole Christian aeon, the age of Pisces now coming to a close.[43] Hence in its most universal sense, the extraction of the blood of the fish would suggest the extraction of life and meaning from the whole Christian dispensation. A precious psychic essence is being separated from the previous form which had contained it. As the dream indicates, the transition from the old form to the new one is dangerous. The blood might clot. In other words, in the process of separating the religious meaning of life from its containment in traditional Christianity, there is danger that the suprapersonal value may be lost entirely. Or, perhaps, the danger of coagulating into fixed form would suggest that the newly released transpersonal energy might become prematurely bound in narrow and inadequate categories of understanding and action.

[43] Jung, C. G., *Aion*, C.W., 9 ii, par. 127 f.

Examples might be political or sociological partisanships, or perhaps, various petty personal fanaticisms in which the container is too small to hold the magnitude and meaning of the suprapersonal life energy. However, the dream implies that the transformation will be successful.

In summary, the blood of Christ represents the primal power of life itself as manifested on the psychic plane, with profound potentiality for good or ill. As a symbol of the fluid essence of Selfhood and totality it contains and reconciles all opposites. If it comes as a fiery influx of undifferentiated energy it can destroy the petrified or undeveloped ego. On the other hand it is the nourishing, supporting, binding, life-promoting energy which flows from the transpersonal center of the psyche and which maintains, validates and justifies the continuing existence of the personal center of the psyche, the ego. As a combination of water and fire, it is both comforting, calming, protecting and also inspiring, agitating and invigorating. It is the essence beyond time which carries and renders meaningful personal temporal existence. It is the eternal column on which the present moment of conscious existence rests. Whenever a sterile, stagnant, or depressing state of consciousness is released by an influx of meaningful images, feelings or motivational energies it can be said that an archetypal dynamism represented by the blood of Christ has begun to operate. Such experiences confirm the reality of the "power for redemption" which is the essential quality of the blood of Christ.

CHAPTER TEN

The Philosophers' Stone

Understand ye Sons of Wisdom, the Stone declares:
Protect me, and I will protect thee; give me my own,
that I may help thee.

—THE GOLDEN TREATISE OF HERMES *

1. INTRODUCTION AND TEXT

A rich and complex symbol of the Self is found in the alchemist's idea of the Philosophers' Stone—the ultimate goal of the alchemical process. Some may wonder what value the fantasies of the alchemists can have for modern empirical psychology. The answer is that these fantasies express symbolically the deeper layers of the unconscious and provide valuable parallels to help us understand the images that emerge today in the depth analysis of individuals. The very fact that the alchemists were psychologically naive and uncritical permitted the symbolic images to manifest themselves without distortion. Jung puts it this way:

> (In order to understand the full range of a symbol's meaning) the investigation must turn back to those periods in human history when symbol formation still went on unimpeded, that is, when there was still no epistemological criticism of the formation of images, and when, in consequence, facts that in themselves were unknown could be expressed in definite visual form. The period of this kind closest to us is that of medieval natural philosophy. . . . It attained its most significant development in alchemy and Hermetic philosophy.[1]

Jung says at the conclusion of *Mysterium Coniunctionis:*

* Atwood, M. A., *Hermetic Philosophy and Alchemy,* reissued by the Julian Press, New York, 1960. p. 128.
[1] Jung, C. G., *Alchemical Studies,* C.W., 13, par. 253.

Alchemy . . . has performed for me the great and invaluable service of providing material in which my experience could find sufficient room, and has thereby made it possible for me to describe the individuation process at least in its essential aspects.[2]

The goal of the individuation process is to achieve a conscious relation to the Self. The goal of the alchemical procedure was most frequently represented by the Philosophers' Stone. Thus the Philosophers' Stone is a symbol for the Self.

Fragmentary descriptions of the nature and attributes of the Philosophers' Stone are scattered throughout the voluminous alchemical literature. A full study of the phenomenology of this image would require the sizable task of collecting these scattered materials. However, my purpose in this chapter is much more modest, and for this purpose I was fortunate to find in a single text a fairly full and detailed description of the Philosophers' Stone.

The text I shall use is found in the prolegomena to an anthology of English alchemical texts edited by Elias Ashmole and published at London in 1652.

It reads as follows (with spelling modernized):

(1) (The mineral form of the Philosophers' Stone) hath the power of transmuting any imperfect earthy matter into its utmost degree of perfection; that is, to convert the basest of metals into perfect gold and silver; flints into all manner of precious stones; (as rubies, sapphires, emeralds, and diamonds, etc.) and many more experiments of the like nature. But as this is but a part, so it is the least share of that blessing which may be acquired by the Philosophers' Materia, if the full virtues thereof were known. Gold I confess is a delicious object, a goodly light . . . ; but, as to make gold is the chiefest intent of the alchemists, so it was scarce any intent of the ancient philosophers, and the lowest use the adepti made of this Materia.

(2) For they being lovers of wisdom more than worldly wealth, drove at higher and more excellent operations: And certainly he to whom the whole course of nature lies open, rejoiceth not so much that he can make gold and silver, or the devils to become subject to him, as that he sees the heavens open, the angels of God ascending and descending, and that his own name is fairly written in the Book of Life.

[2] Jung, C. G., *Mysterium Coniunctionis*, C.W., 14, par. 792.

(3) Next, to come to the Vegetable, Magical, and Angelical Stones; the which have in them no part of the Mineral Stone . . . for they are marvelously subtle, and each of them differing in operation and nature because fitted and fermented for several effects and purposes. Doubtless Adam (with the Fathers before the flood and since) Abraham, Moses, and Solomon, wrought many wonders by them, yet the utmost of their virtues they never fully understood; nor indeed any but God the Maker of all things in heaven and earth, blessed for evermore.

(4) For, by the Vegetable (Stone) may be perfectly known the nature of man, beasts, fowls, fishes, together with all kinds of trees, plants, flowers, etc. and how to produce and make them grow, flourish and bear fruit; how to increase them in colour and smell, and when and where we please, and all this not only at an instant . . . but daily, monthly, yearly, at any time, at any season; yea, in the depth of winter . . .

(5) Besides the masculine part of which is wrought up to a solar quality, and through its exceeding heat will burn up and destroy any creature, plant, etc., that which is lunar and feminine (if immediately applied) will mitigate it with its extreme cold: and in like manner the lunar quality benumbs and congeals any animal, etc. unless it be presently helped and resolved by that of the Sun; for though they both are made out of one natural substance, yet in working they have contrary qualities: nevertheless there is such a natural assistance between them, that what the one cannot do, the other both can and will perform.

(6) Nor are their inward virtues more than their outward beauties; for the solar part is of so resplendent, transparent lustre, that the eye of man is scarce able to endure it; and if the lunar part be exposed abroad in a dark night, birds will repair to (and circulate about) it, as a fly round a candle, and submit themselves to the captivity of the hand . . .

(7) By the magical or prospective Stone it is possible to discover any person in what part of the world soever, although never so secretly concealed or hid; in chambers, closets, or caverns of the earth: For there it makes a strict inquisition. In a word, it fairly presents to your view even the whole world, wherein to behold, hear, or see your desire. Nay more, it enables man to understand the language of the creatures, as the chirping of birds, lowing of beasts, etc. To convey a spirit into an image, which by observing the influence of heavenly bodies, shall become a true oracle, and

yet this is not any ways necromantical or devilish; but easy, wondrous easy, natural and honest.

(8) Lastly, as touching the angelical Stone, it is so subtle that it can neither be seen, felt, or weighed; but tasted only. The voice of man (which bears some proportions to these subtle properties) comes short in comparison. Nay the air itself is not so penetrable, and yet (oh mysterious wonder!) a Stone, that will lodge in the fire to eternity without being prejudiced. It hath a divine power, celestial and invisible, above the rest and endows the possessor with divine gifts. It affords the apparition of angels, and gives a power of conversing with them, by dreams and revelations; nor does any evil spirit approach the place where it lodgeth. Because it is a quintessence wherein there is no corruptible thing, and where the elements are not corrupt, no devil can stay or abide.

(9) S. Dunston calls it the food of angels, and by others it is termed the heavenly viaticum; the tree of life; and is undoubtedly (next under God) the true . . . giver of years; for by it man's body is preserved from corruption, being thereby enabled to live a long time without food; nay 'tis made a question whether any man can die that uses it. Which I do not so much admire, as to think why the possessors of it should desire to live, that have those manifestations of glory and eternity presented unto their fleshly eyes; but rather desire to be dissolved, and to enjoy the full fruition, than live where they must be content with the bare speculation . . .

(10) That there is a gift of prophecy hid in the red Stone, Racis will tell you; for thereby (saith he) philosophers have foretold things to come, and Petrus Bonus avers that they did prophesy not only generally but specially; having a pre-knowledge of the resurrection, incarnation of Christ, day of judgement, and that the world should be consumed with fire; and thus not otherwise than from the insight of their operations.

(11) In brief, by the true and various use of the Philosophers' Prima Materia (for there are diversities of gifts, but the same spirit) the perfection of liberal sciences are made known, the whole wisdom of nature may be grasped, and (notwithstanding what has been said, I must further add) there are yet hid greater things that these, for we have seen but few of his works.

(12) Howbeit, there are but a few stocks that are fitted to inoculate the grafts of this science on. They are mysteries incommunicable

to any but the adepti, and those that have been devoted even from their cradles to serve and wait at this altar.[3]

Elias Ashmole, the author of this text, was not a practising alchemist. He was a scholar of wide learning with particular interest in alchemy and astrology and had gathered a large collection of books and manuscripts on these subjects. A personal note of interest was his relation to the alchemist William Backhouse. The alchemist adopted Ashmole as his spiritual son. "This was a signal event in Ashmole's life—one which he felt placed him in the long line of true sages."[4] Two years later Backhouse, seemingly on his death bed transmitted further secrets to Ashmole. Ashmole wrote in his diary that Backhouse "told me in syllables the true matter of the Philosophers' Stone, which he bequeathed to me as a legacy."[5]

Ashmole's description of the Philosophers' Stone is undoubtedly a compilation of the qualities of the Stone as described in the numerous alchemical texts with which he was familiar. Ashmole collected these scattered items, compounded them into an organic whole by passing them through his own rich imagination and then gave them expression in his quaintly charming style.

Ashmole describes the Philosophers' Stone as though it were four different Stones which he calls respectively, the Mineral Stone, the Vegetable Stone, the Magical Stone and the Angelical Stone. In our text these four categories divide the power of the Stone into different modes of functioning for purposes of description, but there is a deeper meaning than this. Throughout alchemy, the symbolism of the number four plays an important role. Fourness was considered to be the basic ordering principle of matter. In the beginning of the world, prior to creation, there was only the *prima materia* which was without form, structure or specific content. All was potential, nothing actual. In the act of creation the four elements, earth, air, fire and water were separated out from the *prima materia*. It is as though the cross of the four elements had been imposed on the *prima materia* giving it order and structure and bringing cosmos out of chaos.

[3] Ashmole, Elias (editor) *Theatrum Chemicum Britannicum*, A Reprint of the London Edition 1652, with a new Introduction by Allen G. Debus. Johnson Reprint Corporation, New York and London, 1967.
[4] Ibid., p. XXIX.
[5] Ibid., p. XXIX.

In order to produce the Philosophers' Stone, the four elements must then be reunited in the unity of a quintessence. The original whole and unified state of the *prima materia* is thus restored in the Philosophers' Stone on a new level. These ideas have many parallels in the process of psychological development, particularly four as a symbol of wholeness. The fourfold nature of the Philosophers' Stone immediately relates it to the fourfold mandala images of the Self and indeed we have alchemical pictures of the Stone which are in the form of mandalas (*Picture 51*). In psychological terms we usually consider the number four to refer to the four psychic functions, thinking, feeling, sensation, and intuition. However, this interpretation is by no means adequate to cover the full meaning of fourness. The four elements for instance cannot be equated with the four functions. It seems rather that the structuring pattern of fourness can emerge in a variety of contexts to bring order and differentiation to experience. But always it carries the implications of fulfillment or completion.

Although Ashmole speaks of four different Stones, in the discussion which follows the actions of the different aspects of the Stone shall be considered as deriving from single, unitary Philosophers' Stone.

2. TRANSFORMATION AND REVELATION

The first paragraph of the text begins as follows:

(1) (The mineral form of the Philosophers' Stone) hath the power of transmuting any imperfect perfection; that is, to convert the basest of metals into perfect gold and silver; flints into all manner of precious stones; (as rubies, sapphires, emeralds, and diamonds, etc.) and many more experiments of the like nature. But as this is but a part, so it is the least share of that blessing which may be acquired by the Philosophers' Materia, if the full virtues thereof were known. Gold I confess is a delicious object, a goodly light . . . ; but, as to make gold is the chiefest intent of the alchemists, so it was scarce any intent of the ancient philosophers, and the lowest use the adepti made of this Materia.

According to the alchemical view, metals in the earth went through a gradual, natural process of growth. The base metals such as lead were immature, early forms. Very slowly they would mature and grow into the noble metals, gold and silver. The alchemists thought they could hasten the natural growth process

Picture 51. THE ULTIMATE GOAL AS A MANDALA, Alchemical Drawing.

by the procedures of their art. This idea is an obvious projection onto matter of the fact that natural psychological growth is fostered by paying attention and "working on" psychic content.

Gold and silver were considered "noble" metals because they were incorruptible, they were not subject to rust or corrosion. Thus they carried the qualities of unchanging consistency and eternity. Similarly, the experience of the Self in the individuation process conveys to the ego the characteristics of reliable stability which make it less subject to regressive decomposition. These ego qualities result from increasing awareness of and relationship to the transpersonal or "eternal" dimension of the psyche which is an important aspect of the experience of the Self.

Turning lesser matter into gold can also have a negative aspect, e.g., as presented in the legend of King Midas. He was granted his wish that everything he touched would turn into gold but then was dismayed to find that his food became inedible. This story pictures a condition of identification with the Philosophers' Stone which is inimical to life. Man cannot live by eternal verities alone, he also needs bread, i.e., personal, temporal satisfactions.

The text tells us that the Stone converts flints into precious stones. Precious gems represent values, items which are treasured for their beauty and worth. Flints are dull, ordinary material but quite hard. They would represent the banal, "nitty-gritty" aspects of life. Understood psychologically this capacity of the Stone refers to the ability of the integrated personality to perceive meaning and value in the most ordinary and even disagreeable of happenings. Likewise, inferior, "base" aspects of oneself will be seen to contain value. Since beauty is in the eye of the beholder, it is a change in the perceiving attitude which brings the transformation.

Ashmole feels obliged at this point to inform us that the making of gold and jewels is the least of the Stone's powers. Although we are taking his description symbolically, he is taking it literally. He is like a dreamer describing his dream while still asleep in it, whereas we are trying to understand the meaning of his dream from the standpoint of waking consciousness.

Goldmaking we are told, was not the intent of the ancient philosophers. This statement corresponds to the widely-expressed idea in alchemical works that, "our gold is not the common gold" but is "philosophical gold." What is confusing is that after saying this the authors then proceed to talk about fires, flasks, and chemical procedures in the laboratory. The only explanation is that the alchemists themselves were confused. They were looking for a "philosophical" or spiritual content in a chemical procedure and this was doomed to failure. However, in their failure, the alchemists left us a rich heritage of symbolic material which describes the phenomenology of the individuation process.

Reference to the ancient philosophers brings up the whole question of the meaning of the term Philosophers' Stone. Philosopher means lover of Sophia or Wisdom. A stone is matter in one of its hardest forms and connotes solidity, permanency and stubborn factuality. The Philosophers' Stone thus symbolizes something like concretized or actualized wisdom. In *Aurora Consurgens* [6] wisdom personified as *Sapientia Dei* is specifically equated with the Philosophers' Stone. However, the Stone means more than wisdom meant to the philosophers just as the Stone means more than the figure of Christ means if understood in the usual purely spiritual sense. Jung's comment about the Stone's relation to Christ is relevant here since Christianity took over the one-sided spirituality of Platonic and Stoic philosophy:

> . . . The symbol of the stone, despite the analogy with Christ, contains an element that cannot be reconciled with the purely spiritual assumptions of Christianity. The very concept of the "stone" indicates

[6] von Franz, Marie-Louise (editor) *Aurora Consurgens,* Bollingen Series LXXVII, Princeton University Press, 1966.

the peculiar nature of this symbol. "Stone" is the essence of everything solid and earthly. It represents feminine *matter*, and this
concept intrudes into the sphere of "spirit" and its symbolism . . .
The stone was more than an "incarnation" of God, it was a concretization, a "materialization" that reached down into the darkness of
the inorganic realm or even arose from it, from that part of the Deity
which put itself in opposition to the Creator . . .
We may therefore suppose that in alchemy an attempt was made
at a symbolical *integration of evil* by localizing the divine drama of
redemption in man himself.[7]

Paragraph two continues:

(2) For they being lovers of wisdom more than worldly wealth,
drove at higher and more excellent operations: And certainly he
to whom the whole course of nature lies open, rejoiceth not so
much that he can make gold and silver, or the devils to become
subject to him, as that he sees the heavens open, the angels of
God ascending and descending, and that his own name is fairly
written in the Book of Life.

This paragraph is similar in tone to a passage in *The Hermetic
Museum*:

Neither be anxious to ask whether I actually possess this precious
treasure. Ask rather whether I have seen how the world was created;
whether I am acquainted with the nature of the Egyptian darkness;
what is the cause of the rainbow; what will be the appearance of the
glorified bodies at the general resurrection . . .[8]

In both passages the experience of revelation is considered to be
the important thing.
Our text contains three biblical references. The first is in the
twenty-eighth chapter of Genesis where it is said Jacob dreamed
"that there was a ladder set up on the earth, and the top of it
reached to heaven; and behold, the angels of God were ascending
and descending on it" (RSV).
Jacob's ladder symbolizes the ego-Self axis as discussed earlier
(p. 37) (*Plate 5*). The ascending and descending angels correspond
to the alchemical procedures of *sublimatio* and *coagulatio*.[9] Sub-

[7] Jung, C. G., *Mysterium Coniunctionis*, C.W., 14, par. 643.
[8] Waite, E. A. (Transl.), *The Hermetic Museum*, London, John M. Watkins,
1953, Vol. I. p. 8.
[9] Cf. Jung, C. G., *Psychology and Alchemy*, C.W., 12, par. 65 f.

Plate 5
JACOB'S LADDER by William Blake

limatio, psychologically, is the process of raising concrete, per-
experiences to a higher level, a level of abstract or universal
Coagulatio, in contrast, is the concretization or personal realization
of an archetypal image. For the ascending and descending angels
to be visible would mean that the personal ego-world and the
archetypal psyche are seen as inter-penetrating. Blake expresses
this state in his lines:

> To see a world in a grain of sand
> And a heaven in a wild flower,
> Hold infinity in the palm of your hand
> And eternity in an hour.
> *(Auguries of Innocence)*

Of interest also is the fact that a stone was concerned with
Jacob's dream. He had used a stone as a pillow and after the dream
when he realized that the place ". . . is none other than the house
of God, and this is the gate of heaven," he set up the stone for
a pillar. Jung suggests that Jacob's stone which marks the place
where "upper" and "lower" unite may have been considered as
equivalent to the Philosophers' Stone.[10]

The second biblical reference is found in Luke 10:19-20 where
Jesus says to his seventy messengers: "Behold, I have given you
authority to tread upon serpents and scorpions, and over all the
power of the enemy; and nothing shall hurt you. Nevertheless
do not rejoice in this, that the spirits are subject to you; but
rejoice that your names are written in heaven." (RSV). The third
reference is the term "book of life" which is found in Revelation
20:15, "and if any one's name was not found written in the book
of life, he was thrown into the lake of fire." (RSV).

In Chapter six I have discussed the psychological meaning of
having one's name "written in heaven" or in "the book of life." It
refers to the realization that one's individuality or personal identity
has a transpersonal, *a priori* origin and justification for being.
Such an experience is the definitive solution to an "identity crisis,"
to use a currently popular term. It is also the answer to lesser conditions of alienation, unworthiness and inferiority.

The text tells us that the Philosophers' Stone has a revelatory
capacity. It opens up "the whole course of nature," reveals the
connecting links between the personal and transpersonal (earth
and heaven) dimensions of the psyche, and makes evident that
one's personal ego has a "metaphysical" foundation and hence

[10] Jung, C. G., *Mysterium Coniunctionis,* C.W., 14, par. 568.

an undeniable right to exist in all its uniqueness. These effects correspond closely to the effects of an encounter with a symbol of the Self that may emerge in dream or fantasy in the course of psychotherapy.

For example, a woman with an alienation problem had this dream: *An orphan child was placed at my doorstep at night. It seemed that it had an umbilical cord which reached into heaven. I felt completely fulfilled when I discovered it. I knew my purpose in life.*

The umbilical cord reaching to heaven is an explicit image of the ego-Self axis. The theme of the orphan comes up as a description of the Philosophers' Stone. On the mandala he carved on a stone at Bollingen (*Picture 52*), Jung carved the following words deriving from alchemical quotations concerning the Philosophers' Stone:

> I am an orphan, alone; nevertheless I am found everywhere, I am one, but opposed to myself. I am youth and old man at one and the same time. I have known neither father nor mother, because I have had to be fetched out of the deep like a fish, or fell like a white stone from heaven. In woods and mountains I roam, but I am hidden in the innermost soul of man. I am mortal for every one, yet I am not touched by the cycle of aeons.[11]

The text proceeds:

> (3) Next, to come to the Vegetable, Magical, and Angelical Stones; the which have in them no part of the Mineral Stone . . . for they are marvelously subtle, and each of them differing in operation and nature because fitted and fermented for several effects and purposes. Doubtless Adam (with the Fathers before the flood and since) Abraham, Moses, and Solomon, wrought many wonders by them, yet the utmost of their virtues they never fully understood; nor indeed any but God the Maker of all things in heaven and earth, blessed for evermore.

The chief content of this paragraph is that Adam and other ancient worthies were possessors of the Philosophers' Stone. This is a common assumption in alchemical texts and it was thought, for instance, to account for the longevity that was enjoyed in those early days. In Judeo-Christian myth, the early patriarchs were considered to be almost semi-divine ancestors. They were in immediate contact with the source of being. God spoke to them and

---

[11] Jung, C. G., *Memories, Dreams, Reflections,* edited by Aniela Jaffe, Pantheon Books, New York, 1963, p. 227.

Picture 52. THE BOLLINGEN STONE.

shared his purposes. They are eternal archetypal figures who continue to live in paradise. It is appropriate that they should have possessed the Stone. The psychological parallel is that experiences of the Self are often accompanied by an aura of antiquity. A specific aspect of the phenomenology of the Self is its essentially timeless, eternal and hence ancient quality. It conveys the sense that one is participating in a process of the ages which relativizes the vicissitudes of the here and now.

3. THE FERTILITY PRINCIPLE

The text continues:

> (4) For, by the Vegetable (Stone) may be perfectly known the nature of man, beasts, fowls, fishes, together with all kinds of trees, plants, flowers, etc. and how to produce and make them grow, flourish and bear fruit; how to increase them in colour and smell, and when and where we please, and all this is not only at an instant . . . but daily, monthly, yearly, at any time, at any season; yea, in the depth of winter . . .

The Stone is here described as the growth and fertility principle. This aspect of the Stone corresponds to the saying of Jesus, "I came that they may have life, and have it abundantly." (John 10:10 RSV) An explicit identification of Christ with the fertility principle is found in an apocryphal legend concerning the flight into Egypt. On the way to Egypt, Joseph, Mary and Jesus met a farmer sowing wheat. The infant Jesus picked up a handful of seed and threw it by the wayside. Instantly it grew, ripened and was ready for reaping. As Joseph and his family hid in the tall wheat a group of Herod's soldiers came looking for them. "Have you seen a mother and child?" asked a soldier. "Yes," said the farmer, "I saw her as I was sowing this wheat." "That must have been months ago," said Herod's soldiers and they went away [12] (Picture 53).

Also Osiris embodies the principle of life and fertility. An Egyptian Coffin text says;

> I am the plant of life
> Which comes forth from Osiris,
> Which grows upon the ribs of Osiris,

[12] Gaer, Joseph, The Lore of the New Testament, New York, Grosset and Dunlap, 1966, p. 626.

Picture 53. THE MIRACULOUS GROWTH OF WHEAT, *Très Riche Heures de Jean, duc de Berry.*

> Which allows the people to live,
> Which makes the gods divine,
> Which spiritualizes the spirits, . . .
> Which enlivens the living,
> Which strengthens the limbs of the living.
> I live as corn, the life of the living, . . .
> I am life appearing from Osiris.[13]

In antiquity the fertility principle occasioned a great deal of worship. Sexual symbolism played a large part in these rites since sexuality is obviously the source of life and a means by which the transpersonal purposes of Nature make man their instrument. The womb, the breast and the penis are thus apt symbols for the life principle itself which in the words of our text brings forth all forms of life and knows "how to produce and make them grow, flourish and bear fruit."

[13] Clark, R. T. Rundle, *Myth and Symbol in Ancient Egypt*, New York, Grove Press, 1960, p. 118 f.

Considered psychologically, the growth-promoting qualities of the Stone refer to the fact that the Self is the *fons et origo* of psychic existence. Life, growth and fertility are expressions of libido or psychic energy. This aspect of the Stone is connected with the alchemical symbolism of the *benedicta viriditas*, the blessed greenness, which has links with Aphrodite, the spirit of vegetation and the Holy Ghost. (Cf. p. 213)

The fertility aspect of the Stone appears at times in dreams. For instance a young man who was going through a life transition and was rather too-closely involved with transpersonal energies dreamed that where he walked the grass grew thicker and greener in the path of his footsteps. Another man had the following dream: *I see a man with a phenomenally long penis. He was a young man and yet he seemed to be my grandfather. The penis was like a pipe and put together in sections. In order to get around he took off the sections and carried them in a specially fitted box.*

This figure is immediately identified as an aspect of the Self by the fact that it is paradoxically both young and old, i.e., transcends the category of time. The Philosophers' Stone is frequently described in such paradoxical terms. The huge penis refers to the creative or fertility principle which we are discussing (*Picture 54*). Its size, which goes far beyond human proportions, indicates its archetypal or suprapersonal nature. The fact that it is built in sections and has an artificial or constructed quality is reminiscent of the phallus of the reborn Osiris. Following his dismemberment, the original phallus was the one fragment which could not be found. Isis therefore replaced it with an artificial, wooden one with which Horus was conceived. Conception by a wooden phallus is a strange, non-human happening. It thus alludes to a transpersonal process beyond human or ego understanding. It perhaps points to *psychic* conception by a symbolic image rather than concrete reality.

4. THE UNION OF OPPOSITES

The text proceeds:

(5) Besides the masculine part of it which is wrought up to a solar quality, and through its exceeding heat will burn up and destroy any creature, plant, etc., that which is lunar and feminine (if immediately applied) will mitigate it with its extreme cold: and in like manner the lunar quality benumbs and congeals any animal, etc. unless it be presently helped and resolved by that of

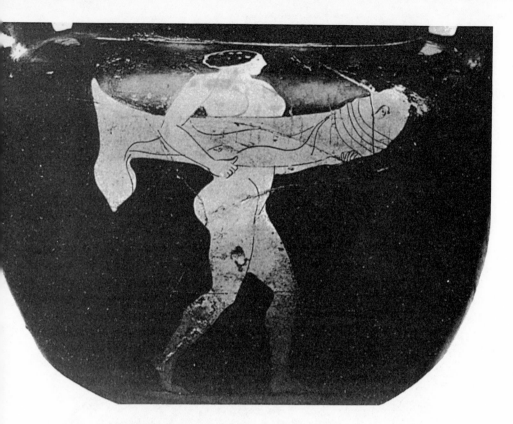

Picture 54. THE REGENERATIVE SYMBOL OF THE HALOA FESTI-
VAL, From a Greek vase.

the Sun; for though they both are made out of one natural substance, yet in working they have contrary qualities: nevertheless
there is such a natural assistance between them, that what the
one cannot do, the other both can and will perform.

We are here informed that the Philosophers' Stone is a union
of two contrary entities, a hot, masculine, solar part and a cold
feminine, lunar part. This corresponds to what Jung has demonstrated so comprehensively, namely, that the Self is experienced
and symbolized as a union of opposites. The Philosophers' Stone
is often described as a *coniunctio* of Sol and Luna. Many alchemical
pictures attempt to depict this paradox (*Pictures 55 and 56*).

The text also describes the negative and dangerous qualities
which each of these parts can have when it operates alone. The
solar part when encountered by itself is destructive because of its
excessive heat and intensity. This is reminiscent of Psyche's second

Picture 55. THE SUN-MOON HERMAPHRODITE.

Picture 56. UNION
OF SUN AND
MOON—SULPHUR
AND MERCURIUS.

task in the myth of Amor and Psyche. Venus had ordered Psyche to get a wisp of wool from a special flock of sheep with golden fleece. A friendly reed growing by the river gave Psyche this advice:

> . . . (do not) at this hour approach those terrible sheep. For they borrow fierce heat from the blazing sun and wild frenzy maddens them, so that with sharp horns and foreheads hard as stone, and some times even with venomous bites, they vent their fury in the destruction of men. But . . . (when) the heat of the noonday sun has assuaged its burning, and the beasts are lulled to sleep by the soft river breeze . . . and, when once the sheep have abated their madness and allayed their anger, go shake the leaves of yonder grove, and thou shalt find the golden wool clinging here and there to crooked twigs.[14]

Neumann comments that "the rending golden rams of the sun symbolize an archetypally overpowering male-spiritual power which the feminine (ego) cannot face." [15] Neumann interprets the whole Amor and Psyche myth from the standpoint of feminine psychology and certainly it is the woman who is most vulnerable to the destructive effects of one-sided solar power. However the problem also applies to men.

The one-sided solar component of the Philosophers' Stone in its destructive aspect is encountered psychologically either internally or externally in projection. Externally it may be experienced as a scorching by the fiery affect of another person. Internally it may be encountered when one becomes identified with and consumed by a fiery anger emerging from the unconscious. In either case there are damaging psychic effects from which it takes time to recover. Moderate or mitigated quantities of solar libido are creative, fructifying and life-promoting, but a one-sided excess is inimical to psychic life.

The text tells us that the lunar part of the Philosophers' Stone when encountered by itself may also be destructive because its extreme cold "benumbs and congeals." The classic example of the benumbing, paralyzing aspect of the negative feminine principle is the myth of the gorgon Medusa. To look at her turns one into stone. The man's ego is the one more vulnerable to this effect. For example I once heard of the case of a young scientist who

[14] Neumann, Erich, *Amor and Psyche*, Bollingen Series LIV, Princeton University Press, p. 43 f.
[15] Ibid., p. 99.

was enthusiastically involved in some important research. One day his mother came to visit him in his laboratory. She looked around and uttered some depreciatory remark concerning the value of what he was doing. That did it! It was enough to destroy the man's relation to his work for several days. His libido had been "benumbed and congealed." He was relieved only when anger at the situation broke through to consciousness, i.e., when the solar component of the Philosophers' Stone resolved the one-sided effect of the lunar component.

The congealing, benumbing effect of the lunar quality is an extreme form of the capacity of the feminine principle to promote *coagulatio*. Images and urges of a spiritual nature which would prefer to soar unfettered by the earth are obliged by the feminine Eros principle to become related to personal, concrete reality. If the ego is too far removed from such reality it will experience the encounter with the feminine as a paralyzing crash to earth.

It can be quite helpful to realize that the damaging effects of the dangerous lunar power and the destructive solar power are, nevertheless, aspects of the Philosophers' Stone. When one is recuperating from the effects of an encounter with either of these potencies, it helps in maintaining one's orientation and perspective to know that what he is suffering from is the Stone itself. Anyone who would seek the Philosophers' Stone is bound, repeatedly, to be a victim of one of its partial aspects. These happenings constitute the alchemical operations which gradually bring about the transformation. But the operations are on ourselves. *We* experience the *calcinatio* of the solar fire or the benumbing *coagulatio* of the lunar power. In the midst of these rigors it is immensely helpful to know that they are part of a larger, meaningful process.

The next paragraph speaks of the positive qualities of the solar and lunar components of the Stone:

(6) Nor are their inward virtues more than their outward beauties; for the solar part is of so resplendent, transparent lustre, that the eye of man is scarce able to endure it; and if the lunar part be exposed abroad in a dark night, birds will repair to (and circulate about) it, as a fly round a candle, and submit themselves to the captivity of the hand . . .

The positive aspect of the solar principle of masculine, spiritual consciousness derives from the fact that it is light-producing. Everything becomes clear, shining and transparent in the intensity of its illumination. The experience of this aspect of the Self may carry considerable numinosity and is generally accompanied by light symbols—brilliant illumination, shining countenances, haloes, etc. William James comments on the frequency of light phenomena, which he calls photisms, in the experience of religious conversion. He quotes the description of such a case as follows:

> All at once the glory of God shone upon and round about me in a manner almost marvelous . . . A light perfectly ineffable shone in my soul, that almost prostrated me on the ground . . . This light seemed like the brightness of the sun in every direction. It was too intense for the eyes . . . I think I knew something then, by actual experience, of that light that prostrated Paul on the way to Damascus (Picture 21). It was surely a light such as I could not have endured long.[16]

In the course of analysis, illuminations of a lesser magnitude sometimes occur and are associated with characteristic dream images. Examples of such images can be found in the dream series published by Jung in Part II of *Psychology and Alchemy*, e.g., 7, 19 and 20 in that series. The experience accompanying these images is an expansion of awareness and increased understanding. It is an encounter with an aspect of the Self and hence very impressive. However, since only one side is constellated the typical symbols of wholeness are not explicitly stated.

The text also speaks of the positive aspects of the lunar part. What the moon means psychologically is very difficult to convey adequately in words. Erich Neumann has made a splendid effort to do so in his paper "On the Moon and Matriarchal Consciousness" [17] which I warmly recommend. In this paper he writes:

> It is not under the burning rays of the sun but in the cool reflected light of the moon, when the darkness of consciousness is at the full, that the creative process fulfills itself; the night, not the day, is the time of procreation. It wants darkness and quiet, secrecy, muteness, and hiddenness. Therefore, the moon is lord of life and growth, in opposition to the lethal, devouring sun. The moist nighttime is the time of sleep, but also of healing and recovery . . . It is the regenerat ing power of the unconscious that in nocturnal darkness or by the light of the moon performs its task, a *mysterium* in a *mysterium*, from out of itself, out of nature, and with no aid from the head-ego.[18]

---

[16] James, William, *Varieties of Religious Experience*, New York, Modern Library, Random House, p. 246 f.

[17] Neumann, Erich, "On the Moon and Matriarchal Consciousness," *Spring*, Analytical Psychology Club of New York, 1954, p. 83.

[18] Ibid., p. 91.

The text tells us that the lunar part of the Stone will attract birds at night and cause them to accept captivity willingly. Birds as elusive intuitions or spirit-potentials are thus brought into reality by the lunar mode of being which is so well described by Neumann. We also have expressed here the theme of the taming of the wild creature. A parallel is the motif of the unicorn who can be tamed only in the lap of a virgin (*Picture 57*). In alchemy, the unicorn symbolized Mercurius, the elusive spirit difficult to grasp and contain. In one text the unicorn turns into a white dove, another symbol for Mercurius and also for the Holy

Picture 57. VIRGIN TAMING A UNICORN,
Alchemical Drawing.

Ghost.[19] Thus the virgin who can tame the unicorn will be synonymous with the lunar portion of the Stone which brings birds willingly into captivity. These images refer to a certain attitude engendered by the lunar or Yin aspect of the Self which brings wild, free but undisciplined urges into relation to reality and into submission to the transpersonal totality of the personality. It is the taming of wild willfulness which thinks it is sufficient unto itself. An actual woman may serve this function for a man. She must be virginal in the symbolic sense described by Esther Harding [20], i.e., one who belongs to herself and functions as an independent feminine being uncontaminated by masculine attitudes.

In alchemy the unicorn in the lap of the virgin was clearly associated with the dead Christ in the lap of Mary.[21] This brings the whole idea of the incarnation of the Logos into this symbolism. Incarnation is an aspect of *coagulatio*. The alchemists were concerned with how to coagulate, capture or fix the elusive mercurial spirit. One way represented pictorially was to transfix the mercurial serpent to a tree or nail it to a cross just as was done to Christ (*Picture 58*). Tree and cross are feminine symbols and hence equate with the virgin's lap and the lunar aspect of the Stone. These images defy facile explanation but they surely have to do with the *realization* of the psyche as a concrete entity which is brought into effective, particularized existence by the lunar aspect of the Stone.

5. UBIQUITY

Paragraph seven continues:

(7) By the magical or prospective Stone it is possible to discover any person in what part of the world soever, although never so secretly concealed or hid; in chambers, closets, or caverns of the earth: For there it makes a strict inquisition. In a word, it fairly presents to your view even the whole world, wherein to behold, hear, or see your desire. Nay more, it enables man to understand the language of the creatures, as the chirping of birds, lowing of

[19] Jung, C. G., *Psychology and Alchemy*, C.W., 12, par. 518.
[20] Harding, M. Esther, *Woman's Mysteries*, New York, C. G. Jung Foundation, 1971, p. 103 f.
[21] Jung, C. G., *Psychology and Alchemy*, C.W., 12, par. 519.

Picture 58. THE CRUCIFIED SERPENT,
Alchemical Drawing.

beasts, etc. To convey a spirit into an image, which by observing
the influence of heavenly bodies, shall become a true oracle, and
yet this is not any ways necromantical or devilish; but easy, won-
derous easy, natural and honest.

Nothing can be concealed from the Stone, all is open to its
view. It is ubiquitous (*Picture 59*). The Stone is thus equivalent
to the all-seeing eye of God. In the fourth and fifth visions of
Zechariah there is an interesting parallel to our text. In the fourth
vision Zechariah sees a stone with seven eyes upon it (Zechariah
3:9). In the fifth vision he sees a golden lampstand on which

Picture 59. UBIQUITY OF THE STONE,
Alchemical Drawing.

are seven lamps. An angel tells him: "These seven are the eyes of Yahweh; they cover the whole world." (Zechariah 4:10 Jerusalem Bible). Jung states that certain alchemists interpreted these passages to refer to the Philosophers' Stone.[22] The seven eyes of God would correspond to the seven planetary spheres and in alchemy to the seven metals. They are the seven steps on the ladder of transformation.

The eye of God was a prominent image in ancient Egyptian religion. A coffin text says: "I am the all-seeing eye of Horus, whose appearance strikes terror, Lady of Slaughter, Mighty one of frightfulness." [23] This passage reflects the usual attitude of the ego upon encountering the experience of the eye of God. It is an anxious attitude in which one is afraid that his sins of unconsciousness will be found out and judged. Since nothing can be hidden from the Philosophers' Stone, the Stone will be felt as a dangerous threat by any one who is trying to evade full self-awareness.[24] The Stone can see all because it symbolizes the complete, integrated personality which will have no hidden, split-off aspects. For the same reason it permits the understanding of the birds and beasts, which represent man's intuitive and instinctive wisdom. The image of the eye of God suggests a unified source of consciousness (vision) within the unconscious. It perhaps also alludes to the phenomena of synchronicity. The eye as a circle is sometimes a feature of mandalas, e.g., Jung's Bollingen Stone is in the form of an eye with a *pupillus* figure (Telesphorus) within the pupil (*Picture 52*). The eye of God is a pictorial expression of the statement, *Vocatus atque non vocatus Deus aderit* (*Picture 60*).

Finally this paragraph tells us that the Stone can "convey a spirit into an image, which by observing the influence of heavenly bodies, shall become a true oracle." To convey a spirit into an image must refer psychologically to the capacity of the unconscious to express a vague undifferentiated mood or affect in some specific fantasy image. This happening is what we seek in the process of active imagination. To bring an emerging unconscious content

---

[22] Jung, C. G., *Psychology and Alchemy*, C.W., 12, par. 518.

[23] Clark, *Myth and Symbol*, p. 221.

[24] "Divine Wisdom . . . is the union wherein God eternally sees Himself, He being that union Himself. In the Love, the Light of God, that mirror is called the Wisdom of God; but in the Wrath it is called the all-seeing Eye." Boehme, Jacob, in *Personal Christianity, the Doctrines of Jacob Boehme*, edited by Franz Hartmann, New York, Frederich Unger Publishing Co., p. 48.

Picture 60. THE EYE OF GOD, 16th Century Woodcut.

into consciousness, the immaterial must be clothed in matter, the disembodied, or better the not-yet-embodied, must undergo incarnation; a spirit must be caught in some discernible form in order to become a content of consciousness. This is one aspect of the alchemical operation of *coagulatio.* Dreams perform this function as do active imagination and other forms of imaginative creative expression. Our text says it is the Philosophers' Stone which performs the transformation of spirit into image. This corresponds to the old statement that dreams come from God. In other words, the image-making power of the psyche derives from its transpersonal center, the Self, and is not a function of the ego.

C. A. Meier has reported a modern dream which is an exact parallel to our text. The dream reads as follows:

> I am lying on a couch; on my right, near my head, there is a precious stone, perhaps set in a ring, which has the power to make every image that I want to see visible in a living form . . .

Meier associates the couch to the *cline* or bed on which the patient slept when he visited the ancient shrines of Asclepius in the hope of receiving a healing dream. He speaks of the precious stone as a symbol of the Self and says that it "also fulfills the function of the crystal ball in prophecy, that is, it serves as a 'yantra' (charm) for the visualization of unconscious contents." [25]

[25] Meier, C. A. *Ancient Incubation and Modern Psychotherapy,* Evanston, Northwestern University Press, 1967, p. 56.

Our text adds that the image, when it is related to the influence of the heavenly bodies, becomes an oracle. The heavenly bodies, as planetary factors, would refer to the transpersonal forces, the archetypes of the collective unconscious. The idea seems to be that when one experiences the image-making power of the unconscious in context with an understanding of the archetypal dimension of the psyche he is given access to an oracular, i.e., a broader, ego-transcending wisdom.

Paragraph eight continues:

> (8) Lastly, as touching the angelical Stone, it is so subtle that it can neither be seen, felt, or weighed; but tasted only. The voice of man (which bears some proportions to these subtle properties) comes short in comparison. Nay the air itself is not so penetrable, and yet (oh mysterious wonder!) a Stone, that will lodge in the fire to eternity without being prejudiced. It hath a divine power, celestial and invisible, above the rest and endows the possessor with divine gifts. It affords the apparition of angels, and gives a power of conversing with them, by dreams and revelations; nor does any evil spirit approach the place where it lodgeth. Because it is a quintessence wherein there is no corruptible thing, and where the elements are not corrupt, no devil can stay or abide.

Here again we are presented with the paradoxical nature of the Stone. It is so invisible, diffused and rarefied that we have no way of perceiving it but by taste. On the other hand it is a stone, so solid and unchangeable that eternal fire cannot weaken or crumble it. This is the theme of the stone which is not a stone which goes all the way back to Greek alchemy.[26] Ruland says, "The Stone which is not a stone is a substance which is petrine as regards its efficacy and virtue but not as regards its substance."[27]

The Philosophers' Stone is a symbol of the center and totality of the psyche. Hence the paradoxical nature of the stone will correspond to the paradoxical nature of the psyche itself. We speak of the reality of the psyche but how many have the perceptive faculties to "taste" its real presence. If that oft-referred-to "man in the street" were to read this chapter, would he think that I was talking about anything real? Probably not. The majority of those that term their vocation psychology are not aware of the reality

[26] Berthelot, M. P. E., *Collection des Anciens Alchemistes Grecs*, reprinted by Holland Press, London, 1963, I, III. 1.

[27] Ruland, Martin, *A Lexicon of Alchemy*, transl. by A. E. Waite, London, John M. Watkins, 1964, p. 189.

of the psyche. It is considered to be behavior, conditione
rological reflexes or cell chemistry, but the psyche itself is
In the words of our text "it can neither be seen, felt, or v
For those who can perceive reality only in those terms, the ps,
will not exist. Only those who have been forced by their own
development or their own psychogenic symptoms to experience
the reality of the psyche know indeed that although it is intangible
yet it is "petrine as regards its efficacy." The fullest realization
of this fact comes as the fruit of the individuation process.

The text further tells us that the Stone "affords the apparition
of angels, and gives a power of conversing with them, by dreams
and revelations." This is an elaboration of the image-making capacity previously mentioned. To be in contact with the Self brings
awareness of transpersonal meanings, here symbolized as converse with angels.

The paragraph concludes with the statement that no evil spirit
can approach the Stone, "Because it is the quintessence wherein
there is no corruptible thing." Psychologically speaking, an evil
spirit or demon is a split-off complex with an autonomous dynamism
which can possess the ego. Its existence is perpetuated by a re-
pressive ego-attitude which will not accept the split-off content
and integrate it into the personality as a whole. Awareness of the
Self and the requirement of the total personality eliminate the
conditions under which autonomous complexes can survive. The
quintessence is the fifth unified substance that results from the
union of the four elements. It corresponds to the unified personality
which gives equal consideration to all four functions. A single function operating arbitrarily without the modification and correction
of the other functions is devilish. As Jung puts it: "Mephistopheles
is the diabolical aspect of every psychic function that has broken
loose from the hierarchy of the total psyche and now enjoys independence and absolute power." [28] As did Christ, the Stone casts out
devils, i.e., partial aspects of the personality which try to usurp
the authority of the whole.

6. SPIRITUAL FOOD AND THE TREE OF LIFE

Our text continues:

> (9) S. Dunston calls it the food of angels, and by others it is termed
> the heavenly viaticum; the tree of life; and is undoubtedly (next
> under God) the true . . . giver of years; for by it man's body is

[28] Jung, C. G., *Psychology and Alchemy*, C.W., 12, par. 88.

preserved from corruption, being thereby enabled to live a long
time without food: nay 'tis made a question whether any man can
die that uses it. Which I do not so much admire, as to think why
the possessors of it should desire to live, that have those manifestations of glory and eternity presented unto their fleshly eyes; but
rather desire to be dissolved, and to enjoy the full fruition, than
live where they must be content with the bare speculation . . .

This paragraph presents several ideas which require elaboration.
The stone is called "the food of angels." Ordinarily one doesn't
think of angels as requiring food. However, perhaps their condition is analogous to that of the dead spirits in the underworld
as found by Odysseus. In order to bring forth the spirits he was
obliged to sacrifice two sheep and pour out their blood which
would attract the spirits who are hungry for blood.[29] This is
an interesting image which expresses how libido must be poured
into the unconscious in order to activate it. Evidently something
similar happens with angels, they need the food of the Philosophers' Stone in order to manifest themselves to man. Food is a
symbol of *coagulatio*. Thus the idea might be that the eternal,
angelic realm is concretized or brought into temporal existence
via awareness of the Self.

The term "food of angels" also has a scriptural reference. Referring to the manna from heaven sent to the Israelites in the
desert, Wisdom 16:20 says, "You gave the food of angels, from
heaven untiringly sending them bread already prepared, containing every delight, satisfying every taste." (Jerusalem Bible). "The
food of angels" is here equivalent to "Bread from Heaven" and
in the sixth chapter of John this term is applied to Jesus who
says: "I am the Bread of Life; he who comes to me shall not
hunger, and he who comes to me shall never thirst." (John 6:35
RSV). The Catholic liturgy uses these texts as references to the
Eucharist which leads us into the next characterization of the stone.

The stone is also called "the heavenly viaticum." The viaticum
is the Eucharist administered by a priest to a dying man. The
word originally referred to money or necessaries for a journey.
It derives from *via*, road or way. The journey a dying man takes
is out of this world into heaven. The same note of death is struck
later in the paragraph when Ashmole wonders why anyone with
the Philosophers' Stone should want to stay alive. Thus the stone
promotes a kind of death to the world, i.e., a withdrawal of
projections.

[29] Homer, *Odyssey*, Book XI.

Picture 61. THE ALCHEMICAL TREE.

To call the Stone viaticum means that it has been equated
with the body of Christ as prepared by transubstantiation in the
mystery of the Mass. Melchior, an early Sixteenth Century alchemist, made the comparison explicit. He described the alchemical
process in the form of the Mass, with the alchemist in the role of the
officiating priest.[30] In addition to Melchior, Jung has presented
many other examples of the alchemists' tendency to equate the
Stone with Christ.[31] Here we see an early effort of the individuation
principle, based on the primacy of subjective experience, to take
over and assimilate the central value of the prevailing collective

[30] Jung, C. G., *Psychology and Alchemy*, C.W., 12, par. 480.
[31] Ibid., par. 447 ff.

religious tradition. A similar situation exists today between analytical psychology and religion. For those who no longer find
traditional religious forms meaningful, analytical psychology offers
a new context in which to understand the transpersonal symbols,
a context which is appropriate to the most developed aspects of
modern consciousness.

The Stone is also called "the tree of life." This refers to the
second tree in the Garden of Eden. After Adam had eaten from
the tree of the knowledge of good and evil he was expelled from
the Garden "lest he put forth his hand and take also of the tree of
life, and eat, and live forever." (Gen. 3:22 RSV). The tree was
henceforth guarded by the cherubim and a flaming sword which
turned every way. The Stone will thus correspond to something
that man was once close to, but having come to consciousness
(awareness of opposites, the knowledge of good and evil) he has
been separated from it. The individual's relation to the Self evolves
in this fashion. As discussed in Part I, originally the nascent ego
is contained in the state of unconscious Selfhood, the primordial
condition of totality which Neumann has called the uroborus. With
the emergence of ego consciousness comes painful separation from
unconscious wholeness and the immediate relation to life symbolized by the tree of life. The ultimate goal of psychic development then becomes the recovery of the lost state of original wholeness, this time on the level of conscious realization.

The Philosophers' Stone was not uncommonly described as a
transcendent tree (*Picture 61*). Thus it relates to the well-known
symbolism of the World Tree or the Cosmic Tree. Just as Christ
was the second Adam, so his cross was thought of as the second

tree, the tree of life (*Picture 62*). An alchemist describes the Philosophers' Stone in these words:

> On account of likeness alone, and not substance, the Philosophers
> compare their material to a golden tree with seven branches, thinking
> that it encloses in its seed the seven metals, and that these are
> hidden in it, for which reason they call it a living thing. Again, even
> as natural trees bring forth divers blossoms in their season, so the
> material of the stone causes the most beautiful colours to appear
> when it puts forth its blossoms.[32]

[32] Jung C. G., "The Philosophical Tree," in *Alchemical Studies*, C.W., 13,
par. 380.

Picture 62. CHRIST THE SAVIOUR IN THE TREE OF LIFE.

Strange and impressive trees appear in modern dreams and drawings. Jung gives a number of examples in his essay, *The Philosophical Tree*.[33] A patient in the midst of a major transition (resolution of the transference) dreamed that a huge tree came crashing to the ground and as it fell he heard a high-pitched, unearthly shriek. This dream has an interesting parallel in a text describing the Philosophical Tree as the inverted tree, "The roots of its ores are in the air and the summits in the earth. And when they are torn from their places, a terrible sound is heard and there follows a great fear." [34] The Philosophical Tree could undergo death and rebirth much like the Phoenix. This dream could thus suggest that the whole personality was undergoing a developmental transformation.

7. THE ONE IN THE ALL

The text continues:

> (10) That there is a gift of prophecy hid in the red Stone, Racis will tell you; for thereby (saith he) philosophers have foretold things to come, and Petrus Bonus avers that they did prophesy not only generally but specially; having a pre-knowledge of the resurrection, incarnation of Christ, day of judgement, and that the world should be consumed with fire; and thus not otherwise than from the insight of their operations.

The Stone's capacity for prophecy means that it is connected with a transconscious reality which is beyond the categories of space and time. This corresponds to the phenomenon described by Jung which he calls synchronicity. One of the ways that it may occur is by a meaningful coincidence between a dream or other psychic experience and some future event. Jung gives a number of examples in his essay on synchronicity.[35] Such experiences are most likely to occur when the archetypal level of the psyche has been activated and they have a numinous impact on the experiencer. The text specially mentions pre-knowledge of the resurrection, incarnation of Christ, day of judgment, etc. These are definitely transpersonal, even cosmic happenings. The implication would seem to be that the Stone transmits knowledge of a

[33] Ibid., par. 304 ff.
[34] Ibid., par. 410.
[35] Jung, C. G., *The Structure and Dynamics of the Psyche*, C.W., 8, par. 816 ff.

suprapersonal structure or ordering of things which is inherent in the universe itself, quite outside the structuring principles of ego consciousness, namely, space, time and causality.

Jung speaks of this transpersonal ordering principle as self-subsistent meaning and reports several dreams which apparently allude to it. One of them is as follows:

> *The dreamer was in a wild mountain region where he found con-tiguous layers of Triassic rock. He loosened the slabs and discovered to his boundless astonishment that they had human heads on them in low relief.*[36]

The term triassic refers to a geological period about 200 million years ago long before man had evolved. Thus in the dream the advent of man was prophesied, so to speak. In other words man's existence was predetermined or inherent in the inorganic substrate of the world.

A patient once brought me a similar dream: *The dreamer was exploring a sea cave examining various attractive stones polished by the tides. To his great surprise he came upon a perfectly formed figure of the Buddha which he knew had been created solely by the natural forces of the sea.* Such dreams suggest that pre-determined order, meaning and consciousness itself are built into the universe. Once this idea is grasped, the phenomenon of syn-chronicity is no longer astonishing. Surely it is not without sig-nificance that in both of these dreams the human form has been imprinted by nature on a stone. In fact I would consider both dreams to be referring specifically to the Philosophers' Stone, the same stone which our text tells us has the power of prophecy.

> (11) In brief, by the true and various use of the Philosophers' Prima Materia (for there are diversities of gifts, but the same spirit) the perfection of liberal sciences are made known, the whole wisdom of nature may be grasped, and (notwithstanding what has been said, I must further add) there are yet hid greater things than these, for we have seen but few of his works.

For the first time the text uses the term *prima materia* as synony-mous with the Philosophers' Stone, and this is done in a passage which emphasizes the various and diverse aspects of the Stone. On the first view it would seem that the end is being confused with the beginning. The *prima materia* is the original first matter which must be subjected to lengthy procedures in order finally

[36] Ibid. par. 945.

to transform it into the Philosophers' Stone, the goal of the opus. But such ambiguities are characteristic of alchemical thought just as they are characteristic of the symbolism of the unconscious.

Descriptions of the *prima materia* emphasize its ubiquity and multiplicity. It is said to have "as many names as there are things" and indeed Jung in his seminar on Alchemy mentions 106 names for the *prima materia* without beginning to exhaust the list. In spite of its diverse manifestations the sources also insist that it is essentially a unity. Our text makes the same point: "there are diversities of gifts, but the same spirit." Thus the Philosophers' Stone, the end of the process, has the same multiplicity in unity as does the original stuff at the beginning. The difference is that it is now a Stone, i.e., concrete, indestructible reality. It is perhaps significant that the beginning of the alchemical process is referred to in this penultimate paragraph of the description of the goal. It suggests that a cycle is completed, the end is a new beginning in the eternal *circulatio,* and that the Stone, like Christ, is both Alpha and Omega.

In psychological terms the theme of unity and multiplicity involves the problem of integrating the conflicting fragments of one's own personality. This is the essence of the psychotherapeutic process. The goal of this process is to experience oneself as *one;* but also, the impetus to make the effort seems to derive from the unity that was there *a priori* all the time. Our text implies that unity once achieved must break into new multiplicity again if life is to go on. In the words of Shelley:

> The one remains, the many change and pass;
> Heaven's light forever shines, earth's shadows fly;
> Life, like a dome of many-coloured glass,
> Stains the white radiance of eternity . . .[37]

Our text concludes:

> (12) Howbeit, there are but a few stocks that are fitted to inoculate the grafts of this science on. They are mysteries incommunicable to any but the adepti, and those that have been devoted even from their cradles to serve and wait at this altar.

This passage confirms an observation which has been gradually forming itself in my mind. It is my impression that those who go farthest in the process of individuation almost always have had

[37] Shelley, P. B., *Adonais,* II 460-463.

some meaningful and indeed, decisive experience of the unconscious in childhood. Jung's childhood experience is an excellent example of this. What often seems to happen is that the inadequacies of the childhood environment or the child's adaptational difficulties, or both, generate a loneliness and dissatisfaction that throw him back on himself. This amounts to an influx of libido into the unconscious which is thereby activated and proceeds to produce symbols and value-images which help consolidate the child's threatened individuality. Often secret places or private activities are involved which the child feels are uniquely his and which strengthen his sense of worth in the face of an apparently hostile environment. Such experiences, although not consciously understood or even misunderstood and considered abnormal, leave a sense that one's personal identity has a transpersonal source of support. They thus may sow the seeds of gratitude and devotion to the source of one's being which emerge in full consciousness only much later in life.

The text says this science can be taught only to a few. The knowledge of the archetypal psyche is indeed available only to a few. It derives from inner subjective experiences which are scarcely communicable. However, the reality of the psyche is beginning to find witnesses for itself. The Philosophers' Stone is a symbol for that reality. There is a healing power in the images that cluster around this symbol. It is a potent expression of the source and totality of individual being. Whenever it appears in the process of psychotherapy it has a constructive and integrating effect. It is truly a pearl of great price.

This symbol developed over a period of fifteen centuries. It was enriched through the efforts of countless devoted men who were gripped by its numen. They worked largely alone, as individuals, without the supporting containment of an institution. They encountered dangers both from without and from within. On the one hand there were greedy princes and heresy hunters, on the other hand were the dangers of solitude and the activation of the unconscious which it brings. This history itself testifies to the power of the *Lapis Philosophorum*, a power capable of enlisting the energies of so many talented men into its service. It is a grand symbol which has at last come within the reach of modern understanding.

Picture 63. THE END OF THE WORK.

INDEX

A

Abednego, 116
Abel, 43ff
Abraham, 44
acceptance, 40
active imagination, 78f, 84, 285
Adam and Eve, 16ff, 21ff, 43, 79, 207
Adam and Eve, Expulsion of, *illus.*, 19
Adam's rib, 16
Adler, Alfred, 36, 171
Adler, Gerhard, 118, 185, 187f, 191
affinity, 38
Agnus Dei, 234
Ahab complex, 234
Aidos, 31
alchemical drawing, 75, 215, 217, 266, 280, 282, 283
alchemy, 102f, 251ff
alcoholism, 56
Alice's Adventures in Wonderland, 175
alienation, 7, 12, 42ff, 62; figure of, 43; from God, 64; individual and collective, 48; neurosis, 56, 58; symptoms of, 107
alter ego, 159
altriusm, 15
Amasis, 32
Amor, 32
Amor and Psyche, 277
amplification, 100, 114
amputation, 145f, 214ff
analogy, 114
anamnesis, 39
anger, 14
anima, 15, 38, 100
Anima Mundi, 213
Anima Mundi, illus., II
animistic beliefs, 111
animus, 15, 38
Annunciation, The, illus., 72, 123
Anselm, 55
Anthropos, 173, 207f
anxiety, 56
aphar, 206
Aphrodite, 274
a priori existence of ego, 157
aqua permanens, 239
Aquinas, Thomas, 218
archetypal figures, eternal, 272
archetypal images, 64
archetypal psyche, 3, 11, 130, 138, 146
Arjuna, 210
Arnold, Matthew, 68
arrogance, 11
ashes, 206
Ashmole, Elias, 261, 264, 267, 288

Attis, 209
Atum, 127
Augustine, Saint, 34, 60, 163, 173f
Aurora Consurgens, 218, 220
authority, 25; figure, 29
autonomy, 244
autos-da-fe, 237
avarice, 63
avidya, 34
axis, ego-Self, *see* ego-Self axis
Aztec Sun God feeding on human blood, *illus.*, 241

B

Bacchae, 236
Baptism of Christ, *illus.*, 147
Baynes, H. G., 13, 182
beatitudes, 34, 136ff
beginning, return to the, 205
benedicta viriditas, 213f
Berthelot, M. P. E., 204, 286
Bernini, 70
Bhagavadgita, The, 210
"Bird in Space," 221; *illus.*, 222
Bird writing with Christ's blood, *illus.*, 255
birds, 284
birth of consciousness, 18; *illus.*, 222
black, 23
Black Elf, 211f
Blake, William, 79, 85
blood as glue, 229; as milk, 232; as nourishment, 231f; of the pascal lamb, 233f; as semen, 233; symbolism, 229
blood of Abel, 228
Blood of Christ, 225ff; *aqua permanens*, 252; attributes of the, 246; *calcinatio* and *solutio*, 251; *elixir vitae*, 252; image of, 226f, 233f; mythological parallels, 251; process of sacrifice, 243; in modern psyche, 254; redemptive power of, 246, 248
blood of the communion meal, 230f
"blood of the covenant," 229f
blue, 248f
Bradley, F. H., 15f, 169
Brancusi, 221
Brand, Dr. Renée, 154
bread, 206
Bread of Life, 288
breast, 273
Breughel, 27
Buddhism, Tibetan, 182
Budge, E. A. Wallis, 213
Bunyan, John, 52ff
Burnet, John, 3

C

Cain, 43ff
calcinatio, 206, 251, 278
Calypso, 115
Cannon, W. B., 61
capitalism, 68
Carlyle, Thomas, 62
Carpocrates, 136
Castor, 166
categories of existence, suprapersonal, 60
chalice, 235, 240, 246
Chalice of Antioch, *illus.*, 236
chance, 101
chaos, 4
child, 143f
childhood, 5, 11; alienating, 98
Christ, 13, 23, 102, 112, 122, 131, 133, 138,
    149, 150, 155, 183, 187, 253ff; as Alpha
    and Omega, 294; as God and man, 241;
    imitation of, 134; as Paradigm of the
    Individuating Ego, 131ff; priest and
    victim, 242; self and ego, 241
Christ as cluster of grapes, *illus.*, 237; crushed
    as a grape, *illus.*, 240
Christ in the Garden, *illus., Plate 4*
Christ the Savior in Tree of Life, *illus.*, 291
Christ's blood saving souls from Purgatory,
    illus., 247
Christian myth, 152, 154
Christian tradition, 63
Christopher, Saint, 98
Chrysostom, 245
church, 115, 163
circle, 4ff, 37f, 188ff, 211f, 255, 284; *see*
    mandala
circulatio, 245, 294
Clark, R. T. Rundle, 127, 213, 273, 284
Clement of Alexandria, 232
coagulatio, 268f, 288f
collective unconscious, 3, 100
communism, 65, 68
communion, 230, 231
compensation, 33
concupiscence, 35, 91, 175, 246, 251
concretistic fallacy, 149
confessional, Catholic, 64
conflict, 24, 68; intrapsychic, 137
coniunctio, 239, 258; lesser and greater, 249;
    masculine and feminine, 223; of Sol and
    Luna, 275f
conscious assimilation, 139
consciousness, 7, 25, 84, 145; evolution of,
    116; light of, 129
conscious realization, 103
continuum, 178
Cosmic Tree, 290
cosmogony, 170
cosmos, 101
Creator, 4
crime, 21, 26

cross, 4, 9, 135, 150, 264
crucifixion, 139, 149, 150, 152, 248
Crucifixion, within field of force, *illus.*, 139;
    and dismemberment, *illus.*, 141
cup, 231f; *see* chalice

D

Daedulus, 26
Danae, 70; *illus., Plate 2*
Daniel, Book of, 116
Dante, 46
Dark Night of the Soul, 52, 81, 150
death, 199f, 224
death and rebirth experience, 87
"death flower," *see* Narcissus
deflation, 36
deity, 10
delusions, 13; of psychotics, 111
Demeter-Kore myth, 205
demon, 287
depression, 56, 153, 200
depth psychology, 69, 133, 136
desires, concupiscent, 175
desirousness, 11, 204
despair, 42, 44; suicidal, 82
destiny, transpersonal, 245
Deuteronomy, 228
Deuteros Anthropos (Gk.), 207
devil, 23, 54, 229, 287
dialectic, 7, 187
dialogue, 78
Diamond Sutra, 201
differentiation, 158
Dionysus, 162, 235, 237, 248f
Dioscuri, myth of the, 166
Discobolus, 72
Discus Thrower, The, 72
disgrace, 149
Diskobolos, *illus.*, 74
dismemberment, 139, 141, 176
Dismembered Man, *illus,* 217
dispersal, 174
dissociation, 20
dissolution, 249
Divine Comedy, The, 46
Djed column, 221
dogma, 65
Dominicans, 243
Donne, John, 93
Doresse, Jean, 134, 172
Dorn, G, 253
Dove transmits divine, *illus.*, 124
dragon, 251
dreams, 84ff, 118ff, 125, 174f, 199ff, 248ff;
    compensatory, 89; of flight, 27; Icarus,
    27, 28; metaphysical, 199; numinous,
    84; transition, 21ff
drives, compulsive, 160
duality, 20, 191; *see* two
Dunston, S., 263

dust, 206
dynamism, 65

E

East of Eden, 44
Ecclesiasticus, 93
Eckhart, Meister, 243
Ecstasy of St. Theresa, The, *illus.,* 73
ego, 3, 4f; alienated, 161; birth of the, 129; conscious, 121, 209; development, 153; germ, 6; impotence of the, 216; the individuated, 96; inundation of the, 132; non-inflated, 34; paradigmatic model, 156
ego-Self alienation, 117; permanent, 55
ego-Self axis, 6, 7, 11, 12, 37, 40f, 52, 54, 58f, 69, 125f, 129, 186, 270; restitution of the, 56
ego-Self identify, 40, 102; separation, 5, 6, 36; union, 5f
Eleusian mysteries, 204
Eliade, Mircea, 221
Elihu, 88
Elijah, 49
Elijah being fed by ravens, *illus.,* 50
Eliot, T. S., 47, 64
elixir of life, 4
elixir vitae, 235, 252
Eliphaz, 84
Emerson, Ralph Waldo, 33, 101
emotional deprivation, 59
empathy, 170
emptiness, 136ff
End of Work, *illus.,* 296
energy, constructive, 143; extra-personal, 11; psychic, 274
Energy Law, Central Source of, 60
Enneads, 166, 169
environment, childhood, 295; hostile, 295
envy, 63
Epimetheus, 24
Epiphanius, 173
erection, 72
Erman, Adolf, 209
Eros, 249; principle, 278
Esau, 70
Eucharist, 288
Euripedes, 236
Eve, 16ff, 20ff, 207; Gospel of, 170
Evelyn-White, Hugh G., 8
evil, integration of, 268
evolution of human figures in children's drawings, *illus.,* 9
eye of God, 282ff; *illus.,* 285
existentialism, 48
experience, childhood, 295
exteriorization, 174
Ezekiel, 233

F

fairy tales, 188
faith, 57
"Fall of Icarus," 27; *illus.,* 28
fall of man, 16
fallacy, concretistic, 110ff; reductive, 110ff
fanaticism, 65
fate, 76
field of force, 139
fire, 164, 204, 216
Fire of God, fallen from Heaven, *illus.,* 79
Fire rains from Heaven, *illus.,* 83
fish, 258
Fitzgerald, Edward, 237
five, symbolism of, 219, 287
Flagellation of Christ, *illus.,* 151
flight, 27
folk wisdom, 63
food, spiritual, 287ff
"food of angels," 288
Fordham, Michael, 5, 37
four, 179, 188; elements, 264f; functions, 265; legs, 108
fragmentation, inner, 174
Frazer, James G., 100, 209, 213, 223
Freud, Sigmund, 36, 113
Friars Minor, 243
fruit, 18
frustration, 42, 224

G

Gaer, Joseph, 272
Galileo, 198
Garden of Eden, 16, 18, 21f, 24, 58, 79; as a Circle, *illus., Plate 1*
Genesis, 16, 206
Gethsemane, Garden of, 150, 253
Giant, The Awakening, *illus.,* 203
Ginsberg, G., 20, 214f
gluttony, 63
gnosis, 18, 221
Gnostics, 18, 164f, 171f, 180, 207
goal, symbols of the, 195ff; ultimate, as a mandala, *illus.,* 266
God, 15f, 18, 54f, 57, 70, 78, 85, 101f, 122, 137, 150; God-image, 65, 68; vengeance of, 15; will of, 34
Goethe, 47
gold, philosophical, 267
Golden Bough, The, 100, 212
grape symbolism, 240
grapes of wrath, 237
green, 213f
growth of wheat, miraculous, *illus.,* 273
guilt, 21, 246

H

Hades, 162, 204, 227
Hagar, 44

Hagar and Ishmael in the Desert, *illus.*, 45
hallucinations, 111
happiness, 61
Harding, M. Esther, 183, 281
Harnack, Adolph, 202
heart, 256
heavenly, viaticum, 262
Hebrews, 18
Hegelian formula, 211
Hera, 30, 151
Heracles, 252
Heraclitus, 3
hermaphrodite, 17f
Hermaphrodite, Sun-Moon, *illus.*, 276
Hero, birth of the, 129
Herodotus, 31f, 209
Hesiod, 8, 204
hexagon, 216
Hildegard of Bingen, 213
Hippolytus, 164
Hölderlin, 37
Holy Ghost, 122, 164, 181, 213, 255
homeopathy, 98f
homeostasis, 61
Homer, 204, 288
homoousia-homoiousia conflict, 155
hostility, 134
"hot rodder," 29
humility, 15
hybris, 18, 25f, 31, 65, 152, 226
"Hymn to Demeter," 204
"Hymn of the Pearl, The," 119

I

Icarus, 26f
I Ching, 104
Id, 113
identity, ego-Self, 6, 12f, 15; objective, 3;
    subjective, 3
idolization, 68
illegitimacy, 58f
illness, psychological, 12
imago Dei, 3
impotence, 114, 216
incarnation, 166, 173, 232, 281, 285
individual, 162f; being an, 153ff
Individuation as a Way of Life, 105ff
individuation, 7, 26, 96; crisis, 150; process
    of, 103; process and goal, 193; the quest
    for, 131
infantile-omnipotent assumptions, 36
infantilism, 97
inferiority complex, 56
inflation, 7, 14f, 62; heroic, 30; negative, 15
Ino, 115
intercourse, 72
Isaac, 44
Isaiah, 238
Ishmael, 44
Israelites, 49, 233
ivy, 209
Ixion, 30, 150, 152; Bound to the Wheel,
    illus., 30
Inge, W. R., 184

J

Jacob, 70
Jacob's dream, 269; *illus.*, 71; Jacob's ladder,
    268; *illus.*, *Plate 5* ; Jacob's stone, 269
James, Henry, 14
James, William, 49, 52, 279
Jeremiah, 223
Jerusalem Bible, 238f
Jesus Christ, 55f, 132ff, 138, 142, 146, 149f,
    153, 158f, 172; beatitudes of, 63
Joachim of Floris, 183
Job, 76f, 78f, 81f, 87ff, 91ff, 95f, 115
Job complex, 234
John, Gospel of, 217
John of the Cross, Saint, 49, 81, 150
Jonah, 70, 76, 187
Jonas, Hans, 119, 123, 159, 172
Jung, C. G., 3f, 16, 33, 38, 49, 52, 69, 76f,
    81, 88, 89, 94, 101, 103, 109, 112, 114,
    116, 117, 118, 131f, 135, 142, 145, 152,
    154, 155, 157ff, 160, 163, 174ff, 179ff,
    182, 184f, 188ff, 190ff, 194ff, 204, 211,
    213f, 216, 219, 223, 226, 235, 239f, 245,
    253, 261, 269ff, 279, 281, 284, 287, 289f,
    292ff
justification, 57

K

Kabbalah, 208
karma, collective, 220
Kellog, Rhoda, 8
kenosis, 138
Kheprer, 213
Kierkegaard, 22, 48
King, 144
kingdom of heaven, 145, 207
Kluger, Rivkah Schärf, 91, 93
Koan, 201
Krishna, 210

L

Lao-Tzu, 36, 187
lapis, 160
Lapis Philosophorum, 295
Last Supper, 245
Legge, Francis, 221
libido, 82, 234, 274; investment, joint, 231;
    solar, 277
light symbolism, 129, 200, 250, 279
limbo of despair, 150
lion, 251
lion with paws cut off, *illus.*, 177
lithos ou lithos, 206
liturgy, Catholic, 288
Liverpool, 176
Liverpool mandala, *illus.*, 177
Logos, 207f, 208, 217f, 232, 249;
    feminine personification of, 204
loneliness, 171
Lord's Prayer, The, 94
love, 170
Lucifer, 93

Luna, *see* moon
lunar power, *coagulatio,* 278
lust, 11, 63
Luther, Martin, 56
Lyndus, Joannes, 216

M

magic, primitive, 100
man, ideal, 134
mandala, 4, 6, 9, 17; image, 31, 37f, 129,
    152, 176, 189ff, 265
Manichaaean eschatology, 223
manna, 49, 288
Manna, Israelites gathering, *illus.,* 49
Marduk, shrine of, 127
Mary, 70, 123
Mass, the, 64, 290; ritual, Roman Catholic,
    231f, 288f
Mathers, S. L. MacGregor, 208
Matthew, 145
maturity, 5
May, Dr. Rollo, 57
Maya, doctrine of, 117; veil of, 210
meaning, abstract, 108; subjective, 108
meaninglessness, 107
Mead, G. R. S., 173, 208, 250
Medusa, 277
Meier, C. A., 285
melancholia, 15
Melchior, 289
Melville, Herman, 46
Mercurius, 13, 248, 251, 280
Mercury, 186
Meshach, 116
Messiah, 238, 239; complex, 14
metals, "noble," 266
metanoia, see repentance
metaphysics, empirical, 197; and unconscious,
    197ff,
Michelangelo, 72, 202
microcosm, 158
Midas, King, 266
midlle age, 7
milk, 231ff
mirror, 154f, 159, 162
misery, 61
Mithra, 187, 202
Moby Dick, 266
monachoi, 172
Monad, 163ff, 169f, symbolism, 175
Monadology, 167
Monogenes, 170f
moon, Sun-moon Hermaphrodite, *illus.,* 276;
    Union of Sun and Moon, *illus.,* 276
Mosaic Law, 133
Moses, 70
mourning, 136
multiplicity, 172ff
murder, 44
Murray, Gilbert, 31

mysterium, 94
myth, 16; Christian, 150ff, 243, Judeo-
    Christian, 270; Mithra, 202; and
    religion, 69ff; and ritual, Hebrew, 230
mythology, 3, 65

N

Napoleon, 13
narcissism, 161
Narcissus, 161f
nature, mystical communion with, 11
Nazism, 65
Nebuchadnezzar, 116
Nekyia, 161
Nemesis, 26, 31, 161f
nest symbol, 209
Neihardt, John G., 212
Neumann, Erich, 4, 38, 167, 245, 277, 279
neurosis, 52
New English Bible, The, 136
Nietzsche, F., 27, 69, 249
Nirvana, 117
Nō drama, Japanese, 200f
"noble savage," 11
nostalgia, 7, 11
nous, 171
number symbolism, Pythagorean, 180, 184,
    192
numinosum, 52, 82, 94
numinous encounters, 117

O

"Ode on Intimations of Immortality," 10
Odes of Solomon, 231
Odysseus, 228, 288
Odyssey, 115
Omar Kháyyam, 236
omnipotence, 15
omphalos, 20
"One," the, 165ff; *see* Monad
only-begotten, 171
Ophites, 18
opposites, 274ff; union of, 4
oracle, 286
orgasm, 72
Origen, 145, 155, 173
original man, 8
orphan, 163, 270
Orpheus, 237
orthodox views, 88
orthodoxy, 225
Osiris, 139, 209, 213, 221, 272
Otto, Rudolph, 94f

P

Painting of a Patient, *illus., Plate 3*
Pandora's Box, 24

Paracelsus, 186
Paraclete, 242; synonymous with blood of
    Christ, 243
paradigm of the ego, Christ as, 154
paradoxes, 165
Paramandenda, Swami, 210
paradise, 8, 11
Paradise as a Vessel, *illus.*, 17
parent-child relationships, 39, 88
parental rejection, 39, 55
participation mystique, 65
paschal lamb, 233
passion, 251
Paul, Saint, 55, 76
patient's drawing, *illus.*, 74
penis, 273f,
Penitence of David, The, *illus.*, 57
Pentheus, 237
perfection, 135
permissiveness vs. discipline, 12
Perry, John Weir, 13
Persephone, 202, 204f
Perseus, 70
personality, individuated, 68; non-inflated,
    63; wholeness of, 142; perversion,
    polymorphous, 11
petra genetrix, 202
Peuch, Henri-Charles, 223
Phaeton, 29f; complex, 29
phallic symbol, 221
phallus, 274
Pharaoh, 234
Philip, Gospel of, 173
Philosophers' Stone, 206, 220, 252f, 260ff,
    275; as Alpha and Omega, 294; as eye
    of God, 282ff; as fertility principle, 272;
    as *homo totus,* 254; nature and
    attributes of, 261ff; paradoxical nature
    of, 286; as *prima materia,* 293; in
    prophecy, 292; symbol of Self, 261; as
    tree of life, 290; as viaticum, 289
physical fact, 112
physical phenomena, 112
philosophy, Platonic, 267
philosophy, Stoic, 267
Physis, 204, 208
Pietá, 72
Pieta, *illus.*, 75
piety, 142
pillar, symbolism of, 221
Pinedo, Ramiro de, 238
Pisces, 258
Pistis Sophia, 221, 250
Plato, 8, 162, 165, 170, 180, 204, 236
Pleiades, 90
Plotinus, 166ff
Plutarch, 238
pneuma, 204
polarization of opposites, 20
pole, symbolism of, 221, 223
Pollux, 166

Poimandres, 207
Polycrates, 31f
potency, 114
pragmatism, psychological, 143
pride, 63
prima materia, 102f, 160, 211, 263ff
Primal Man, 207
primitive, 101; image of the 11; symbolical,
    11
projection, 174; animus, 28; phenomena, 120;
    psychological, 133; of the Self, 104
Prometheus, 16, 24
protoplasm, 174, 175
provisional life, 13
psyche, 6, 89, 204; autonomous reality of,
    111; as image maker, 285; individual, 3,
    225; modern, 154; unconscious, 114
Psyche, 277
psychic, energy, 56, 109; facts, 112; health,
    43; identification, 133; life, 158;
    meaning, 101; inner states, 133;
    sustenance, 143; totality, 129; wound, 12
psychic stability, reestablishment shown in
    child's painting, *illus.*, 10
psychological development, 61; oral, anal and
    genital, 183; reorientation, 107
Psychological Types, 158
psychology, analytical, 121, 131;
    behavioristic, 133; child, 5f; Christian,
    55; Freudian, 113; modern, 114
psychopathology, 114
psychosis, 13; overt, 149
psychotherapy, 62, 107; Jungian, 113
psychotic melancholia, 54
Puer Aeternus, 14
purgatory, 246f
pyramid, 127; Mayan, *illus.*, 128
Pythagoreans, 164

Q

quaternity, 179, 182, 189, 191, 193

R

racism, 65
rage, 116
Raphael, 258
Rawlinson, George, 32
reality, archetypal, 11; encounters, 12; of life,
    84; spatio-temporal, 162
Red Sea, 252
redemption, 103
redness, 23, 238, 239, 248f
Regenerative symbol of Haloa Festival,
    illus., 275
religion, 3; collective, 69
reminiscence, theory of, 119f
repentance, 42, 53, 91
repression, 20, 146
Republic, 236

resentment, 96
revelation, 199, 269
"Rhythm of Education, The," 183
"Rite of the Crown," 63
rites, 65
ritual, 63
"Robe of Glory," 159
Ross, Nancy Wilson, 201
roundness, 8f
Rousseau, 11
Ruland, Martin A., 219, 286

S

sacrifice, arrangements of, 244; blood, 228;
    God-God, 244; God-man, 244; man-God,
    244; man-man, 245; psychological
    implications of, 243
sacrificial attitude, 96
St. Anthony and St. Paul being fed by a
    Raven, *illus.*, 53
St. Christopher carrying Christ as Sphere,
    illus., 99
St. Paul, Conversion of, *illus.*, 77
Salt, 186
sanctuaries, Semitic, 223
Sapientia Dei, 218
Sarah, 258
Satan, 78, 91, 93f; *see* devil
Satan tempting Christ within circle,
    illus., 148
Satori, 201
scintilla, 164
scorn, 149
Search for Meaning, The, 107ff
Self, 3, 4, 31, 38, 96, 97; *a priori*, 171;
    awareness of the, 48; encounter with
    the, 62ff, 95
self-acceptance, 40, 146
Self-archetype, 78
self-assimilation, 245
self-criticism, 153
selfhood, transpersonal reality of, 257
self-realization, 153
self-recollection, 174
self-regulation, 61
self-righteousness, 86
semen, 233
separateness, acceptance of, 131
separatio, 134f
Sermon on the Mount, 136
serpent, 15ff, 23, 79, 167; crucified, *illus.*, 282
seven, 193
sexual problems, 210
sexual symbolism, 273
sexuality, 18, 76, 273
shadow, 38f, 85, 87, 91, 142, 200, 235, 240,
    245, 249
Shadrach, 116
shame, 31
Shelley, Percy B., 294

sin, 38f, 55; as inflation, 34
"single ones," 172
six, 216
Skeat, Walter W., 163
sloth, 63
Smith, W. Robertson, 230f
Sol, *see* sun
solar fire, *calcinatio* of, 278
solipsism, 15f
solitaries, 172
Solomon's Seal, 216
Sophia, 102, 204, 218, 221
square, 4, 211f
Splendor Solis, 215
star, 159
Star of Bethlehem, 122
status quo, conscious, 70; psychological, 79
stealing, 21
Stein, L., 130
Steinbeck, John, 44
stone, 206, 223
Stone, Angelical, 263f, 270; Magical, 262,
    264, 270; Mineral, 261, 264, 270;
    Philosophers' (*see* Philosophers' Stone);
    Vegetable, 262, 264, 270, 272
Stone, Bollingen, *illus.*, 271
Stone, Ubiquity of, *illus.*, 283
strife, 186
sublimatio, 268ff
Sullivan, Harry S., 109
sulphur, 186
superstitious, 101
suicide, 44
Sun, the, 3, 176
sun-wheel, 72; varieties of the three-footed,
    illus., 76
super-order, 60
superstitions, 111
Suzuki, D. Y., 201
swamp, primordial, 116
sword, 21
symbiotic relationships, 26
symbol, function of the, 107, 109
"Symbolic Life, The," 117ff
symbolic imagery, 110; life, 109; meaning,
    130
symbolon, 130
symptoms, psychic, 256; psychosomatic, 56;
    as degraded symbols, 50ff
synchronicity, 293

T

taboo, 33; -s, 63
Tao Te Ching, 187
tarot cards, 81
Teilhard de Chardin, Pierre, 105, 158
temptation, 147
Tertullian, 145
tetragrammaton, 208
Thomas, Gospel of, 134, 170

Thompson, Francis, 70
three, 184, 188; (*see* triads, trinity)
"Tibetan world Wheel, The," 189
Tillich, Paul, 198
Tobias, 258
Tolstoy, 49, 51f, 81
torture, 37f
totality, 186, 188; trinitarian, 186;
    unconscious, 162
Tower, The, *illus.*, 82
transference, 59
transpersonal categories, of existence, 64;
    dimension, 64; experience, 64; powers,
    11, 101; psyche, 144; totality, 241
transvestism, 114f; sacerdotal, 115
traumatic childhood, 54
treasure-house, 220
tree, alchemical, *illus.*, 289
tree of life, 17, 263, 287
triadic symbolism, 76
triads, masculine and feminine, 185
Trinity, 179ff
trinity symbolism, 179f, 182, 185ff, 188f, 191,
    193
trinity of matter, 216; of spirit, 216;
    Teutonic, 185
Trismosin, Solomon, 215
twelve, 193, 208f
two, 184

U

unconscious, collective, 3
unconscious existence, a priori, 158
unconscious identification, 103
Unconscious, Metaphysics and the, 197ff
unconsciousness, 25
understanding, 170
unicorn, motif of the, 280
Union of the Sun and Moon-Sulphur and
    Mercurius, *illus.*, 276
uniqueness, 157
unitary reality, 96
unity, 172ff
universality, 157
urges, protoplasmic, 175
uroborus, 4, 7, 167, 184
Uvae Hermetitis, 240

V

Valentinian speculation, 171
values, projected, 143
Varieties of Religious Experience, 50, 52,
    54, 279
Vaughn, Henry, 235
Vaughn, Thomas, 62
vegetation spirit, 209, 212f, 272, 274
Veil of Maya, 210
Venus, 277
verities, eternal, 266
via negativa, 163

viaticum, heavenly, 263
victim, 15
violence, 42, 44
Virgin taming Unicorn, *illus.*, 280
virtue, 142
"Visions," 135
visualization, 285
Von Franz, M.-L., 14, 218, 267

W

Waite, A. E., 186, 208, 225, 253
Waste Land, The, 47
"Water of Life, The," 188
wheel, 31, 35
wheel of life, 34; *illus.*, 35
white, 23, 239
White, V., 180
Whitehead, A. N., 183
wholeness, 13; archetype of, *see* Self
widow, 163
Wilde, Oscar, 33
wilderness, 50, 70
Wilhelm, Richard, 104
will of the ego, 145
Willoughby, Harold R., 63
window, 170, 175f, 178
wine symbolism, 237ff
Wisdom, 93, 218; *see* Sophia
wise men, 129
womb, 273
Wordsworth, William, 10, 122, 159
works, 57
world-ego, 209
world navel, 4, 20; see *omphalos*
World Soul, The, *illus.*, II (frontispiece)
World Wheel, Tibetan, 189
wrath, 63; God's, 238
"writer's block," 22

Y

Yahweh, 18, 20f, 24, 38, 43, 70, 82, 89, 91,
    93, 95, 215, 228f, 233f, 252, 284;
    complex, 14;—answers Job from
    whirlwind, *illus.*, 90;—frightens Job with
    glimpse of Hell, *illus.*, 86;—shows Job
    the Depths, *illus.*, 92
Yama, 189
yellow, 248f
Yggdrasil, 21
Yin, 281

Z

Zechariah, 282, 284
Zen Buddhism, 63
Zen Koan, 201
Zeus, 24, 30, 70
"Zeus, Tower of," 164
Ziggurat, 127; Great Ziggurat of Ur,
    illus., 127
Zodiac, signs of the, 90, 209
Zosimus, 204